CLOSE TO THE WIND

Pete Goss

CLOSE TO THE WIND

CARROLL & GRAF PUBLISHERS, INC.
NEW YORK

First Carroll & Graf edition 1999

Carroll & Graf Publishers, Inc.
19 West 21st Street
New York, NY 10010-6805

Library of Congress Cataloging-in-Publication Data is available.
ISBN: 0-7867-0607-4

Manufactured in the United States of America

Contents

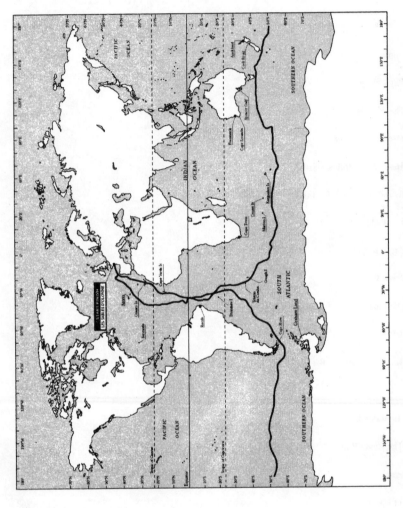

My route in the Vendée Globe, 3 November 1996 – 23 March 1997

CLOSE TO THE WIND

Prologue

If the Southern Ocean represents the consummate challenge for any long-distance sailor, then the Vendée Globe is the pinnacle—one man, one boat against the elements. Competitors must sail nonstop and completely unassisted around the world. The sailors leave Les Sables d'Olonne on the French coast in early November. The course takes them through the Bay of Biscay, the horse latitudes, the doldrums, the long sweep around the Atlantic High, down to the southeast below the Cape of Good Hope and then into the vast desolation of the Southern Ocean. As they push further and further south towards the Horn, they will face storm after storm and will often venture within the northern limit of iceberg drift. It is the ultimate test of man and vessel across the last great wilderness. Over the centuries many sailors have perished here.

Once round Cape Horn there are still 1,000 miles or so to sail before competitors leave the clutches of the Southern Ocean, cross the vast expanse of the Atlantic and, finally, return to Les Sables d'Olonne. They will have been alone at sea for between three and a half and four and a half months.

I set my heart on taking part in a single-handed, round-the-world race in 1986. It was to be ten long and hard years before I achieved that goal when I competed in the 1996 Vendée Globe. In the event, mine was to be more than a yacht race. I faced challenges I never knew existed and at times it became a struggle for survival.

Don't ever think the Vendée was a single-handed race. As the skipper of the boat, I was proud to be part of a large family that designed and built *Aqua Quorum*. Without them I could never have made my journey, and I thank them all. This book is an account of that voyage and the events leading up to it. I hope I have done justice to all those who helped me achieve my dream.

1
BEGINNINGS

The British Steel Challenge. Winter 1992.
Somewhere in the Southern Ocean.

I set to work on the forestay fitting. I was sitting far forward, my legs over the side . . . a huge wave swept in from behind . . . the bow settled as the crest bore down. I felt the water reach my feet, my knees, my waist . . . the wave gathered its shoulder under the hull . . . she started to move, water gently tugging at my legs, pulling at me. A bow wave formed around my chest and when it came the acceleration was frightening . . . I was looking down the front of the biggest wave I had ever seen . . . a whoop of wild exhilaration rose from my clenched guts and I wondered how it would be to return one day and sail single-handed on the lightest, fastest, most high-tech boat I could muster. I wanted to surf down one of these waves to see how fast I could travel and discover what would happen at the bottom.

In 1964, when I was three, I was taken to Plymouth to watch the start of the second Observer Single-handed Transatlantic Race (OSTAR) from there to Newport, Rhode Island. This most famous of yacht races marked the birth of single-handed competition and was the brainchild of Blondie Hasler, an ex-Royal Marine. My family and I had gone out in my grandfather's old motor-sailer to wave the fleet out of Plymouth Sound. Of course,

I had no idea at the time what an influence Hasler—a short, bald man with a ruddy face—and his tiny junk-rigged Folkboat *Jester* were to have on my life. Hasler had risen to fame after he led a daring exploit during the Second World War, when ten marines canoed under cover of darkness up the Gironde river to Nazi-occupied Bordeaux, where they sank several ships at the harbour quayside by attaching limpet mines to them. They were known thereafter as the Cockleshell Heroes—'cockleshell' being the term given to any small, light boat.

I called out to wish Hasler good luck and he shouted something back, which was lost in the general din. I was too young to grasp the enormity of what those yachtsmen were pitting themselves against. Thirty-seven days later—an eternity to a three-year-old—my father, John, told me Hasler had made it, and the magnitude of what he had achieved sank in. I was hooked from that moment on and often dreamed of someday setting out on a similar adventure. It was always the sea. Throughout my early childhood I made crude sailing ships out of boxes and broom handles, and set sail on imaginary voyages of discovery.

I also have vivid recollections of my first Channel crossing from Plymouth to Treguier with my father when I was quite young. We planned the menu, studied charts, prepared the boat and checked the weather forecast prior to departure. It was a hard trip and the feelings of achievement and pride when we made landfall were fantastic. I felt as if I had taken a step into the unknown and come out on top—although in truth my father did most of the work. But before long the Channel was not enough and I wanted more. It was the first of many steps that were eventually to lead to the somewhat larger challenge of the Vendée Globe thirty or so years later.

I was born on 22 December 1961 in Yealmpton, Devon. My father was a consultant in tropical agriculture who worked abroad on two-year projects, supervising development schemes in Aden, Australia, Pakistan and Saudi Arabia. I suppose my up-bringing was a little unconventional. We lived in the bush in Aden for a while in the 1960s, where at times my father had to go to work in a mine-proof Jeep with a machine gun mounted on the back. It was a pretty wild time—one of our bedrooms had bullet holes up the wall and we had to have armed guards round the house at night. Access from the outside world was by Dakota, which had to land on the beach—we burned old car tyres to show our position and the wind direction. It was an unstable period in the country, with much talk of revolution. We had a small cata-maran hidden on the beach, with an escape route from the house via a *wadi* (dried-up water course), should things get really bad. The plan was to pile us all on board and sail out to meet one of the oil tankers passing up and down the Red Sea. They were exciting times and good fun, particularly as I was at an age when danger has no meaning. Travel and adventure were becoming a way of life. I believe that the greatest lottery in life is your parents. You aren't able to choose them and yet they are the ones who have the job of establishing the principles with which you set out in life. After that, it's up to you. My parents taught me that I could do anything I wanted to and I have always believed it to be true. Add a clear idea of what inspires you, dedicate your energies to its pursuit and there is no knowing what you will achieve, particularly if others are inspired by your dream and offer their help.

Generally, children whose parents were working abroad were sent to boarding school. However, my mother Sally wanted her family around her, and so opted to keep her four boys—my elder brother Richard, younger brothers Martin and Andrew, and me—at home and teach us herself using a correspondence course. Now that I have children of my own I understand what she achieved;

she wasn't a teacher, yet she managed it and managed it well. To my mind, we were very lucky and privileged: not every youngster is able to travel the world and stay in other countries long enough to get under the skin of the local culture.

By the time I was fourteen years old I was back in England and my last two years of education were at a public school in Plymouth. I hated every second of it. It was the first time I had been subjected to the restrictions and disciplines of daily school routine—I found the going hard. I can remember one geography lesson during which we were studying the agricultural system of a country where my family and I had lived for two years. I knew that what was being taught was out of date, but when I tried to explain that things had changed, that progress had been made since the text book had been published, I was told to shut up and listen—we were studying for an exam on the book. Well, sod you, I thought. From that point on I switched off, kept my own counsel and wasted a very good educational opportunity—something that I have since regretted. I left school as soon as I could at the age of sixteen.

I was fourteen when I first met Tracey, who is now my wife and mother of our three lovely children Alex, Olivia and Eliot. Tracey was thirteen years old at the time and she laughs now when I say that from the moment we met I knew we would marry some day. Our first encounter took place in *Sanuk*, my family's wooden sailing dinghy. I needed a crew to help me take part in a race organised by my local sailing club in Cornwall, and she was the only one available. She wasn't too keen as she couldn't sail, but I promised that all she would have to do was pass me the sandwiches. The race was a distance of three miles or so. We forgot the sandwiches, worked hard together and won the race. We've been good friends ever since.

After I left school I worked on a local farm for a time while I

looked around for something a little more exciting. The chance
came along in the shape of the Royal Maritime Auxiliary Service
tugs that worked out of Plymouth. I landed a job as a ship's boy
and loved it—it was an active life and I was good at the work.
The crew were a jolly, roustabout bunch and, to cap it all, the
wages were good. A whole new world was opening up.

I may have done a lot of travelling, but in other ways my life
had been a fairly protected one. Alcohol was high on the crew's
agenda and I did my best to keep up with the older, more seasoned hands on their wild runs ashore. I struggled to last the
course on these sessions but usually ended up sleeping in a corner.

The job and the crew taught me a lot about life. The men may
have played hard, but they also worked hard—and well, too. I
came to realise that the principles enshrined in good seamanship—
hard-won values developed and handed down over many years
of experience—are standards by which you can run your life. If
you see that a job needs doing, do it; when you do the job, do it
well; and accept no standard but the highest. At sea you never
know when you might need to call on your equipment in a crisis
and you can't afford to have it let you or anyone else down. Don't
get caught in a corner, always think ahead and make sure that
you have an alternative plan. My time on the tugs also made me
appreciate the power of the sea and to view it with a professional
eye, rather than with the dewy-eyed enthusiasm of an amateur.

I was on the *Robust* when she was called out to help during
the ill-fated 1979 Fastnet Race in which fifteen yachtsmen died.
While we missed the worst of the storm, we did witness its after-
math, and a very sobering experience it was. In my view, many
of those lives were lost due to a lack of discipline and an ignorance of basic safety practices. The design and construction of
many of the yachts in the race were not up to the job and a
number of easy years had lulled crews into a sense of compla-

cency. Some crews had no training or disciplined routines in place, and in some cases did not even meet each other until the day of the race. Several of the new boats were simply unseaworthy because designers had shaved away at safety margins in the interests of speed. We came across a number of empty yachts that had been abandoned for life rafts, with subsequent loss of life. If only the crews had remained on board, some of those men would probably have survived. Many a crew has abandoned the safety of a yacht too soon. Unless the craft is on fire or sinking beneath you, you should stick with it—a vessel, even one that is dismasted or stricken in some other way, is much more seaworthy than a life raft. It is also easier for Air Sea Rescue crews to spot a yacht in a rough sea than to see a tiny inflatable. The experience was a sobering reminder that the sea is boss, and the sorrowful sight of those abandoned yachts has stayed with me ever since.

I had two years with the tugs and loved every minute of it. I was a bit wild and always in trouble, so I'm not sure that I contributed a great deal beyond my immediate responsibilities. The pay was amazing for a teenager still living at home. Once, when we were called out to a burning gas tanker, I earned £900 in one week. However, I made the most of it, as you do at that age, and all I had to show after two years was a bicycle. The job was great and I have some good memories, but it wasn't long before I became restless and yearned for something more adventurous.

Several of the crew were ex-Royal Marines and I found that I had an empathy with them. They did their job with whatever was at hand. I listened open-mouthed to their war stories and tales of antics ashore and decided that this was the life for me. I went to my local recruiting office in Plymouth and signed up for nine years in the Royal Marines.

One of the sergeants who introduced us to the joys of life in the Marines cut an impressive figure. He looked like Desperate

Dan of schoolboy-comic fame. Hair sprouted from his nose and ears, curled up from his chest to escape the confines of the collar around his neck, and protruded from cuffs enclosing mighty wrists. His glare was so fierce that we raw recruits couldn't meet it as it made its slow, penetrating and disdainful pass over us, putting the fear of death in to us. His gravelly voice, roughened on a thousand parade grounds, commanded our total concentration: 'I ain't no fuckin' Einstein, but I do know Newton's theory of shit,' he growled. 'Shit runs downhill and from where I'm stood, you're at the bottom of the valley.'

Great, I thought. I'll have some of this. Whatever it takes to get a green beret, I'll do it. You pour as much shit down your hill as you like. I'll do whatever it takes to get to the top, look back and push over the next load. An hour's intensive exercise later I had learned that climbing out of that pit was to be no easy task. The honour of wearing a green beret was indeed going to be hard-earned. However, I loved the training and couldn't get enough of it. It was the first time I had encountered something to command my full attention and energy.

My first assignment was Commaccio Company, an internal security unit based in Arbroath, Scotland. We were responsible for protecting nuclear weapons bases, and oil rigs. This was what I had joined up for—having lots of fun, while at the same time working in a very professional organisation. We were extremely fit, always on the move, and forever training and preparing for the worst.

After about two years in Commaccio Company I was called in to see the boss, who told me about a job with the new Royal Marines Sail Training Centre in Plymouth. He felt I was the man for the position. I decided to go for the interview because at least I would get a trip home out of it. And so started a long and happy stint at the Sail Training Centre, where my early aspirations to a career in sailing were reinforced. There were two of us on board the sail training vessel: Terry Judge, an old-timer who had many years' experience, and me. It was an unusual situation in that we had command of a yacht on which the crew might range from new recruit to major-general. As lower deckers, Terry and I had to bridge both command and age gaps to ensure that our crew, many of whom had not met each other before, pulled together. Oddly enough, the higher or lower the rank, the easier the man was to deal with. It was the middle ranks, fighting for the next step up the ladder, who often proved a handful. Still, we never had any problems that couldn't be solved and I was able to learn the first principles of man management.

The interesting thing about an offshore trip on a small boat is that you untie more than the boat when you slip the mooring. The trappings and pretensions of rank and authority are soon stripped away. There's nowhere to hide, and it can be a raw experience for some. Natural leaders come to the fore, and a pecking order emerges which is not necessarily the one in place prior to departure. What is important is that everyone feels they are making a contribution, whatever their skill or ability. This promotes a mutual respect which evolves into a healthy team spirit where rank ceases to matter. If it is your turn to clean the toilet—and this includes the skipper—then clean it you will.

We covered thousands of miles, and eventually we were running our own expeditions as far afield as the Baltic and the Mediterranean. For several months at a time we were away from base working as an independent unit. Having become a skipper in my own right, I developed a pride in how things should be done. I found that I thrived on the responsibility, particularly when I was under pressure or when things were going wrong. It was an incredible opportunity and I made the most of it as mile upon mile passed under the keel, each one slowly turning me into a professional seaman. For all the educational books, courses and videos, you can't duplicate time before the mast.

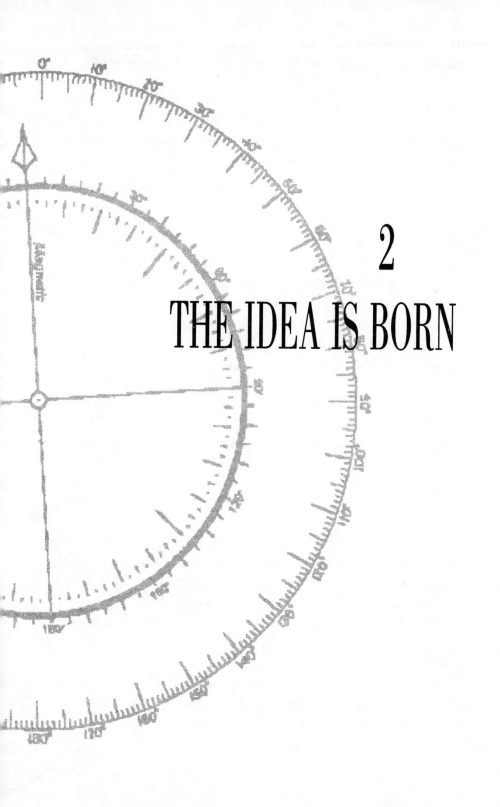

2

THE IDEA IS BORN

In 1986 when I was twenty-four years old, I was in the middle of the Atlantic in my first ocean yacht race, the Carlsberg Two-handed Transatlantic from Plymouth to Newport, Rhode Island. I was sailing a Royal Marines yacht called *Sarie Marais* with fellow Royal Marine and long-time friend, Chris Johnson. It had been a tough trip. During the early hours one morning a storm was raging and I was down below bailing. The noise was terrific as the wind shrieked through the rigging and the hull slammed against the heavy seas. The ship was taking a pounding—and so was its crew. My tired mind was drifting when it hit me that this was the best thing I had ever done. I was exhausted but I had never felt better—and suddenly I knew what I had been put on this earth for. There and then I decided to go it alone and do a single-handed, round-the-world race. I felt such conviction that I spoke it out aloud. I wanted it, I knew I could do it, and from that moment on it never left my mind.

Sarie Marais had been handed on to the Royal Marines by the Navy. She was a Doug Peterson-designed OOD 34, a production sloop—and a pretty tired one at that. In common with most service yachts, she had been looked after but had had a hard life—that had taken its toll on the structure of the vessel, despite a comprehensive refit. It was Chris and I who were to bear the consequences.

I was serving at the Sail Training Centre in 1985 when *Sarie Marais* was adopted. She fell under the auspices of my CO Colonel Lamb, who wasn't sure how to use her—apart from the fact that he felt she should do something to be remembered by now that she was part of the Corps. My direct boss Sergeant Graham Tongue telephoned me while I was on a sailing expedition in the Baltic to ask me if I would like to do a transatlantic race. My answer was a rather dazed 'yes'. I couldn't believe it. I was finally to get my chance at a big one.

The days spent preparing the boat for the race were carefree ones. We had the might of the Marines behind us for a start; we were on a wage; we could use the resources of the sailing centre; and, because it was classed as a military exercise, we didn't even have to take any leave. For all that, we earned it—as does everyone in the Marines—by working extremely hard. Chris and I concentrated on the boat, completing hundreds of training miles during which we got to know *Sarie Marais* and each other inside out.

Soon, *Sarie Marais* had had her refit and we were ready—except that we hadn't opened the books on astro-navigation. No worries—we had a satellite navigation system on board and we threw the books below to consult if the system gave up the ghost. This was a race that we wanted to sail from the cockpit, not from the chart table. And, if the worst came to the worst, we were bound to hit America provided we kept following the sunset. Once we got there we could always ask a fisherman whether we should turn left or right. Actually, we ended up following the vapour trails of aircraft flying from London to New York. When it was overcast we relied on Concorde—if the sonic boom came from the north we tacked up, and if it boomed to the south we tacked down. It still amazes me to think of it.

Chris, who had boxed in the Corps, was a character. He had a big lump on his forehead as a result of being hit with a bottle during a night ashore. The lump had a life of its own and would swell up to twice its normal size if the weather was about to change. It was to become our early warning system of approaching storms. We knew there was a big blow on the way when, during one watch change, Chris came on deck with a real throbber—the best yet. When we checked, the other signs were there too: the barometer was falling and a big swell was setting in from the west.

The storm developed and gave us a beating. One enormous wave swept the boat and I found myself wrapped around the backstay and suspended about six feet above the deck. I have made it a rule since always to clip on with a safety line. Any fool can drown—that's the easy bit.

Poor old *Sarie Marais* gave her all for the twenty-four hours that the storm blew. However, it was just too much for her and I suspect we pushed her a bit too hard. First, the structural frames in the bow cracked—to such an extent that the bow section flexed so much that the forehatch kept springing open, flooding the boat with gallons of water. Next, cracks appeared in the deck—first by the chainplates, and eventually running aft along the deck for about six feet. By now the hull was flexing so much that gaps of up to an inch were opening and closing near the bulkheads and we had to be careful where we put our fingers. A large split developed in the hull under the engine and the rudder felt loose. It was a hard storm.

When finally the storm passed we bailed the boat reasonably dry and set things as straight as we could. To celebrate reaching the halfway point we had a bit of a party, opened a bottle of champagne and presents that family and friends had wrapped up for the occasion. Soon the wind dropped away to a flat calm and, exhausted from the storm, we both fell into a deep sleep.

I was woken by a strange floating sensation. It felt very odd and I opened my eyes with a start to find that the water inside the boat was above knee level. To keep the weight of the boat to a minimum, we had removed the metal water tank and replaced it with several two-gallon plastic containers that, as soon as they became empty, were stowed under my berth. As water leaked into the hull and the level rose, so did the containers—and so did I.

As the trip progressed, Chris and I continued to bail, gradually clearing the boat. Then, to our horror, we discovered that the source of the leak now seemed to be in the area around the keel fastenings rather than the forehatch. We feared that the damned thing was about to fall off. And now the engine wouldn't start, which meant that our autopilot couldn't be used. We consulted a chart to establish what options we had. For a start we were not going to retire; we were here to do a job and do it we would. Newfoundland was the nearest land so we decided to head in that direction and, if the boat was still in one piece by the time we arrived, we would carry on down the American coast to Newport and the finish.

The next step was to prepare for the worst—we made sure the life raft was ready in the cockpit, along with a grab bag containing extra essential gear. We worked out the best place for the off watch man to sleep, and who would do what in the event of a disaster. With that we sailed on and settled into a rather tedious routine. Up to a force four the helmsman could keep the incoming water at bay by working the bilge pump at the same time as steering. Any wind stronger than that and whoever was off watch had to help by bailing from down below up into the cockpit, from where the water would then drain away—we were extremely fit by the end of the race.

The boat was flexing so much by this time that if you sat in the companionway with your elbows resting on either side of the hatch, they would go up and down by about an inch with each flex. Our diet was dictated by whichever cupboard or drawer would open—most were jammed shut by the distortion of the hull. The more that was thrown at us the harder we worked. Nothing was going to get us down and there was no doubt in our minds that we were going to cross the finishing line. After all, we were representing the Corps.

The state of *Sarie Marais* was worsening by the day. We only just made it, by cutting corners in the interests of speed. We had one frightening moment when, getting a bit too cocky for our own good, we cut in so close to the Nantucket shoals that I found myself helming in breaking seas. It was blowing about a force six. I could see the bottom between waves, and sand was being deposited in the cockpit. Very sobering and a lesson I am the better for learning. Never get cocky at sea—it ain't over until the mooring lines have been made fast.

When we arrived at Newport we were delighted to hear that we had come second in class despite all our troubles. We lifted poor old *Sarie Marais* out to check the damage to the keel and it promptly fell off. You don't get much closer than that. The poor old lady had given her all and would not be sailing back home. It was sad to see her abandoned there. I don't think there is anything we could have done for her—she was an old boat being asked to do more than she was capable of. Perhaps we could have been easier on her during the early part of the race, but this would only have put off the inevitable.

Sarie Marais gave me my apprenticeship and I shall never forget her for it. Having made the decision during that voyage to compete in a single-handed, round-the-world race, I now had a clear goal and it was up to me to make it happen. From now on, every decision I took outside my private life would be based on that ambition. Whenever I was faced with a choice, I would only have to ask myself what was in the best interests of my goal, and a clear answer would usually present itself.

My newly found sense of purpose would call for a lot of tolerance on Tracey's part, however much I tried not to let it encroach on our private lives. Before I set off on *Sarie Marais* I had sold my van to pay for her air fare so that she could join me in America, and I eagerly awaited her arrival so that I could share my new dream. At that time we were living in an old terraced house in Torpoint, Cornwall. We had put all our effort and money into reroofing, plumbing and rewiring it, doing most of the work ourselves. In fact, I was still working on the wiring at two in the morning on the day of the race because I didn't want to leave Tracey without power while I was away.

As soon as she arrived in America I told her my plan and she was immediately supportive. If that was what I wanted to do, then she was right behind me. We went on to have a great holiday. I remember one occasion in a rough waterfront bar full of fishermen when Tracey, with a twinkle in her eye, started a drinking competition. I couldn't believe it—we were going to be slaughtered. The opposition sent over a couple of 'real American drinks'. I think the first was called a 'Mud Slide', the second was a 'B52'. Thinking on our feet we sent back a 'real Cornish drink'. It consisted of a double whisky, crème de menthe, sherry, gin, rum, a dash of lemon and Coke. 'Goddamn, you guys really drink this shit over there?' We only just won.

I had yet to demonstrate that I could sail single-handed, and I decided to enter the next Carlsberg Single-handed Transatlantic Race (CSTAR) from Plymouth to Newport in two years' time. I would need time off, so when I returned to Britain I put my case to the Royal Marines, with the help of Lieutenant Paul Morris, who had heard about my plans when he was on a sail training course I was skippering. Paul knew his way around the system and was to help with getting sponsorship and preparing the boat. The Marines were fantastic. First, they agreed that I could stay in my job provided I put promotion on hold; second, they agreed to stand by me and give me time off to compete as long as I raised the money and built the boat in my own time. The reality was that my boss Graham Tongue used to let me slip away if things were getting tight. Graham was a valuable source of advice throughout my time in the Corps. He is an amazing organiser with a lot of sailing behind him, from one of the first Whitbread races to experience in early multi-hulls.

I now began in earnest to plot a long-term strategy. Here I was, a young Royal Marine with no money. I had never sailed single-handed before, yet I was proposing to put a team together to design and build a high-tech yacht which I would race round the world. It was a tall order. First of all I needed to learn about the commercial world, particularly that of sponsorship. I had seen a number of people take the sponsor's cash and then sail over the horizon without putting much effort into giving value for money. This meant yet another company that would never touch sailing again. It was bad for the sport and I felt it wasn't right for people to complain that they weren't getting enough support from companies if they weren't prepared to make an effort themselves. It was for the sportsmen to provide tangible and measurable results. It doesn't matter to sponsors whether it is an egg-and-spoon race or a yacht race—if it gives them a return, then they'll invest.

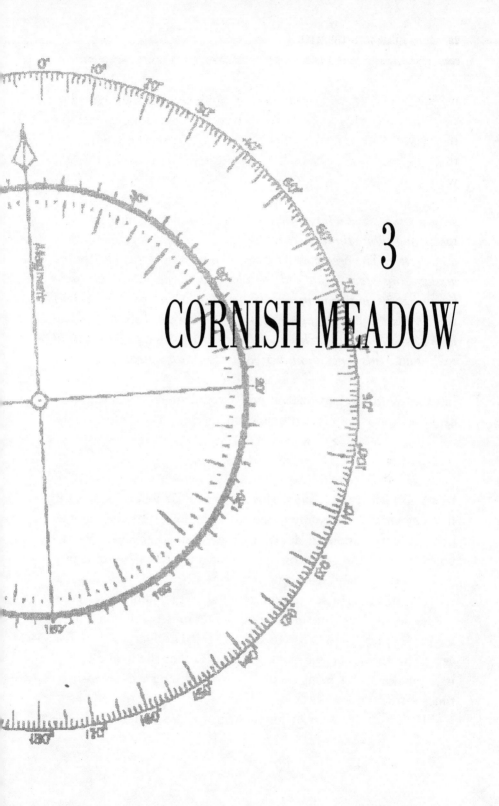

3
CORNISH MEADOW

It is not the critic who counts, nor the man who points out how the strong man stumbles or where the doer of deeds could have done better. The credit belongs to the man who is actually in the arena, whose face is marred by dust and sweat and blood; who knows great enthusiasm, great devotion and the triumph of achievement and who, at the worst, if he fails, at least fails while doing greatly—so that his place shall never be with those cold and timid souls who know neither victory nor defeat . . .

In other words get on with it and screw 'em—don't know who said this, but it's a favourite of mine.

I had no idea what I was letting myself in for when I started in the summer of 1986 to raise money for the 1988 Carlsberg single-handed. I was soon to discover that sailing is the easy part. I bought a second-hand word processor and started write a proposal, immediately regretting my wayward and lazy days at school. I'm embarrassed to admit it now, but I couldn't even compose a decent letter. A simple, two-paragraph covering note took me three hours, with constant visits to the dictionary. When Tracey got in from working at the local post office she would correct it. To make up for being so slow, I worked longer hours—sometimes through the night.

My first choice of boat for the trip was a Sadler Barracuda—

a forty-five-foot, fractional-rigged sloop. A year and many failed proposals later, I realised I was barking up the wrong tree—at £150,000 the Barracuda was too expensive a proposition for an unknown rookie. I was chasing too much money.

I had no choice but to dump a year's work in the rubbish bin and, a little wiser, start anew. I was forever on the phone chasing potential sponsors and following up any leads that might come my way. I scoured newspapers and business magazines in the search for companies that might fit the bill. I sent for their annual reports to find out in more detail what they did. I referred to *Who's Who* and various other publications in the reference library to establish if any members of the board were sailors. Slowly I put a dedicated campaign together. If I felt a particular business was a good prospect, I used a light-box to trace its company logo on the sails and hull of the yacht illustration on the front cover of my proposal and then shaded it in using coloured pencils. I would then send the proposal with a covering letter and a detailed breakdown of how the project could be tailored to them. It looked impressive but cost peanuts, as the Royal Marines' printers ran off copies of the proposal and Tracey and I did the binding ourselves. The cover looked great. A plastic overlay gave it a glossy finish. In total I sent out 2,500 proposals—and I had had to research up to ten companies to find even one worth contacting. It was a mammoth task—and still it didn't work. Many didn't bother to respond, although those that did often said it was one of the best proposals they had seen.

It was a desperate time and not one that I would like to repeat. I was always on the road, chasing meetings. It all seems old hat now, but it was new ground for me and the fact was I still didn't have enough money to buy the fenders, let alone the boat.

My bike was my sole means of transport because I had sold my van earlier that year to buy Tracey's ticket to America. I once rode fifty miles in one day going from meeting to meeting. Before each interview I changed into a blazer and tie, which I carried in a rucksack on my back, and walked into the office as if I had just arrived by car. On one occasion I had a meeting with a rather stuffy managing director, after which I nipped round the back of the building to change for the next leg of the cycle ride. I was stripped down to my underpants and, just as I was pulling on my tracksuit bottoms, the chap walked out the back door on his way to lunch. He shot one startled look at me and legged it. I thought the meeting had gone well, but he never contacted me and refused to take my follow-up calls. I'm not sure if he thought single-handers had funny sexual preferences, but if he did I had obviously supported the theory.

The highlight of this period was when Tracey and I were married on 4 July 1987 at Maryfield Church, Wilcove, Cornwall. The sun shone on the best and wisest thing I have ever done.

As well as taking a huge step in my personal life, I was also about to take a significant leap towards achieving my sailing ambitions—I had found my boat for the CSTAR. She was one of the best designed and constructed boats I have ever sailed—a little twenty-six-foot catamaran called a Firebird. Captain James Getgood had brought her to my attention because he felt that it might be a good boat for an entry in the next Three Peaks Race, a madcap mix of sailing and running up and down mountains, in which I had previously competed. James had led the Royal Marines' entry in the last Three Peaks. We drove down to Falmouth in Cornwall for a test sail with the designer Martyn Smith. Martyn had been chief stress engineer for British Aerospace and had worked on the design for Concorde. He is also a keen sailor and, in my view, a genius. As soon as I stepped on the Firebird I knew she was a thoroughbred. Once the sails were up I could find no bad habits.

She was built by Modular Mouldings, a small company of enthusiasts based in Gweek in Cornwall, and was pure quality. Helming her down the estuary, I was overcome with excitement— I knew I had found my boat for the CSTAR. The fact that she was billed as a day-sailer was irrelevant. In my view she could take on anything. I asked Martyn if he thought she might be up to an ocean crossing. He looked rather startled, thought about it for a while and then said that, with the right sailor on board, he saw no reason why not. I couldn't sit still for excitement and crawled around her visualising what she would be like in a North Atlantic blow. I was completely focused on the CSTAR—the Three Peaks never entered my mind.

I shot through the front door and babbled away to Tracey about the Firebird. She was worried that, in desperation, I was being unrealistic, what with the disappointment of having had to dump a year's work and the feeling that the race was starting to slip away from me. She had a point, so I decided to jot down all the factors that were important to the success of the voyage and then think each one through in detail. I was, after all, proposing a very ambitious entry: at twenty-six feet she would be the smallest catamaran to cross the North Atlantic from east to west—let alone single-handed. Her design was radical and, it had to be admitted, she was never intended for ocean sailing. In addition, being so low in the water, I would be alarmingly exposed to the elements, which can get grim in the North Atlantic.

I was told that I was mad, irresponsible, selfish, inexperienced, bound to drown. I heard it all. It takes a long time for some people to accept something new but, provided you have studied the problem, considered every possible danger and have a decent solution, it's best just to prove your point by getting on with it. One simply has to recognise that progress is about change and development; by definition, attitudes will always follow one step behind. I felt that whatever anyone else might say I probably had the safest boat in the fleet. Being a multi-hull, it wouldn't sink beneath me. The greatest risk was capsize, and if I were to turn the Firebird over it would be no worse than capsizing a beach cat. I wouldn't want that to happen on a sixty-footer at thirty knots—it would be as great a risk to life as a car crash. I had worked out a plan to right the Firebird and although I didn't have the time to test it, I was confident of its success and would just have to have a go if the need arose. The RAF very kindly supplied a four-man life raft in an eight-man valise so that I could accommodate the extra safety gear I felt was necessary. I was extremely fit, I was training on the prototype craft, and would be using the best protective clothing from Musto. I could see no reason, given my determination to succeed, why we shouldn't finish the race.

Most important of all, I felt I would be self-sufficient, something that I have always valued. I would be out there by choice and the responsibility was mine. Under no circumstances did I want my dream to result in having to call on the rescue services and, by so doing, putting them at risk. Although I had an EPIRB (emergency position-indicating radio beacon)—and believe every mariner should carry one in case of dire emergency—I could relate to Blondie Hasler's views on the subject. He hated radios on yachts because he feared that yachtsmen in difficulty would send out distress signals and cause a lot of trouble. He felt it would be more seemly for the chap to die like a gentleman. I believe that no passage should be undertaken with rescue being considered as an option. Modern equipment and methods do not replace basic seamanship skills, they are simply aids—albeit very good ones.

One of the reasons I chose the Firebird was that I believe the weak link in any single-handed operation is the single-hander him- or herself. No matter how much I tried, I could never do the job of a full crew. Therefore, the easier the boat was to sail, the more it would utilise its most limited resource: me. This offered greater potential for success against the bigger yachts which, on the face of it, stood well above my entry. On this basis, I felt competitive, and actually viewed many of the larger boats as easy pickings, unable to perform to their full potential as their greater workload would tire their skippers to the point of collapse. This was a marathon not a sprint, and I could see myself finishing the race as hungry for speed as I had been at the start—rather than grinding slowly over the finishing line. Any necessary sail changes would be done as soon as they were called for, with relatively little energy on my part, rather than waiting for the wind to settle. As the Firebird was so light and well designed, and thanks to the small loads that were being generated, there was minimal risk of damage. In addition, she was just plain fast. Plymouth port control had clocked me on their radar belting across Plymouth Sound at twenty-two knots.

She was also an attractive proposition commercially—the total budget was now down to £30,000, as opposed to the £150,000 needed for the Barracuda, and much of this would be recouped on the resale of the boat. She was definitely going to attract publicity: her revolutionary design was unique and she would be the smallest multi in the race. Having been designed, built and sailed in the West Country, the campaign suddenly took on an identity that local people and businesses could rally round. I started the grind for sponsorship believing that I would eventually get there. There was someone out there who would sponsor me—all I had to do was keep looking. If I was lucky it would be soon; if I was unlucky it would be later. The solution to most things is hard work and as someone once said, 'The harder I work, the luckier I get.'

I contacted everyone I could think of. I sent out proposal after proposal and started to generate publicity. Many people are reticent about approaching the press. I waded in with an open mind and was pleasantly surprised, finding them polite, supportive and genuinely interested in my plans. I explained that I was new to the business of seeking publicity, and was given lots of constructive advice and offers of help. One of the pleasures of these projects is that you meet all sorts of interesting people and dabble in things you would never normally come into contact with.

BBC provided me with a huge break: they were making a documentary illustrating the diversity of the race's entrants. The programme was to follow the fortunes of Denise St Aubyn Hubbard—at sixty the oldest woman in the race—Tony Bullimore and his amazing sixty-foot Formula One trimaran, and me. Tony was someone I admired and I found Denise inspiring. Among her other achievements, she had been a member of the British Olympic diving team and had skippered a Royal Naval minesweeper. I hope that at her age I have a mind as open as hers to new challenges.

The documentary, and support from the local press, gave the project credibility—the fact that people were reading about it meant it would happen. The BBC documentary was pure gold in that sense. Half an hour of prime-time viewing was a real head-turner.

My big break came at last in the form of a phone call from Charles Lovick, an independent insurance broker and vice-commodore of the Royal Western Yacht Club, who had seen my proposal. He would put up half the money and help raise the rest through his contacts. He would be a silent sponsor in return for ownership of the boat. This meant that anyone else coming on board would have a clean, fixed-price contract and *carte blanche* on the publicity—all at half price. I jumped at his offer. All three of us would get what we wanted from the project, and I was halfway there. I put the phone down with a whoop of joy and was so excited I had to go out for a run to calm down!

Proposals were reprinted and I started again with a vengeance. However, months later further sponsorship hadn't come in. I grew desperate—the cut-off date for construction was approaching and I still wasn't able to give the go-ahead to build the Firebird. I couldn't sleep. I would wake up at two in the morning and throw myself at the computer—which by now I could practically make smoke—as I followed up every lead and phone call with proposals and ideas. I would bloody well swamp the place until something gave. We came close to success a couple of times. At meetings I would outline the project and Charles Lovick would start selling it. I was so impressed by his patter that I was almost persuaded to get out my own cheque book at times. Charles knew what businesses were looking for and, as a businessman himself, he spoke the same language. It was a new and fascinating world.

For all that, we were running out of time. Modular Mouldings kept putting back the cut-off date for construction until eventually it got silly. I was being pulled apart. I had half the money, I could taste the race and I knew I could do it. The frustration was like a solid lump in my chest. The only way I could get to sleep was to go out and run myself to exhaustion—only to wake up in the early hours and get back to work. On reflection, I had let it take over my life—not something that I would allow to happen again. I had lost perspective and my quality of life was suffering. One should never forget that it is only a yacht race.

The darkest hour arrived. I rode out to the cliffs at Whitsand Bay and sat on a rock watching the waves roll in. I thought the whole thing through and faced up to the fact that we would have to call it off the next day. Oddly enough, it was a relief. I was emotionally drained and for the first time could relax, feel the sun, and see the birds. It was bliss. I decided I would call Charles and tell him what I think he already knew. I would tell Modular Mouldings it was all off. I would then take some time out before starting again—but this time I would keep things in perspective. The ride home was a relaxed and enjoyable affair. Tracey and I went for a long walk and talked about our future and how we needed to maintain a balance. We wanted to have a family and would need some security. I had decided to pursue a career in sailing and, despite all the setbacks, was still convinced that there was a good future once a foundation had been laid. Tracey is the real hero in all this. She had no doubt that I could do it and never lost faith at any time during the next ten years as we struggled away. Together we have found a way to work in harmony with my racing, as well as bringing up a young family. I compete in one big project every four years and treat my sailing time as work so that we get weekends together whenever possible. We have always insisted that my career should not be at the expense of our family life.

Charles was very understanding and offered to drive down to Modular Mouldings with me. There was someone he felt it might be worth visiting on the way and he said we might as well drop in and see him. I slept like the dead that night and woke up refreshed. I had rationalised the disappointment, deciding to treat the last couple of years as a lesson from which I would benefit for the rest of my life. I walked out to Charles's toot of the horn with a light step, looking forward to seeing Modular Mouldings, even if it was with disappointing news. At least they would be put out of their misery as well.

The person Charles wanted to talk to about the project was Keith Davenport and he had already outlined the campaign to him over the phone. The office was humming with activity as we sat waiting for Keith, who was obviously a busy man. He burst into the room, filling it with enthusiasm and energy, and started to fire off comments and questions. 'For Christ's sake! You must be mad.' 'You look too young—what do your parents think?' 'There are no figures in here for a wage. How will you feed yourself?' 'The Royal Marines? Fantastic!' 'Why hasn't someone sponsored you already?' 'I love kids—would you mind helping with the Wishing Well Appeal?' 'Brilliant! The kids will love it. We'll call it *Ghostbusters*. What do you reckon to that for a name?' Err, yes . . . well . . . 'Great! I'm up for it. Go to it. Order the boat—Charles and I will sort out the money. I think you're nuts, but I love it. Got to go, lots on today.' And he hurried out of the room.

I had never met anyone with such energy. I couldn't get my head round the sudden change in my luck. I had faced so many disappointments up until then that it just didn't seem possible, particularly when delivered like that. Charles grinned. 'We had better get on with it then.'

I spent the rest of the journey in a daze. I was trying to sort out a jumble of emotions and started to worry now about the reaction we might get from Modular Mouldings. We were well past their final cut-off date. It was in their hands. We told them the news and let it sink in. I could bear it no longer. Surrounded in their immaculate shed by rolls of composite cloth and drums of resin, I pointed out that as a team we had thirteen weeks in which to build the boat from scratch, complete a qualifying sail and get to the start fully prepared. It was a seemingly impossible task. 'I'm up for it. Are you?' I asked. There was a short pause as the partners in the company—Bob and Brenda Caraco and boatbuilder of the Firebird Toby Richardson—looked at each other and with one voice said: 'Yes.' We were off!

We piled into their office and scratched out a plan of action. Halfway through the meeting Toby stood up and said: 'Well, I'd better get going. There's a boat to be built.' I knew then that with the team we had we would do it. I don't think Toby left the shed until the boat was finished to his exacting standards. I visited the factory as often as I could to keep a close eye on construction. I needed to know her inside out in case of problems when I was at sea on my own.

It was a heady drive home. I told Tracey the good news and went for a cycle ride to sort out my thoughts and mull through the day's events. I decided not to get too excited until the contract between Charles and Keith had actually been signed. I failed abysmally and stayed up most of the night planning how to make the start in good shape in such a short time. It was so refreshing after two years of disappointment. I seemed to have unlimited energy. I worked late every night, and was up and away early each morning. It was great. We had managed it, thanks to Charles and Keith.

The news was soon out and all sorts of people stepped forward to help. An old lady, who had knitted me a good-luck sweater for the Carlsberg Two-handed Transat, stopped me in the street to say she had started to knit another. 'I'm so worried about your going on this trip,' she said. 'I could cope with your being out there on your own on the two-handed, but how will they tie your other hand behind your back now that you are going to be single-handed? It really isn't right.' I only just managed to hold back a smile as I explained what I was setting out to do and what was meant by the term 'single-handed'.

I am always happy to break down the myths, mysteries and misunderstandings that sometimes exclude outsiders from the true spirit of sailing. It isn't a black art and by no means an elitist sport. I remember once, when I was very young, walking along a pontoon to look at a top racing yacht. I was made to feel uncomfortable and very unwelcome as the crew strutted about like rock stars in designer sunglasses. My own sailing club, Torpoint Mosquito, near Plymouth, is a prime example of how open and encouraging things should be. As a junior member I had helped dig the foundations for a new extension, and assisted with clearing a way for the new slipway. Everyone worked together and it had been great fun, particularly as the senior members put a lot of effort into bringing on the juniors. Those men had a huge influence on me while I was growing up.

I promised myself that if I was ever lucky enough to have a boat of my own it would be open to anyone who was interested.

Final preparations were at last in place and I was towed out to the start. I could hardly believe the moment had arrived but felt absolutely confident. One of the BBC cameramen who had been trailing me for a few days gave me a hug and said, with tears in his eyes: 'It's been good to know you.' He obviously thought I wasn't going to return—and he wasn't the only one who felt it was impossible to survive the race in such a small catamaran.

I was very tired—it had been a hard thirteen weeks and we had only just made it, cutting a few corners in the process. Race safety rules demanded that every boat had a radio. I must confess that I didn't have enough money for one, so we pulled an old, broken one out of a skip one night, shone it up with a little shoe polish and wired up the back light so that the dials gave off a healthy glow. I am ashamed to say that this ploy worked and the race committee were satisfied when they scrutinised the boat. In my defence, I felt that nothing could be allowed to stop me now— and did have a good emergency beacon on board. However, I felt awful about the deception and vowed that, however tight things were, I would never do something like that again. After all, the rules are there for my benefit.

The race was a fantastic experience. I felt completely at home by myself and settled into getting this tiny boat across the Atlantic as fast as I could. Initially we had a real old blow and I just had to run before it as it carried me down to the Azores. It was exhilarating—at one point I was getting speeds in excess of twenty knots with no sails up. Waves were sweeping the boat and on many occasions only my head and the mast showed above the water. I hand-steered for about thirty-six hours—making sure that my mother's fruit cake—which I never go to sea without—was within grabbing distance of the helming position. You can live off it, ballast the boat with it, and I am sure you could plug a leak with it if you had to.

It was with some relief that I pulled through the storm intact and was able to sail in the direction I wanted. I was determined to do well and slept on deck all the way, with the main sheet wrapped round my arm for safety. If I was tired and things were looking a little marginal, I went to sleep wrapped in oilies and thermals, and draped myself across the winches and deck fittings so that the general discomfort and cramp would be sure to rouse me every half an hour or so. I never felt lonely. I missed people, but that's different. I chatted to the boat and established a relationship with it.

At one point the main beam started to come undone. It was making a dreadful noise as it worked loose. I grabbed the special tool kit to tighten up the fitting, only to find that one of the spanner sockets—the one I needed, of course—was missing. The kit had been put on board at the last minute and in the rush I hadn't inventoried its contents. Never again. It took twelve desperate hours with a hacksaw and file to make a new tool for the job, while the boat tried to pull itself apart.

Two days from the finish, at about five in the morning, it became foggy, cold, flat calm and poured with rain. There was a blow on the way and I knew that if I went to sleep I would wake up with the boat upside down. I had been up all night and was on my knees with tiredness. In order to stay awake I sang at the top of my voice and marched around the deck, pausing occasionally to shake my fists skyward and swear at the weather. In the middle of one of these tirades a faint voice called, ' 'Allo.' Astonished, I turned round to find that a fellow competitor, Frenchman Gerard Montariol in his forty-five-foot trimaran *Gauloises IV*, had crept out of the fog and was watching me from a few yards off. How embarrassing! I threw him a can of beer and, after a chat, we decided to have a private race to the finish. I was delighted to have bumped into him because, being without a radio, I had no idea how I ranked. However, here I was in the company of a much larger boat, so I must have been doing all right.

Off we set, the wind blew up as expected and *Gauloises IV* pulled away. *Cornish Meadow* and I kept on plugging—our time would come. Three miles from the finish, the sea dropped to a flat calm with the Frenchman a mile and a half ahead. I was determined not to let the flag down and, stripped to the waist ready for action, I unstowed my paddle. The light weight of *Cornish Meadow* paid off now and I could manage two knots if I put my all into it. About two hours later the gap had closed and we had worked our way to windward in light and fickle winds for one of the most exciting finishes of my life. Neither of us knew until the last minute who would pull it off. However, my vessel was small, light and manoeuvrable and I was therefore able to make the most of every wind change, putting the spinnaker up just before the line to accelerate across his bow and the finish. Fantastic! Not only had we made it, but I came second in class and thirty-fifth out of ninety-five overall and had proved a point. The concept of a light and simple boat had merit for this competition. It was established beyond doubt that a small cat was able to take on the task. Others have since underlined the point.

I stepped off the boat and on to dry land in the sure knowledge that somehow I would fulfil my round-the-world dream. I now knew I could sail single-handed—indeed, I had found the experience thoroughly enjoyable. I had been blooded and had proved to myself that I had the commitment, the determination and the ability to be competitive.

4

ABOUT TURN! QUICK MARCH!

With *Cornish Meadow* and the CSTAR behind me, it was time to think about the next step: the big one, single-handed and round the world. And, of course, a new boat, designed for the job. It all came down to cash. If I were to achieve my dream and build the boat, I needed money—a great deal of it—in the form of sponsorship.

The *Cornish Meadow* adventure had been a success, pleasing my sponsors and attracting loads of publicity. The BBC made an additional documentary based on my experience alone called *Battling the Atlantic*. It was shown twice nationwide, as well as getting air time in Canada, Australia, South Africa and Singapore. Much of the credit for its success must go to the producer Tony Byers, who was to become a trusted friend.

The programme generated additional media coverage, in which I always hammered home what was next on the menu—a round-the-world race. I set out to make myself a successful fundraiser. I felt I had two areas of responsibility toward my sponsors, both past and future. I would always do my best to win the event, of course, but I also needed to engineer a professional and high profile campaign in the run up to the race so that the sponsors got value for money whatever the eventual outcome. Winning should be considered a bonus.

Whenever I got the chance, I chatted to photographers and cameramen to find out what they looked for in a shot. I peered through the lens myself and found out how a sailing boat looked at this or that angle; how certain kinds of light made the vessel look better or worse. I learned that yellow stands out in a fleet of yachts and will attract the camera as it sweeps by looking for something on which to linger. No prizes for guessing what the colour of my next boat would be.

I studied interview techniques, watched the professionals at work and learned how to turn questions into an opportunity to get my message across. Privately, I rehearsed my responses to imaginary questions so as to ensure concise and interesting answers. I dug up quotes that non-sailors could relate to, giving a life to my dream that everyone could understand. I set out to be media-friendly, so that a journalist could invest time in my project and be confident of a good return. I remembered those occasions in the past when I had to deal with pessimists who were convinced that my tiny catamaran *Cornish Meadow* was not going to make it across the Atlantic. I explained my strategy and would finish by saying: 'It's only wind and water.' The phrase caught on and became widely used. It seemed made-to-measure for headlines and, in fact, became the title of a book written about the BT Global Challenge.

My first public speech, however, was a different matter. It was to the members of Torpoint Mosquito SC, and I was terrified at the prospect. On the water, especially after my single-hander, I felt confident and at ease with myself. I told myself not to be so stupid: if I could sail a single-hander across the Atlantic, I could certainly talk to a roomful of people. Of course I could. Well, that was the theory, anyway.

I was dreadfully nervous during the week before and couldn't eat for the twenty-four hours prior to the talk. Only those who are themselves shy can relate to the terror of having to stand up in front of a crowd. However, I knew I would have to do a lot of this sort of thing if I wanted to fund the race, so I steeled myself to go through with it. Happily, once I began to speak, I got into my subject and into my stride. The nerves fell away, my knees stopped knocking and, to my amazement, I found that I was actually enjoying talking to all these people. I now look forward to public presentations and am on top of my shyness.

Life in the Marines was not without its problems at this point. I needed more and more time off from my duties with the Sailing Centre to pursue my new ambitions. My CO was distinctly uneasy about this and I couldn't blame him. However, my project was so much bigger now and I knew I would not be able to pull it all together in my spare time, as I had done in the past. A settlement came at a meeting with General Vaux, during which I had fifteen minutes to put my case. The General listened carefully and gave his approval. The entire project could have been scuppered without his support but, thank goodness, he chose to put his own time and commitment behind me. He even advised me on how to run the campaign and gave me names of potential sponsors.

The next step was to decide on a designer for the boat. I felt that the best man was Adrian Thompson. I had never met him but had admired his boats from afar and my instinct told me that he was right for the job as we seemed to share a similar philosophy on sailing. I set off for Devon, where he lived. I knew exactly what I wanted: a fifty-foot boat with a clean and simple design that would enable me to be more efficient than the bigger boats, thereby winning the class two fifty-footer section and, with a bit of luck, making inroads into class one and the sixty-footers. Adrian, despite being busy with two boats under construction, took time out to see this rookie sailor with big ideas. I didn't know what kind of reception I would receive—he leads his field and is used to having the world's finest knocking on his door.

He is a giant of a man with a ready smile and a relaxed manner, and immediately put me at my ease. I outlined my thoughts on the boat and, feeling a bit cheeky, asked if he would consider designing it for me. His face lit up with an enthusiastic grin. 'I've been waiting for someone like you to walk through that door for the last five years,' he said. 'What you have just described sounds remarkably like an idea for a boat that has been drifting around in my head looking for someone to sail it.' He grabbed a piece of paper and sketched the boat. It was quite uncanny in its likeness to the one I had in mind. Two extremely pleasant hours were to follow as I listened to Adrian talking about the boat and his thinking behind it.

I left knowing that I had found the man who would design my boat—as well as become a good friend. Adrian has the knack of being able to make an incredibly complex design problem seem clear and logical—even to someone like me, who has the brain power of a rocking horse. He is also happy to tackle anything. He produced the composite racing bicycle on which Chris Boardman won the Prologue in the 1997 Tour de France; he developed a new wave-piercing concept that revolutionised powerboat design; and he designed and produced the first aerodynamic composite golf club (which was promptly banned as it knocked the ball twenty per cent further). For all this he retains his humility. In Adrian's eyes life is too good to be taken seriously. If there is no budget and one has to use second-hand bits and bobs to do the job, then that's part of the fun and challenge; a way will be found.

Adrian started out as a farmer. But his life changed dramatically the day he decided to compete in a sailing race around Ireland and Britain. He took out a pile of books on boat design from his local library, disappeared behind his bedroom door and set to. Six months later he emerged with his design, built the boat himself and went on to win his class. *Alice's Mirror* was one of the first water-ballasted boats and the forerunner of a whole new generation of design. Such is the measure of the man. He quickly moved on to greater things, designing and building a trimaran, which also set new standards. His interest in composites, which at the time were practically unknown, helped to develop yachts as we now know them. He was the first to build a maxi yacht without a space frame, using a monocoque structure instead. They are all built that way today. His skills are second to none.

I had my designer and now I needed a professional proposal. Lou Lou Rendal is a family friend whom we had first met in Newport at the end of the 1986 Carlsberg Two-handed Transatlantic. She is rich in public relations skills, and offered to help write the proposal. Once more we were off along that dark and desperate tunnel looking for sponsorship. But people were beginning to believe in my project.

While I was at sea on *Cornish Meadow*, I gave the question of sponsorship and how it affected me as a sportsman much thought. It was my first taste of being responsible to people other than myself for a good result. Sponsorship meant that I had a duty to perform for commercial reasons, as well as for the simple pleasure of competing. It was a weighty responsibility—not only did I owe it to my family and myself to excell in an event, I also owed it to a small army of sponsors. I was fiercely competitive and intended to remain so—but I decided that it must not be for commercial reasons alone. I came to the conclusion that all I could ever do was simply my best. My will to win would get the result, provided I gave it free rein. Most important of all, I vowed that whatever difficulties a race threw at me I would never give up. Retirement would not be an option. The only things that would stop me would be circumstances outside my control: sinking, for example. If I were to give in because of lack of commitment, I would regret it for the rest of my days. As long as I know that I have done my best, if I am beaten over the finishing line I can offer the victor genuine congratulations for a job well done.

I came very close to finding my major sponsor when an insurance company showed interest in my proposal. After many meetings and reports, a vote at board level was all that was required and that, I was told, was a foregone conclusion. The board members had been canvassed and all of them were in favour. It was in the bag, it seemed. Until the phone call from my champion in the company, that is, who broke the news that the financial market had just taken one of the biggest dives in its history. My project was history, too. It had been struck off the company's agenda and would not be going back on in the foreseeable future. It was a crushing blow. I had thought I was home and dry. The fact that it would have been a different story had the meeting taken place a week earlier made it all the more painful. I felt as though fate were against me.

This cruel blow broke my resolve. I had been working so hard and for so long. I continued to do the rounds of potential sponsors for a couple of months but at every turn was told: 'A great project, old chum, but the crash has put the stoppers on sponsorship.'

To add to my troubles, there was an even more pressing matter that needed to be addressed. The end of my nine years' service with the Royal Marines was becoming a daunting reality. I had neglected to give it much thought on the assumption that I had found my sponsor and therefore had a future in place. I had to put my round-the-world ambitions on the shelf and think about life after the Marines. Also, my first child, Alex, was born on 20 March 1989, and Tracey and I were now responsible for the welfare of someone other than each other.

At first it seemed natural that I should look for a job that involved being on the water. I had had a few offers but they just didn't interest me. How could I settle for sail training when what I really wanted was to be taking part in a single-handed, round-the-world race? I began to wonder whether I was in fact an adventurer first, and a sailor second. Perhaps sailing was simply the medium through which I expressed my thirst for excitement. It was the challenge of the oceans that fulfilled my needs. Reluctantly, I decided to give up sailing and train in another area. It was a time of great disillusion: to throw all that work away with nothing to show for it was devastating. I was completely committed as a sportsman and yet I seemed unable to break into the major league.

One of my entitlements when I left the Marines was to go on an employment training course. I decided to treat this as both an introduction to something new and a six-month sabbatical between the services and civilian life. I wasn't ready to make a decision and needed time out to make sure that the next big step was the right one. I opted for a course in carpentry, reasoning that if I had a trade under my belt and a bag of tools I could earn an honest crust anywhere in the world.

At last, in March 1990, the fateful day arrived. I stood in front of the CO; he said a few quick words of encouragement and wished me well for the future. I handed in my ID card. 'About turn! Quick march!' And I was out the door as the next man was being marched in. It was all over, just like that. As I walked away from Stonehouse Barracks in Plymouth I knew had just left a special world full of professional people who had been fantastic to me. Many good memories passed through my mind as I walked home.

I threw myself into the carpentry course. Given the circumstances, it was just what I needed to clear my head. I was learning something new, using my hands, and I had a comfortable routine. To return home at the end of a day and not have to run upstairs and start chasing sponsors well into the night was a relief. I was able to enjoy life again, slowly shedding the disappointment of having failed to raise a sponsor.

However, it wasn't long before the sea started to call again and I changed my course to boatbuilding. I reckoned that I could always get a job in a boatyard and, if I did ever find a sponsor, the knowledge would be invaluable. It was a hard time financially, with my family and I living on unemployment benefit for the duration of the course. The dole can be a dark place—not too good for your self-esteem. Many of those on the course were long-term unemployed who actually looked grey and lifeless as a result. And yet the majority were a great bunch who were simply looking for that chance to prove themselves.

I managed to raise some funds from the local council to charter a catamaran for a long weekend of adventure training. I felt that an outlet was needed to drag these people out of the circumstance in which they had become trapped. The council was great and allowed me to run the trip, provided one of the course instructors, Tom Sizor, accompanied us. Anyone could come if they chipped in £5 towards the food. That is a lot of money when you're out of work, but I wanted them to put a value on what they were about to do, rather than simply see it as just another handout.

It was their trip: they worked out what food to take, studied the charts, decided where to go and took decisions during those three unfettered days. You could feel the sense of purpose and excitement putting a spring back in their step. It was a wonderful weekend. I still see some of them now and they talk about the experience fondly and say how much it meant at the time. We sailed to the Isles of Scilly, where we anchored up for the night prior to making our way home again. It was lovely weather and we took the opportunity to swim off the starboard hull of the boat, where we had rigged the boarding ladder. A bet was laid to see if anyone could swim under the boat from the starboard to the port hull in one breath. An ex-fisherman, who would have a go at anything, jumped at the chance, coming up with his mouth agape as he gasped for air. One of the other lads, unaware of the bet, happened to be relieving himself over the port side at just that moment and the swimmer got more than he'd bargained for.

I enjoy teaching and encouraging people to get that little bit more out of their lives. Sailing, of all the adventure training activities—and I have tried most—seems the one most able to stimulate and engender self-confidence and vitality in those who have had it beaten out of them by life and have perhaps taken a wrong turn. The results that the Prince's Trust and Ocean Youth Club achieve by creating this environment have long convinced me of its worth. It costs hundreds of pounds a week to keep a youth in prison; a square-rigger sail training ship can be run for that kind of sum. It is an idea that keeps scratching away for when I am old and bold.

Shortly after the Isles of Scilly trip with my fellow dole mates, Chay Blyth, the trail-blazing, record-breaking, round-the-world sailor of great renown, advertised for a skipper to train crews, which would be made up of novice adventurers, who would take part in his latest sailing project, the 1992 British Steel Challenge. Chay wanted to break down the elitism of round-the-world sailing and was offering the chance of a circumnavigation to anyone between the ages of twenty and sixty years old. No sailing experience was required. Provided the applicant passed an interview and could raise £14,850 towards their berth over a three-year period, he or she was on for the challenge of a lifetime. Ten vessels would race around the world the wrong way, east to west, against prevailing winds and currents. Each yacht would be crewed by ordinary people who would achieve the extraordinary. Chay, of course, was well qualified to mount this incredible challenge, having become, in 1971, the first man to sail solo and nonstop the wrong way round the world.

The public response to Chay's challenge was swift and enthusiastic. He was inundated with applications from people who had the gleam of adventure in their eyes. He interviewed them one by one and, selected the first batch of 120 people who would take part. Most of the 2,000 or so others who had applied went on to a waiting list for the next Challenge. It wasn't a case of selecting the best. Sometimes the interview lasted only a couple of minutes, and applicants were told immediately whether they had been accepted or not, regardless of their ability or level of fitness. Chay was looking for the right attitude. Training and hard work would take care of the rest.

Many didn't have a clue what they were signing up for. When Jack Gordon Smith, a lettuce farmer, was taken on he thought: 'Great. I'll miss an English winter.' Something we delighted in reminding him of as we later dodged icebergs in the freezing Southern Ocean.

Seventy per cent of those accepted had never sailed in their lives before. On that basis, you could say that the race had little to do with sailing—it was simply the medium through which the crew would realise the challenge of a lifetime. Chay believes that everyone has an element of adventure in them, and it is only that they haven't had the opportunity to develop the relevant skills and knowledge that holds them back.

I read the advertisement for a training skipper with mounting excitement—if ever a job was tailor-made for me it was this one. My own solo round-the-world ambitions were on the back burner for a while, but this was yachting history in the making and I was determined to be a part of it. The race would be a match race: the boats were identical right down to the food, clothing, number of charts and skills on board. It was a race about people and teamwork and embraced every principle I believed in. Unlike many others in the boating world, including the yachting press who voiced doubts as to the wisdom of the venture, I could see no reason why it shouldn't be a roaring success.

I spent ages preparing my CV and was selected for an interview with Chay, who had a reputation for being something of an ogre. I found both him and his vision inspiring. He was no ogre—he was merely brutally honest. He was an ex-paratroop sergeant and spoke in a way I understood and liked. Far better to know where you stand than have to put up with someone who is unable to speak his mind. I felt the interview went well and wasn't surprised to be summoned to a second meeting. However, I was to be disappointed. Chay felt that at twenty-nine, and despite my sail training experience, I was just too young for the job, given that some of the crew were well into their fifties with high-powered business backgrounds and might find working under someone many years their junior difficult to handle. Although I argued my case strongly, I was turned down.

I went back to my boatbuilding course and was patient. I still felt I was the man for the job and was sure that somehow it would work out. A few months later, in August, I received a call asking me if I would consider skippering the Challenge prototype and training vessel during Cowes Week so that Chay could see me at work. The training programme had hit some sort of snag and they were still looking for a skipper. I accepted. Apart from anything else, I was broke and the money was good. It was one of the best week's sailing I have ever had. Here I was skippering a fantastic yacht around the Solent—and at the end of it I was offered the job. Great!

I set out on what was to be one of the most challenging and rewarding three years of my life. My first encounter with the trainee crew was due to start the next morning, and I stayed up all night getting to know the boat and the contents of each locker.

I was eager to establish what these 120 ambitious souls were like. I would then be able to develop a long-term training programme which would aim at getting them working together. They were a delight. For a start, anyone who takes on a new adventure is bound to be a bit special and I found them to be an inspiration. I was to spend many hours over the following months and years with a knowledgeable bunch. I learned something new every day as I chatted during my watch with doctors, fishermen, farmers, solicitors, builders, businessmen and housewives. It was fantastic to be part of such a great family and to watch it mature as each individual found his or her place.

It was a demanding project which called for sacrifices, and placed pressures on both Tracey and me. Once again Tracey's support, encouragement and faith in the project were to prove pivotal—particularly as our second child, Olivia, was born on 1 March 1991, and the Goss family now had two young mouths to feed.

I operated a fourteen-week cycle of six-day courses. Each crew member had to attend one of these courses. Sometimes, if a person was weak in one area or another, then he or she would have to repeat that particular course.

I knew that work time was important to most of them as they were struggling to meet the stage payments of their £14,850 commitment and so I opted to start the courses on a Friday night to cut their time off work to a minimum. I wasn't to spend a weekend with my family for years, stepping ashore for a break from the boat Wednesday afternoon and having Thursday and Friday morning off. And most of this 'free' time was spent writing reports and catching up on the many other aspects of the project.

Chay proved to be a fair but hard taskmaster, and the project seemed to grow as it gained momentum. Still, we were all there because we believed in it.

And so I began to pass on the knowledge of any successful sea passage: that of seamanship. I felt a great responsibility towards the crew. They had placed their lives in our hands, not fully aware of what they were letting themselves in for or the risks that were involved. We had no idea what was waiting for us in the Southern Ocean. I did my best to provide them with the skills and equipment for the task ahead and it was up to them to cope with whatever came their way. I threw myself into a punishing work routine. I often started a training course feeling exhausted, only to find myself uplifted when the crew arrived and filled the boat with their excitement and enthusiasm.

It wasn't long before I realised that I could not stand on the dock and allow them to sail off without me at the end of the training. I had to be with them. I have never asked anyone to do anything that I wasn't prepared to do myself. If I was to train the crew for what lay ahead I needed to know that I would be taking on the thrills and spills shoulder to shoulder with them. Chay understood my feelings and agreed that I could skipper one of the ten boats on the Challenge, and I set to with even greater enthusiasm.

I felt that I was teaching far more than just how to sail a yacht. Knowing how to tie knots and pull sails up and down is only the beginning—it is how you approach problems and assess risks that is important, and these skills only come with experience. My whole training programme was underpinned by attention to safety, which I drummed into my pupils until it came to them as naturally as breathing. All the basics, such as following your safety strop from harness to clip before you undo it to ensure you are not unclipping someone else's, must become automatic and be adhered to come what may, even if you are exhausted, freezing and unable to see or think in the dark and noise of a storm at night. The ocean will work away at the tiniest little chink in the armour. Trusting in yourself and in the integrity of your shipmates will go a long way towards getting you round the world in one piece.

It soon became obvious that what this disparate group of individuals most needed to learn was teamwork; real teamwork that is, rugged and deep-seated enough to last twenty-four hours a day, month after month, rather than a few token hours. When you're thousands of miles from the shore, out of range of assistance and facing everything that nature can throw at you, all you have is each other. You can't opt out. The sea has harsh values which are relentless and non-negotiable.

In those early days, there was the odd individual who seemed to have trouble coming to grips with this idea of pulling their weight. Perhaps it was a company director or a solicitor who had spent so long delegating that they had forgotten how to get on with it themselves. Faced with a simple task, they would stand round with a vague look on their faces as they waited for the job somehow to do itself.

I made it clear that no one was above any task on board and jobs were shared on a rotation basis. Some seemed not to know how to cook even the most basic of meals. I found myself having to pull people back to the galley to clean it again and again, pointing out that, with so many in such a confined space, if the work surfaces were not gleaming the whole crew could go down with a stomach bug. The worst offenders were woken at night and summoned back to the galley to finish the task until they realised that there is only one standard on a well-run boat. Those night calls were most effective.

I remember one chap who, when it was his turn, seemed

incapable of getting down on his knees and cleaning the toilet. On being allocated the task, he made his way down the companionway to the heads and waited until I was doing something else. Then he climbed out of the forehatch, left the boat, and walked away in the hope that someone else would do the job in his absence. I was dumbstruck. I decided that I would throw him off the Challenge if he didn't change his ways. I wasn't worried about the heads, it was his attitude that alarmed me. At sea with a large crew your safety depends on others doing their jobs properly. A simple task left undone can unleash a chain of events that can end up with serious injury and even loss of life.

I found my culprit skulking nearby. I sent him back down to the boat, telling him that he had better give it 'root toot' (make it snappy) as he was now well behind. Half an hour later I found him in the galley with every cupboard open and gear all over the place. I was even more amazed to find that he hadn't even started the heads. His defence was to keep me laughing for days: he couldn't find the bottle of 'root toot' and after the talking-to he had received there was no way he was going to start without it.

There were some frustrating moments but when it came down to it everyone on the Challenge—including my 'root toot' friend— wanted to learn. He eventually developed into a solid crew member, meticulous in all he did.

The lack of experience often showed. There was one occasion when for five days of a six-day course the clement weather had permitted me to back the boat into the marina berth and moor up port side to each evening when we returned. On the sixth day it was blowing a bit and I thought that it would be easier to enter the berth bow first and moor starboard to. We had a few beers and a meal on board and then decided to round off the evening in the pub ashore. Everyone trooped out of the saloon and as I lagged behind to search for my coat I heard a splash and shouts of 'man overboard'. I raced on deck to find one of the crew swimming in the marina off to port. In his experience of boating, you only ever got off a boat on the port side, which he duly did. It was an example of how alien this new environment was to many of the crew.

The interesting thing was the way in which the crew's confidence and aspirations grew as their knowledge increased. To start with they were in awe of the boat and would only tackle a task under close supervision. Their initial ambition was simply to complete a circumnavigation—they didn't really have much idea what the Southern Ocean was all about. They were achievers, all of them, and as their knowledge and sea skills grew so did their aims until, finally, they couldn't wait, not only to take on the Southern Ocean but also to come out of it in first place. It was this spirit that was the catalyst to the whole Challenge.

I broke the training into four phases. The first was an acclimatisation course during which we day-sailed and eased the crew into the basic routines and logistics of life on board. It was also an opportunity for me to get to know them as individuals and for them to feel comfortable with the Challenge, with each other and with me.

I used the first phase of the course—as well as teaching general seamanship, night sailing and so on—to ferret out any problem areas that individuals might have. To this end everyone had to undertake various challenges. For instance, everyone who crewed with me had to reach the top of the mast while the yacht was at sea and under sail. This was a good exercise and built teamwork—the crew had to trust the equipment and their mates, who were on the other end of the rope pulling them up. For many this was a terrifying experience at first. In some cases it took two years of effort to overcome a fear of heights and accomplish the task. Each time they turned up for a course I made them go that little bit further until eventually they triumphed. Those moments of achievement gave me immense satisfaction as I watched them walk away at the end of a course with new-found pride and confidence.

One of the crew I particularly admired was Valerie Elliot. She had twins when she was sixteen years old and had devoted the next twenty or more years of her life to them. By the time she came to us her children had left home and she was a grandmother. Valerie was not very fit or strong and lacked the hardness you need if you are to take on the world's oceans. Her first week on the course was in January and as I walked through the boat explaining life on board—'Always stow your gear; this is your bunk; make sure you use a lee cloth so you don't fall out; here is your life jacket'—I knew that we were in for a real hammering the next day because the pressure was dropping, confirming the force nine to ten winds that had been forecast. Given that we were training for the Southern Ocean, I had a policy of not stopping for anything. I could hardly start a course by saying that it was too rough to go to sea. In any case, many of the crew were keen to cut their teeth on a good gale so that they had some idea of what it was all about.

For a moment, as I chatted to Valerie, I considered staying alongside. But on principle I felt that we had to go out for at least a taste of the action, because to miss it would be counterproductive in the longer term. And so we slipped our mooring and motored from the shelter of the marina, with the clouds flying over Plymouth, driven by fifty-knot winds from the west. We put up the storm jib, put three reefs in the main and, having strapped everything down, including the crew, reached out into the channel, which was a freezing maelstrom of violent seas, spray and gusts.

If anyone was impressed by the conditions, it was me. Most

of the crew were unaware of the dangers and thought it was a hoot as waves swept the boat from end to end. I took them one by one up to the foredeck and introduced them to life in a blow. The freezing temperatures started to bite quickly; the conditions wore them down and after about six hours we put back into Plymouth. The crew were exhausted but wiser for the experience.

That evening, there was a subdued atmosphere on the boat as the realities of the Challenge occupied everyone's mind. If six hours of nasty conditions in British waters fatigued us what would two months in the Southern Ocean do? This was particularly so in the case of Valerie who, by the time we returned, was exhausted and suffering from mild hypothermia. I had to put her in a sleeping bag for three hours, surrounded by warmed-up tins of food wrapped in socks, before she was able to surface for a meal and hot shower. Val dug deep that night and by the morning she had made up her mind. Come what may she was going to see it through. Within six months she was swimming every other day, going to weight training and aerobics classes and running ten miles every Saturday. Sadly, her marriage failed and she was forced to wash dishes at night and take any other jobs she could find to keep up with the payments. Many of the crew rallied round, offering help wherever possible or simply giving moral support. Val completed her training and went on to sail round the world. A remarkable achievement.

At the other end of the spectrum was Mark Lodge, a ceiling fitter from London who had no sailing experience apart from windsurfing. It was obvious from the moment he stepped on board that he was a natural. There was never any doubt that he would be a watch leader. He was to play a major role in getting *Commercial Union* round the world in the 1992–93 Challenge. He went on to skipper *Motorola* into fourth place in the second Challenge, the 1996–97 BT Global Challenge.

If the first phase of training was a series of hard day sails then the second was an even more punishing six-day spell at sea, sailing round and round in circles off Plymouth within a thirteen-mile radius. I wanted to introduce a watch system to the routine of a long passage—without losing the cut and thrust of short, sharp legs. A long and unbroken passage would be as pointless at this stage as teaching someone to drive a car on the motorway, where all you have to do is follow the white line. On this course there was to be no more than a twenty-minute period without a sail or course change, packing it full of practical experience and hard work. I ran it over the winter months. I wanted to knock the romance out of the Challenge right away because it would be a cruel joke indeed for someone to realise as they rounded Cape Horn that it wasn't for them.

For the third phase of the training we made passage from the Solent to the Isles of Scilly or Falmouth. The accent this time was on making good speed and sail-trimming. Everyone took a turn as watch leader—a difficult job at the best of times. It is always tempting to criticise those in charge when things aren't going well, and I hoped that by giving everyone a taste of responsibility it might make them think twice before unfairly criticising those in charge during the race. Watch leaders have a difficult job and they need just as much help and encouragement as everyone else.

The fourth and final phase of the course was interesting in that I wanted to turn the crew's relationship with the boat and the project on its head and see how they reacted. Until now they had always had either me or the mate on deck offering close super-vision; they could always look to us for a steer in the right direc-tion. However, this would not always be the case. Even skippers must sleep and sometimes they need a break from the day-to-day running of the boat so that they can concentrate on tactics. And so on this course I handed responsibility over to the crew, even making them instruct each other in new skills. The best way to learn is to teach.

We started our day at five-thirty in the morning, rowed ashore, went for a three-to four-mile run and ended with some light circuit training. We then cooled off with a swim in the sea before rowing back to the boat for a hearty breakfast and an hour of maintenance. Two of the crew then gave a lecture on their designated subject—be it man overboard, the boat's engine or world weather systems—after which we would put to sea for some punishing sail training, with at times up to thirty spinnaker gybes until we were happy that we had a slick routine. We had a meal at anchor at about nine in the evening and then continued working until one the following morning. An anchor watch ran until five-thirty when the whole process started all over again. It was a hard course, both intellectually and physically, and the crews loved it.

In their 'free' time away from the training boat the crew worked on a fitness programme. Early on in the project we had identified several people who we felt would become mates during the race and we helped them get their Royal Yachting Association Ocean Yachtmaster ticket. There had to be someone on board with the ability to step into the breach should the skipper fall ill or be lost over the side. On top of this, we arranged things so that once the crew for each yacht had been selected they all undertook a specialist course. We had sailmakers, engineers, photographers and riggers. In addition, each vessel had two crew members who had attended a Royal Navy medical course, where they were taught how to stitch up wounds, apply drips and deal with all the other medical problems that might arise during a trip such as ours.

At last the training programme came to an end. The next step was to split the trainees into ten equal teams or crews, taking age, strength and ability into account. We spread the doctors, ensured that each boat had a joker on board, shared out natural leaders and tried to avoid any clashes of personality. We had a cocktail party and the sponsors each pulled their crew out of a hat so that fair play was seen to be done. Just before Christmas I received a call from Chay, who told me which crew would be mine and said that we had Hall & Woodhouse as our sponsor. They are a family-owned Dorset brewery that manufactures Hofbräu Lager under licence in Britain. Our boat would therefore be known as *Hofbräu Lager*. It was an exciting call as it signalled the start of the second phase of training, in which each team had nine months to polish themselves into an efficient racing unit. It would be a critical stage in this race of equals as it would be the only opportunity for us to gain a competitive edge over the opposition. I worked out my long-term strategy with both anticipation and a tinge of regret. Along with the conclusion of the training had come the end of a fascinating period for me and the Challenge family would never be quite the same again now that they were pitted against each other. I had a suspicion at the time that the training would in many ways be harder and more rewarding than the race itself. It certainly provided me with knowledge and experience that would otherwise have been impossible to acquire.

I had my first *Hofbräu* crew meeting in January 1992, in empty accommodation lent to us by the Royal Marines, when I explained how I saw the race being tackled. My team was a good bunch and as the weekend progressed we quickly gelled, thanks to a number of team-building exercises, ranging from dinghy sailing to gym work, a few beers and a lot of talk.

The sponsors and the size of their budget varied enormously. Some were multinationals who had large amounts of money to dish out while others, such as ours, simply didn't have spare resources to throw around. A class system of haves and have-nots developed in the fleet, which was contrary to the original ethos of a race of equals. Many of my crew had put everything into raising their berth fee and had nothing left—to the point where they were unable to purchase decent thermals or sleeping bags. I was adamant that we would either freeze together or be warm together and set up a crew fund through which we planned to raise enough money to ensure that everyone had the required equipment.

While Hall & Woodhouse might not have had a huge budget, they made up for it with spirit and optimism for what we were setting out to do. They were helpful in a multitude of ways. The race had captured the heart of the nation and we found that all sorts of people wanted to help and be involved in some way. We had postcards printed with a picture of *Hofbräu* on the front and details of what we were about on the back, which we sold for £2 each. The purchasers unwittingly did the hard work: they filled in their names and addresses, and we simply returned the cards with a message from Tasmania after we had gone round Cape Horn. The cards were a resounding success. Many people took a handful and sold them on our behalf to friends and family. We also rented a shop in the marina and sold all sorts of items from clothing to posters, mugs to raffle tickets. It took a lot of effort but was well worth it. We made £10,000 in three months and became probably the best kitted-out crew in the fleet. We were certainly the proudest because everything we had was as a result of our own efforts and *Hofbräu* was one of the most well-prepared yachts when we set sail for Southampton.

The race training was hard but enjoyable work. Skippers were in a tricky situation that required a lot of effort and energy in order to keep everyone pulling on the same rope. We had a crew and yet they were our clients; we had a sponsor and yet we worked for Chay; we were responsible for everything and somehow in the middle of all this had to find the time to take sponsors out for hospitality sails day after day. It was a hectic period and because we slept on the boat there was no escape. An endless stream of visitors and crew passed through, all demanding attention.

At the end of the course I gave each crew member his or her specialist area of responsibility and decided to keep my options open as to watch leaders until a later date. Individuals were given jobs that suited their ability—be it a fit young buck in need of the rough and tumble of the foredeck or an older, thinking person on the helm at the back of the boat.

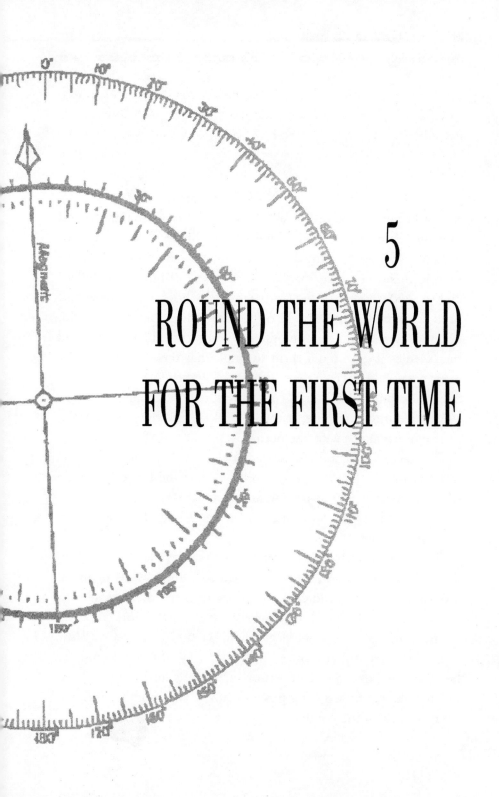

5

ROUND THE WORLD
FOR THE FIRST TIME

The start gun boomed. We were off. Farewell Southampton and England. The British Steel Challenge got under way on 26 September 1992 accompanied by the usual blaze of publicity, the blaring foghorns of the flotilla that ushered us out of the Solent and the good wishes of the British public, whose imagination had been captured by the thought of rookies sailing round the world. The race would take eight months to complete, and as we cleared the Needles it gave me a thrill to think that the next time I saw them we would have circled the globe. The first Atlantic leg from Southampton to Rio passed smoothly for those aboard *Hofbräu*. We settled into a routine, refined our skills and the crew learned to live in harmony with the ocean.

For me, the second leg represented what the Challenge was truly about. At 7,600 nautical miles, it was the longest passage of the race and offered us our first taste of the Southern Ocean and, of course, the notorious, gale-lashed Cape Horn at the tip of South America.

The Southern Ocean is a relentless place. A necklace of deep depressions marches across its surface and huge swells of up to sixty feet high build and circle the globe unchecked. These in turn generate a current which can run as fast as three knots. Add sea temperatures of minus one degree and wind-chill on deck as low as minus thirty degrees; throw in a scattering of icebergs and the fact that the boats and competitors are imprisoned in the grip of this hostile and unforgiving place for up to two months, and you have an idea of the conditions.

After twelve days of pushing south in a competitive drive for the Southern Ocean, we turned right to face a further thirty-eight-day flog from Cape Horn to Hobart, Tasmania. Legion upon legion of waves marched upon us and the wind screamed incessantly in our faces. It was a wild struggle against the elements and I couldn't help being excited by the thought of sailing round the world in the other direction; of feeding off these huge forces instead of constantly fighting against them. The thought put a grin on my face. I would combat the numbing cold of a watch on deck by escaping into my daydreams.

My dreams were banished by a decent blow in the depths of the Southern Ocean. We were halfway between Cape Horn and Tasmania. A loud bang shook the boat followed by a call for 'all hands on deck' and I was jolted from a deep sleep. A surge of adrenalin swept away the cobwebs as I rolled out of my bunk. Someone shouted down the companionway that the forestay had parted. I mentally ran through the problem as I struggled into my oilies. A handful of other boats in the Challenge fleet had suffered the same fate. It was obviously a design fault.

I made way along the foredeck as far forward as I could get. I worked at clearing the mess and started to kick a solution into shape with rigger Mark Steadman at my side. Behind us, of its own accord, the crew was settling into an efficient discipline; a hand was on call with vital equipment; another was relaying messages from halfway down the deck. Down below a fax was being sent off to base; the mother watch was preparing soup and sandwiches to combat the cold, and Mike Kay was on standby in the ship's store. I could call for any item of equipment from a flash light to a jubilee clip and it would be with me in seconds. My crew of rookies had come a long way.

Conditions were not brilliant. *Hofbräu*, despite being such a big, heavy bruiser, was rolling along at a cracking pace under the merest scrap of sail. At forty-two tons it took a lot to push her along so we were amazed to see consistent speeds of fifteen knots on the log as the waves rolled beneath her stern and gave her an effortless shunt.

I set to work on the forestay fitting. I was sitting far forward, my legs over either side of the bow. Without the forestay in my way I had a clear view ahead and it felt as if I was standing on the water. We had a problem. We had to stop the movement of the mast as soon as possible. We couldn't afford to lose it here, and as we struggled away in a controlled frenzy the mast contin-ued to sway with every wave. Suddenly I became conscious of everything going quiet as a huge wave swept in from behind. The helm shouted a high-pitched warning: 'Hold on!' Mark had gone aft to start working on a jury rig and I was on my own. The wall of water was huge and I could feel the heavy boat pause in its headlong rush as it was sucked back into the face of the wave. The stern began to lift and everyone held their breath as the deck became steeper and steeper. It seemed to take an eternity as we rose towards the crest which rumbled its way into the silence that always precedes a big wave. I knew that one of my best helms was at the wheel and could only hope that he would be able to keep us in a straight line. There was nothing I could do. I was in a vulnerable position and would be in deep shit if he lost it.

The bow settled as the crest bore down. I felt the water reach my feet, my knees, my waist and still there was no movement. I was holding on to the nasty end of a forty-two-ton torpedo. A torpedo that was being primed for the most monumental launch. The stern rose higher above my head; the bow seemed to have lost all lift as it was pressed ever further into the water. There was an amazing feeling of power as the wave gathered under the hull—as if an avalanche were about to lose its precarious grip on all that pent-up energy and release it in an agonising split-second.

The moment had come. She started to move, water tugging at my legs, pulling me. A bow wave formed around my chest and when it came the acceleration was frightening. I was in the palm of pure energy. Nothing could be done. I was looking down the front of the biggest wave I had ever seen. I was on my own. I was close to it. It was my wave. Big, grey, mean and so steep that spume fell down its face. It had a fabulous and evil beauty. A whoop of wild exhilaration rose up from my clenched guts and, apart from thinking, 'Fuck me,' I wondered how it would be to return one day and sail single-handed on the lightest, fastest, most high-tech boat I could muster. I wanted to surf down that bastard to see how fast I could travel and discover what would happen at the bottom.

It was a private moment that passed unnoticed by the rest of the crew. The wave decided to let us off as it rolled under the boat and carried its immense energy off into the infinity of the Southern Ocean, searching for something else upon which to vent itself. I watched its back retreat into the oblivion of rain and spray and returned to the job in hand. Thinking about that glimpse, that moment of truth which had re-emphasised my commitment to do a single-handed, round-the-world race, I knew that it could no longer be put to one side. I might just as well get on with the project. I would never be satisfied until it was done. It was like an itch that comes and goes but never disappears completely.

I was in the very arena in which such a race would be fought and could picture the kind of boat, skills and attitude that would be needed. The yacht would have to be very fast and light on the tiller and have the grace to outrun the crushing energy of those great waves, even under autopilot and with me asleep below. It also needed to be reliable, easy to sail, and capable of looking after me should I be ill or injured. I was well aware of the harsh reality of these ocean races: the 1992–93 Vendée Globe, the second in the series, had started just before we reached Cape Horn and I had been following its progress as closely as possible. Considered by many to be the world's toughest yacht race, the Vendée—a nonstop, single-handed circumnavigation—attracts only the hardiest of skippers. I had paid particular attention to Nigel Burgess and Alan Wynne Thomas, who were both flying the flag for Britain. The day after they started we received the sobering news that Nigel had lost his life in a vicious storm in the Bay of Biscay. I had met Nigel and had had the pleasure of getting to know him as a fellow competitor in the 1988 Transat. He was both a gentleman and a kindred spirit. My heart went out to his wife and young family.

The crew of *Hofbräu* excelled themselves, but it was Brian Lister who set the real example. Halfway through the pre-race training he had confessed to a white lie. He was in fact sixty-one years old—one year over the official age limit for entrants—and had recently had a heart bypass operation. He had begged that we judge him on what we had seen to date. Chay decided that since we liked him he ought to stay—after all he didn't choose his date of birth. Brian completed the training and went on to be a tower of strength and wisdom as one of my crew.

Brian was brilliant at the wheel, and always kept the worst off the bow when we were making a sail change. I felt safe when the boat was in his hands. During a particularly bad blow we had had a few problems on deck and Andy Hindley and I had made our way forward to sort out the mess. It must have been blowing up to sixty knots; it was impossible to stand and we were forced to crawl on our hands and knees. As we reached the mast, I looked up to see as steep a wall of water as ever I have witnessed. I shouted a warning to Andy. The wave was too big to avoid. Brian had run out of options and we huddled on the deck, bracing ourselves for the worst. The boat staggered on impact; her struggle to stay level was short lived as she was overwhelmed and lay flat on her side. In the din, clinging to the near-vertical deck, we were dimly aware of the wave crashing into the cockpit. The boat shook with the blow and as the wave roared on we knew instinctively that Brian must have been carried away. It was a chilling moment. I struggled to my feet and, with the words 'man overboard' screaming through my brain, I mentally ran through a pick-up routine which would undoubtedly prove to be futile; a skipper's worst nightmare. The water started to settle and we watched the mainsail emerge from the water. The boom followed. Our eyes were on the spot where Brian should have been. We willed the impossible. The boat struggled up for air. The steering position slowly opened up and a shadowy figure became discernible through the spray. We were euphoric as Brian's little red hat emerged from the foam, shortly to be followed by his hands working furiously on the wheel. He gave us his little smile, stuck his thumb up and carried on steering as if nothing had happened. That's Brian.

Oddly enough, we relished an upset when it came along. It presented a break from the grinding routine. It was during these times that people rose above themselves and excelled against the odds. During long spells the oppressive grey stretches of the Southern Ocean ground the crew down. At times it seemed that all life had to offer was freezing temperatures, bone-jarring motion, endless sail changes and cramped living conditions. Petty frustrations exploded over the most ridiculous issues. The biggest rows during the race were over the fair distribution of ginger-nut biscuits and the sharing out, believe it or not, of M&M sweets. The trick was not to take life too seriously, always see the funny side and never let something brew up until it got out of proportion. We had a team talk every night when we discussed tactics and any other issues, however insignificant they might seem.

During the Southern Ocean leg we had had our share of injuries and at one point became very short-handed. Our mate Jack Gordon Smith was swept along the deck by a big wave and broke his ribs down one side in six places. He was in considerable discomfort and strapped up in his bunk as the boat crashed on to windward. He was out of action right up to Hobart. Sailmaker Becky Slater was effectively removed from the watch system while she struggled to repair a spinnaker which had gone just before Cape Horn. She performed a gargantuan task in the most appalling conditions. At one point I had four of the ten out of the system and yet we still managed to keep the boat going flat out.

We flogged our way on towards Tasmania, nursing our ailing mast every inch of the way. We had managed to come up with a jury rig, which unfortunately parted a few days later. A crack ran halfway round the mast at deck level. It took all our imagination and energy to hold it together with a spider's web of rope, and wedges improvised from timber cut from the furniture below. We crossed the line in third place, a credit to the crew's dedication and hard work. It was a satisfying end to an amazing leg in which we had pulled through the Southern Ocean at its most awe-inspiring and, despite many setbacks.

The finish was a euphoric moment as we crossed the line off Hobart on 5 January 1993. The city gave us an enthusiastic welcome and the party that night was as wild as might be expected. It takes more than a few beers to let off steam after what we'd been through and we went at it with a vengeance. The hospitality was marvellous. Each boat was adopted by a local company and we were royally looked after by the Meadowbank vineyard.

The highlight for me was that Tracey and the children were able to fly out for a three-week break. We rented a flat and enjoyed a home-from-home away from the madding crowd. We were overwhelmed by the support and thoughtful attention, which was summed up by a surprise gift of a basket of toys on our doorstep to welcome the kids from the airport.

I was still following the Vendée as closely as I could and was concerned for Alan Wynne Thomas, who had got into trouble in the Southern Ocean. Details were scant as we tracked his course towards Tasmania and eventual retirement from the race. It transpired that a big wave had knocked his yacht down while he was asleep in his bunk, and slammed him against one of the structural frames. He drifted in and out of consciousness. At one point he came to with his face submerged in the bilges. He was lucky to survive. When he eventually arrived in Hobart an x-ray showed that he had broken all his ribs down one side in a total of seventeen places. Many would not have got through such an ordeal, let alone have managed to sail the equivalent of a transatlantic passage to safety.

The look in Alan's eyes was of pain, exhaustion and the crushing disappointment of having had to retire from the race. I did a few odd jobs around his boat as he recovered in hospital and it made me think long and hard about the design of my own boat for a single-hander. Alan's boat had obviously been picked up and hurled on her side—there was gear all over the place and a lot of damage on deck. I needed to ensure that my accommodation was compact so that if the same fate befell my boat I wouldn't be injured in the process. Gear must be kept to an absolute minimum and spares should be able to double up across a number of areas. Above all, I wanted a boat that would see it through to the end. I didn't want to face the disappointment that Alan, through no fault of his own, was having to cope with.

In the two Vendées so far, the red ensign of Britain had been thwarted. I made up my mind that I would be in the next and third Vendée in 1996 and the red ensign would cross the finish line.

Although we were in Hobart for six weeks, it seemed to pass
in the blinking of an eye what with Tracey and the kids being
there, keeping on top of the refit and making so many new
friends. Strangers visited *Hofbräu* and offered the crew holidays
and the loan of cars and boats. One couple, who heard that we
had missed the festive season, cooked up a full Christmas lunch
with all the trimmings. Tasmania captured our hearts.

It wasn't long before the start gun fired again and we were off
on what was to prove the hardest leg of the race, from Hobart
to Cape Town 5,600 miles away. Sailing the Southern Ocean to
windward had lost its magic. It was cold, rough, the wind was
consistently stronger and the equipment was starting to feel the
pace. However, it was a good leg for us and we were delighted
to finish in second place. A particularly bad blow was encountered
west of the Kerguelen Islands in the Indian Ocean. It inflicted a
lot of damage in the mountainous and unpredictable seas. Gusts
of up to seventy knots were recorded and we continued to battle
away at a creditable nine knots to windward, leaping off the top
of waves and plunging into the troughs with a bone-jarring crash.

On one occasion, despite the conditions that raged outside, we
wedged ourselves round the radio to pick up the fleet positions,
fretting about the odd mile lost or gained. Watch-leader Andy
Hindley stuck his head down the hatch to say that we ought to
tack because the wind was backing. I had to smile. Here we were,
a bunch of so-called amateurs, tacking on the headers in a force
twelve storm and our main concern was making up a few miles
in a race. If that isn't an example of man's capacity for anything,
then I don't know what is.

That night a wave swept the boat with such ferocity that it
bent the stanchions and one of the spinnaker poles resting in its
stowage. The boat took a frightful pounding and for the first and
only time during the race I considered easing up. Indeed, the Ant-

arctic survey vessel *Discovery*, which was in the area, broadcast over the radio to say that they were hove to and had just recorded their biggest wave ever at 110ft.

For many of us, Cape Town marked the end of the adventure and, although the race was as intense as ever, the last leg home seemed an anticlimax to those of us who had come for the challenge. Much time was spent on the side deck mulling over the future while the reality of the race coming to an end started to sink in. Every waking thought for the last few years had been driven by this one purpose and it would be difficult to find something to take its place. I was keen to get home and have more time with Tracey and the children. It felt an age since we had said goodbye to each other in Hobart and I needed a break.

The home leg was our worst from the point of view of speed because we were caught in a twenty-four-hour windless weather system as we desperately tried to cross the doldrums. It was in its way the hardest part of the race as we sat, windless, drifting in the merciless heat, and watched the chance of an overall win slip away. The sails mocked us as, hour upon hour, they relentlessly slatted back and forth in the large and confused swell. Ours had been a good, solid campaign until then, and we had left Cape Town full of optimism. We had had a realistic chance of winning the leg and taking the overall prize. We had worked hard and felt we deserved better luck.

In my view it was our finest hour as a crew. It is easy to be good when you are on top, the true test of a team is what happens when you are down. Everyone worked through their disappointment and accepted the situation. By the time the wind came back, we were 220 nautical miles behind the leaders. Nevertheless, we stuck to our pledge to sail *Hofbräu* round the world as fast as we possibly could. Whatever the final result, minutes still mattered and, thanks to a united effort, we had pulled back to within sixty miles of the leaders by the finish. Although it was our worst leg, at seventh place, I felt it was probably our best, given the windless stretch, and it made our overall position of third place even sweeter. We crossed the line on 23 May 1993 fulfilling everything that we had set out to achieve. Chay's dream had been made reality and I still feel privileged to have helped put it together and, to have seen it through to the end.

I am often approached by budding circumnavigators who ask my advice about getting started. Among other things, I recommend that they consider one of Chay's races as an introduction to the world of ocean sailing. There is no finer apprenticeship. I was lucky to have performed a key role in a ground-breaking project as it had evolved, including the long-term planning, logistics and publicity. I mentally applied the lessons learned to the loosely framed plan on the Vendée Globe that was by now kicking about at the back of my mind.

The race had given me a chance to taste the Southern Ocean and knock the myth out of it. It really was 'only wind and water', just as I had imagined it to be. With this new knowledge I could see myself returning to it with a much more aggressive approach. It is one of the last great wildernesses and being there makes me feel incredibly alive.

6

THE ROAD NOT TAKEN

Two roads diverged in a yellow wood,
And sorry I could not travel both
And be one traveller, long I stood
And looked down one as far as I could
To where it bent in the undergrowth;

Then took the other, as just as fair,
And having perhaps the better claim,
Because it was grassy and wanted wear;
Though as for that, the passing there
Had worn them really about the same,

And both that morning equally lay
In leaves no step had trodden black.
Oh, I kept the first for another day!
Yet knowing how way leads on to way,
I doubted if I should ever come back.

I shall be telling this with a sigh
Somewhere, ages and ages hence:
Two roads diverged in a wood, and I
I took the one less travelled by,
And that has made all the difference.

Robert Frost

Back in England I stepped ashore with the impression that people were listening to me but not really hearing—the usual feeling after a long time at sea—and, with the British Steel Challenge over, I felt displaced for quite some time. Tracey and I had spent all the family savings on the Hobart holiday and the real world beckoned mercilessly in the form of the mortgage and a thousand other bills. I badly needed to make some money and so, within a couple of weeks, I was off again—this time heading up a five-boat entry in the Tall Ships race from Newcastle to Bergen in Norway, which was to take me away for a further seven weeks. Meanwhile, Chay, delighted with the success of the first, launched the next Challenge race campaign—which this time would be known as the BT (British Telecom) Global Challenge—and as soon as I returned from Norway I was plunged into the preparations for the new crew's training programme.

I felt I had more to offer this time and I was keen to take on the training again. I was also concerned that the new crew might be lulled into a false sense of security due to the success of the first race and the immense amount of publicity that it had generated. We had all been very lucky in the Southern Ocean and I felt obliged to ensure that the new crew didn't treat it lightly. Unfortunately, in the eyes of many of them the main objective was to gain a good result—getting round the course was almost taken for granted. It was interesting to see how this new attitude attracted a different kind of person. I refined the original training programme and recruited Andy Hindley, who had excelled on

Hofbräu and was by now an extremely competent sailor and good friend, to act as mate.

Before the start of the first Challenge race Chay had taken me aside and said that he would be looking for someone to fill his shoes eventually and that I was in with a chance. At first it appealed to me, for it would be an exciting job and offered a future in sailing without the usual hand-to-mouth existence. This latter point was particularly attractive as my family could certainly use some security. There was just one snag: as the Challenge business grew, so it lost its intimacy and the feeling that I was making a difference slowly eroded. I had been promoted from training manager to a shore-based job where I was responsible for coordinating the many and complex programmes for all the boats—a role that wasn't really my cup of tea. However hard I tried, I just couldn't become the corporate type. All the same I found myself in the middle of office politics, where people jockeyed for power and where the most mundane things, such as job titles, were immensely important. This, for someone who had just come back from battling through the Southern Ocean, not caring what his title was but just wanting to get the job done, was very tiresome. I had expected to find more teamwork, with everyone pulling together to improve things. It seemed as though I spent the next few months sitting at my desk gazing out the window, thinking about the Vendée—and looking down that big wave.

Our third child, Eliot, was born on 24 June 1994. The Goss household now numbered five. I was in a quandary: on the one hand, here I was with a great future ahead; I was at home every evening with Tracey and our children and was even beginning to get weekends off. On the other hand, the job was strangling the life out of me—and the Vendée out of my life.

It was time to act. As soon as I could I asked Adrian Thompson to come up with a preliminary design. We discussed my thoughts in the light of my Southern Ocean experiences and looked at both fifty-and sixty-foot options so that we could get a handle on relative performances and costs. I still held the view that a smaller and lighter option had merit. While Adrian worked on the design, I addressed the problem of getting enough money coming in to put food on the table. I didn't want to leave Chay shorthanded during the sailing season and so I decided to see my job through to the end of the summer. Meanwhile I would set up a stand-alone business in my spare time that would support me while I sought sponsorship.

Now that I had decided to go it alone I needed a steady income as well as sponsorship, and it dawned on me that there was a way to combine the two. Thanks to the British Steel Challenge, I was now being asked to give motivational, leadership and team-work presentations. The fee could be as high as £500. It was perfect. I arranged sponsorship meetings around the presentations and each time I stood before a group of businessmen I was also addressing a potential sponsor. I never failed to plug the Vendée. I was also asked to run team-building sailing courses, and to arrange corporate hospitality days, where I chartered a yacht and took a group of business people for a sail.

Finances were tight but I felt I had enough potential business in place to justify the gamble without too much risk to the family. Will Stephens, one of the crew for the BT Global Challenge and an accountant, very kindly offered to do my books for me. Tony, my father-in-law, built an office in the garage so that my work wouldn't invade the house. Pete Calvin and his business partner Steve Whittell supplied a computer loaded with all the software that I could wish for. Pete and his brother Dave had signed up for the Challenge because they wanted to follow in the steps of their older brother Mike, a sports reporter who worked for the *Daily Telegraph*. Mike had joined *Hofbräu* for the race from Rio to home and had written some gripping stuff. They were all to prove indispensable friends and allies of the Vendée project. And once again Lou Lou Rendal helped out with a proposal. My plan began to take shape.

Perhaps it was all going too well. However, life had a couple of nasty surprises up its sleeve. The first came along when a business tycoon contacted me to say that he wanted to learn to sail single-handed as he had an ambition to do some long-distance solo voyaging. Fine, I thought. I could involve him in my own project as it developed and eventually take him on a transatlantic passage before setting him on his way. It wasn't a commitment to be undertaken lightly, so I suggested we meet and talk further, which we did. His credentials seemed good and he was keen. I was impressed by the chap and I agreed to take him on when my project was properly under way.

He contacted me again a week later, bubbling with enthusiasm. He wanted to go even further by helping to kick-start the Vendée programme. He proposed that we set up a joint company in which he would invest £100,000. We would each hold fifty per cent of the shares, he said. Not only would he get his training, but he reckoned he could smell a healthy profit at the end of it all. He also said that he had spoken to a number of his contacts and was confident that they would supply additional sponsorship. It meant that I could soon leap into my venture full time. I agreed. The lawyers were instructed, and it seemed that we were on the way.

At the same time as the businessman appeared on the scene, I was also approached by a company who wanted to set up a supporters' club. The club was to be a central point around which their hundred or so clients would rally, each contributing £1,000. The company saw the scheme acting as a catalyst for business between them all. In fact, they said, they had already operated a similar club which had been extremely successful. All I had to do in return was plaster loads of names on the finished boat, give a few talks to the club and send back updates to them during the race. For £100,000, it seemed a good deal. We met and agreed on the details. The Vendée drew closer.

It was time to say goodbye to Chay and the British Steel Challenge. As I wrote my letter of resignation, I could feel a great weight lifting from my shoulders. I realised how unhappy working in an office had made me feel. All the same, my time with the Challenge had been fantastic and I owed Chay a great deal. Chay, if a little miffed, was very supportive. He thought I was mad but understood what I wanted to do—in a similar situation he would have done exactly the same. I was owed a month's leave and he proposed that I take it immediately so that I could consolidate my first step. He offered me the use of his office facilities if I needed them and he would help out with a bit of work here and there to keep me going during the lean periods.

Chay's single-minded determination is often perceived as rudeness. He can be as grumpy as hell and yet when you have worked with him for a while there is no hiding the generous and open character that lurks behind the façade. He has done more for sailing than any other person I know.

I headed for home full of excitement. I was once again in charge of my own destiny and, as hard as it might become, I would see it through to the end. Tracey and I treated ourselves to a bottle of wine that night to celebrate—I was out on my own at last.

My priority during that first month was to get as much presentation and hospitality sailing work as possible, cement the deal with the businessman and also launch the supporters' club. I began to feel a little uneasy about the tycoon—each time we spoke on the phone, the terms of our agreement seemed to change slightly and his enthusiasm seemed to be dwindling. Added to this, the company which wanted to start the club was beginning to express doubts. I became nervous but had no choice but to plough on.

Adrian Thompson suggested that Gary Venning was the man to build the boat. I contacted Gary, a mildly spoken West Countryman with a sharp wit. I explained my ambitions, and was realistic about the fact that we would possibly have to start construction without sufficient funds to complete the boat. Gary asked a lot of perceptive questions, accepted the financial realities of the project and agreed to do the job. Despite having helped build many top boats, this would be the first he could call his own. He told me he had been waiting for a challenge like this one. When we parted that day I promised to let him know the expected start date. He was to prove a very patient man.

My month's leave was now up and still the two big sponsor schemes were not in place. I was having misgivings as my last pay cheque came and went. And then the bombshell. The businessman phoned me and, to my astonishment, told me that the deal was off. I have no idea why he changed his mind. To this day I am at a loss to know why he pulled out.

The next blow came when the company behind the supporters' club idea, despite having reassured me verbally, also pulled out. No reason was offered apart from an excuse about the timing not being right. It floored any chance of the boat's construction in the foreseeable future and underlined what I had already come to believe: business talk is just that, talk. Nothing is fact until a signature is on the dotted line. If anything fuelled my resolve it was these two instances. I might not piss down the businessman's legs if his feet were on fire but I will always be grateful for the lessons these two disappointments taught me.

My whole strategy had hinged on the promised funds. Our

savings had been spent on the project and a mortgage payment was due. I was furious with myself for having trusted someone so blindly and vowed never again to allow myself to be so vulnerable. Tracey and I sat down for a team talk. This was war: we would bloody well put a British entry in the Vendée Globe, whatever it took. This would be my last shot at the damned thing and if I failed I would not set foot on a yacht again, let alone think about single-handed, round-the-world events. Everything was at stake; even my love of the sea was in the balance.

The battle commenced. We sold the car, cancelled payments into the only pension scheme we had, sent back the television set so that we needn't buy a licence, and Tracey once more went to work at the post office. I rolled out of bed early and worked late into the night seven days a week. At one point, when I was desperate, a cheque for £1,500 arrived from Pete Calvin and Steve Whittell with a note saying: 'Thought this might come in handy. Keep it up, mate. We're right behind you.' Dave Calvin was also there during the dark hours; he would shove a roll of banknotes into my pocket, 'to feed the kids', when we met. It was one of the grimmest times of my life and yet there are many fond memories, thanks to those who stood by us.

Gary Venning patiently accepted the inevitable delay to the construction start date. Adrian Thompson was as supportive as ever; he never lost hope and told me not to worry about design fees. He just wanted to see me do the race. The selflessness of all these people strengthened my own determination to pull it off.

It was a daily struggle to keep at least a token momentum to the project. Work trickled in and I began to travel the country, giving talks wherever I could and, finding that one thing led to another, generally picking up a little extra work as a result. It might be another talk, or perhaps a hospitality day later in the year. My travel expenses were usually paid for so I tried to set up meetings with companies in the same area either side of the talk to save money. Staying in a hotel or bed and breakfast on these extra nights away was out of the question, given the state of our finances, so I spent many a night sleeping on railway platforms. When morning came I would have a quick wash in what was always a cold and smelly public toilet before getting back out into the corporate jungle. On one occasion I was so broke that, apart from some biscuits, I didn't eat for two days. Whenever I felt like a treat, such as a newspaper or a bar of chocolate, I would stop and think of the project. The need for a treat would soon go away.

Slowly things improved and in 1995 I began to do some work with the BT Global Challenge. This was mainly thanks to Kim Fitzsimmons, who worked for BT and had become a good friend. She had organised a phone and fax machine for my office in the garage and was forever plugging my ambitions and suggesting people who might be worth following up. She bubbled with enthusiasm—and if anyone held the BT Global Challenge together it was Kim. She seemed to work an eighteen-hour day. On many occasions I would call in the early hours with the intention of leaving a message on her answering machine, only to have her pick up the phone—on one occasion at 3 a.m.

By the end of the year I was able to start saving—albeit small amounts—towards the boat. I was also able to take a small wage out of the company. It was sorely needed. We were lucky to have Tracey's mother Jean on our side. She is a postwoman whose working day starts at 4.30 a.m. with a hard slog on her round come wind or rain. Despite this she would come to our house and babysit for three afternoons a week so that Tracey could go to work. Without this practical help, and her unstinting support whenever we needed an extra day here and there, we would never have managed.

Each time I had a meeting with a potential sponsor I told them about the other goodies I had on offer: talks, days on board a yacht, and so on. I was back to the same old sponsorship grind, with the target of bashing out at least one sponsorship package every day. I chartered yachts for corporate hospitality, which I skippered myself. I often used *Maiden*—the boat sailed round the world by Tracy Edwards and her female crew—and ran her out of the same marina as the BT Global Challenge so that I could juggle the day's sailing and the talks together. Nick Booth—a professional skipper and a good buddy—acted as mate and, amongst other things, greeted the guests on their arrival with a drink and a briefing on safety. I would give my morning talk to the BT Global Challenge guests in the meantime, and sprint down to Nick as soon as I could get away, untying *Maiden* as I jumped aboard. The day's sail would conclude at about 6 p.m. I would then be off to give an evening talk or to try and catch up with my mail and bash out a few more proposals. On one occasion when I had a talk in Birmingham, I ran from the boat, just made it in time for pudding, had them rolling round the aisles with a few funnies and eventually got away at about 1 a.m. An hour's sleep in the car, a quick shower in the marina—and a similar day started all over again.

That year I was asked by the Rover car company to run a three-day team-building course for twenty-five people. While I was working out the details, another company, 3M, made a similar request. The problem was that they both wanted the event to be on the same date. I proposed that I run a joint course in the form of a regatta centred at Cowes on the Isle of Wight. I was determined not to lose the business because it would represent a major financial contribution to my Vendée project.

The companies agreed to the idea. Me and my big mouth. I now had a major event to organise on my own, as well as keeping up with everything else. I chartered eight boats from Sunsail, Musto supplied the clothing, and I recruited some skipper mates. I had a manic time trying to keep up with all the details, from prizes to insurance, arranging artwork for logos on the clothing to establishing individuals' sizes for oilies and so on.

In the middle of all this I flew over to the Isle of Man, where Adrian Thompson lives, for a final design meeting with him. He was, as ever, an inspiration. We decided that the only way to go was to have a swing keel. Until then most boats in open events such as the Vendée carried water ballast to replace the crew, who on a racing boat would normally be sitting on the windward rail. At times this meant pumping up to four tons of water to windward. We felt it was illogical to build a light structure and then pump a load of water into it. If we could hydraulically swing the keel to windward we would have the power and stability of a water-ballasted boat without the penalty of the weight. It would be breaking new ground.

We decided to, in addition, introduce asymmetric dagger boards to improve the boat's upwind performance. This proved to be a master stroke on Adrian's part. We also looked at the merits of a fifty-foot boat over a sixty-footer and decided to opt for a fifty because, being much lighter, it would be more efficient in that it would make best use of its most limited resource: the crew. In fact, the weight factor was so significant that I decided against a roller furling system for the headsails and went for hanked-on sails instead. This would make for harder work, but would reduce the weight of the rig and at the same time give me a spare set of sails below—a crucial ingredient in an endurance race such as the Vendée.

An additional factor in deciding on a fifty-footer was that a new sixty would have cost £200,000 more to put in the water— given my budgetary constraints this meant either a blistering new fifty or a second-hand sixty. There was no choice, particularly as we felt that we had a chance to pull off victory in a fifty. 'Just design the fastest boat possible,' I said to Adrian. 'Finding the money to build it is my problem.' I told him that speed should be his guiding light, and not to worry about accommodation or creature comforts. I went back to the mainland and the Rover/ 3M regatta feeling optimistic and excited about the Vendée.

The day before the regatta I had to talk at a conference in Leeds, which would pay an amazing £1,000. As soon as I could get away I drove back to Southampton like the wind, ran into a supermarket and bought food for sixty people. The next day was full of frantic preparation as we signed the boats over and had a skippers' briefing. The 3M party were the first to arrive and, having briefed them, we handed them over to their skippers and bedded them down for the night. Next the crew from Rover arrived and we went through the same procedure a second time. I flitted from one group to the other trying to make it all work.

The following morning ushered in torrential rain and a force seven blow right on the nose. Conditions were bad but the course had a tight schedule and I had no choice but to follow it. The crew were pretty amazing: it was cold, wet, many were seasick, and yet they still managed to fight their way through it. They may not have particularly enjoyed it at the time, but they certainly felt good about the achievement once they were alongside for the night. As for the prospect of repeating the experience the next day, many were actually considering jumping ship. I gave a pep talk that night and, buoyed up by a bellyful of beer and an excellent weather forecast, we fell into our bunks and slept like the dead.

I looked out of the hatch with some trepidation the next morning to find a wonderful day. Someone was on my side after all. The regatta turned out to be a resounding success. I paid the lads and leapt into the car to drive to Southampton. That same night I had another course starting on an eighty-five-footer—we were to set sail on the tide and push off for four days of hard offshore sailing. I could hardly carry my bag down the pontoon, let alone find the energy for a course. I was so tired at the end of the sail that I had to stop three times at the side of the road to sleep during the drive home to Plymouth. I walked through the door knowing that by the end of the next day I would have to have cleared up my mail and posted a further eight proposals if I was to keep up with my sponsorship target.

I decided at this point to set up a limited company as a vehicle to run the campaign. I needed a steady income and work in place so that I didn't always have to start from scratch. I wanted a central rallying point which marshalled all the expertise that built up during each campaign, and prevented it from slipping away once the race was over. It would be great if sponsors could roll from one campaign to the next, so that the experienced team who worked with me on one project would simply turn its attention to the next rather than being disbanded. I was also keen to improve the lot of Gary and the lads—here were some of the best boatbuilders in the country and as soon as the vessel was out of the build shed door they would have to go back to picking up work wherever they could, very often outside boatbuilding itself.

With Will Stephens's help I established Maritime Challenges Limited, and was immediately confronted with a new and often frustrating world. I didn't even know what a purchase order was. Before putting my first invoice in the post I checked it three times, phoned Will to ensure I had got the Value Added Tax right, and posted it with some trepidation. Tracey and I joked that the Vendée would be a holiday after this punishing schedule.

Aqua Quorum takes to the water in ideal conditions

Above left Sailing my first yellow boat in Thailand, aged about six

Above Learning the ropes from my father at our local sailing club, Torpoint Mosquito

Left I joined the Royal Marines at eighteen and loved every minute of it

Marrying Tracey was the best thing I ever did: our wedding on 4 July 1987

Setting out in *Sarie Marais* with Chris Johnson in 1986

Cornish Meadow was my first full project: the 1988 Carlsberg single-handed transatlantic race

The British Steel Challenge 1992–93. Guess who's driving? The ten crew members are hidden under the breaking wave

Later, we spot our first iceberg in the Southern Ocean

Hofbraü on the 1992–93 British Steel Challenge with Cape Horn in the background...

...a triumphant Brian Lister (left) crosses the line at sixty-two years old. He made us all feel humble

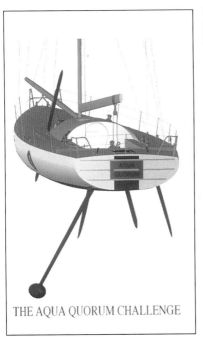

THE AQUA QUORUM CHALLENGE

The computer-generated design for *Aqua Quorum* showing the revolutionary swing keel on maximum power

Working with Adrian Thompson, *Aqua Quorum*'s designer

The plug for the boat was completed in December 1995. At one time, that seemed as far as we'd ever be able to go

I made frequent visits to the build shed as I needed to know the boat inside out

A cabinful of electronic equipment

Some of the two tons of lead for the keel donated by local friends

My parents sealing my food for the Vendée in watertight packs

Some of the build team pose in front of the boat: l to r: me, Alun Strickland, Gary Venning, Keith Fennel, Nick Booth

Aqua Quorum is lowered into the water. Before any fittings were added, she could be picked up by six people

Joanna Lumley made our day when she named the boat at London's St Katharine's docks in March 1996

7
BEGIN IT NOW

*Until one is committed, there is hesitancy,
the chance to draw back, always
ineffectiveness.*

*Concerning all acts of initiative (and
creation), there is one element of truth, the
ignorance of which kills countless ideas and
splendid plans – that moment one commits
oneself, then providence moves all.*

*All sorts of things occur to help one that
would never otherwise have occurred. A
whole stream of events issues from the
decision, raising in one's favour all manner
of unseen incidents and meetings and
material assistance which no man would
have dreamed could have come his way.*

*Whatever you can do or dream you can,
begin it. Boldness has genius, power and
magic in it.*

Begin it now.

Goethe

I had saved the princely sum of £7,000. It was just enough to build the wooden plug for the boat and I gave a relieved Gary the green light. It was November 1995, and he had been growing concerned that time was running out if he was to be ready for the Vendée. He laughed when I told him that if I didn't manage to raise any more cash we would have to call the whole thing off, have a plug-burning party and dance round the bonfire. Suddenly I wasn't just another dreamer walking round with a proposal. Things were really happening.

Once again the Royal Marines – this time in the shape of Major John Spencer, who has played a generous and supportive role in all that I have done – came to my rescue by lending us a building in which to work. Composite boats are exciting to build because, thanks to the wooden plug, you very quickly see the shape of the vessel. A one-off design such as ours begins with the production of a male plug. During construction a laser sight is used to check that it is true. It is then covered with a Teflon skin which, much like a nonstick frying pan, offers a form upon which the 'real' boat can be laid up in resin and composites. Once the resin and laminates of carbon fibres and Kevlar have been applied they can be cured in a heat tent, safe in the knowledge that the Teflon will allow the hull to be released from the plug without sticking. Once cured, the plug is chopped up from within the finished hull to leave what is known as a monocoque structure. It is very light and immensely strong, thanks to having a rounded shape and no joins. Amazingly, six burly men could lift the 50ft-long bare hull.

But all that was in the future. Meanwhile, Gary and I stood quietly in the middle of the large, dusty and very quiet building. It was hard to know where to start, difficult to imagine anything taking shape there. The weight was mainly on Gary's shoulders; he would have to take that empty space and fill it with one of the world's most technologically advanced boats. All he had to hand was enough cash to build the wooden plug and my blind faith that somehow I would raise the rest of the money as we progressed. We found a couple of brooms and set to cleaning the place. With each sweep of the broom thoughts and ideas seemed to gel as we slowly formed a plan of action. One of the first things we did was to find out where the kettle was for the first of many cups of tea that would be drunk over the coming months. Time spent in thought over a cuppa is seldom wasted.

We needed a hard-working and enthusiastic hand to help build the plug. To our great good fortune, Alun Strickland, a school friend of Gary's, decided to take the post. Alun came on board out of a real interest in boatbuilding – it certainly wasn't for the money as we were all on a minimum wage. He proved a quick learner and could turn his hand to anything. He is also one of those rare people who can work for hour upon hour without complaint and will always see a job through to the end. He was later to discover that he had an allergy to the resins used in the hull but he refused to give in to it. He borrowed a full NBC (Nuclear, Biological and Chemical) suit to protect himself and carried on working.

The build shed was perfect for the job. It had been a service bay so it was already set up as a workshop. We painted the floor, borrowed a laser sight and took delivery of the plug materials. We were ready for the off and Gary started to construct the plug, hoping to finish it by early January. I wanted a picture to take to the Earls Court Boat Show, visual proof of positive progress to show the outside world.

We couldn't simply build a boat, bung it in the water and expect it to deliver the goods without a decent work-up. Apart from anything the boat was very radical and it would take a while for me to get the best out of her. I decided to use the 1996 Europe 1 Single-handed Transatlantic Race as my training run. It would be the perfect test as it promised to be tough on both boats and competitors as they flogged to windward in the North Atlantic. It made sense: I would have a competitive fleet to cut my teeth on, the race started in my home port of Plymouth, and, after having sailed back, I would have three months before the Vendée start to make any modifications that might be needed.

It was a tight timetable full of risks but I had to do everything in my power to pull it off. Excuses just aren't my style. It's no good sitting around looking at your navel and forever discussing the meaning of the universe. I believe in rolling up your sleeves and getting on with the job. My attitude to life was unwittingly summed up at a conference where the talk I had given was followed by an American-style presentation. The speaker bounded on stage exuding a practised confidence. He had a healthy glow that was all slicked into place with lashings of hair oil which caught the spotlight perfectly. He seemed rattled by the fact that my talk had gone down well and he chose to kick off by using me as his foil. 'Pete,' he said in a soothing and persuasive voice, 'an incredible story, but let me ask you this: is this glass half full, or is it half empty?' He held a glass aloft which had water lapping away around the halfway mark. The floor was his. I was obviously being primed like a lamb for the slaughter and it would be all the sweeter for timing. 'Think about it,' he continued. 'Half full or half empty. Take your time, Pete. It's important.' The room fell silent. This was obviously a loaded question and people began to squirm uncomfortably in the ensuing silence while I tried to formulate a diplomatic answer. I repeated the question out aloud, as if grasping for inspiration. 'Is the glass half full, or is the glass half empty? Well, I say drink the bastard anyway.' My answer came from the heart, it was me. The rafters rang with laughter.

Gary started his work programme and said that, while he could make savings in many ways, there was one area where there was no room for negotiation: we would use 3M sandpaper. It might be a bit more expensive but its quality would ensure a better job and save money in the long term. 'Right, 3M sandpaper it is,' I agreed. I called Tony Durant who by now, thanks to the regatta I had run for his staff in conjunction with Rover, had become a friend of the project. Tony was in charge of 3M's accounts and had contacts in all of the company's factories across the country. I had met most of these chaps at the regatta and they were already on our side. It wasn't long before all types of product started turning up at our door. Sandpaper, breathing masks, masking tape, electrical connectors, vinyl and so on. More and more 3M products came to light that we could make good use of. By the end of the build we had used sixty-one different products in the boat.

Tony called me up to head office to meet one of the company's senior executives, Bob McDonald. We hit it off straight away. Bob was full of energy and enthusiasm and had an infectious sense of humour that never failed to give me a boost when our paths crossed. He immediately saw that the project had great potential for 3M and decided that he would not only supply products free of charge but that the company would also become a cash sponsor. Things were starting to roll and time would show that the project would never have made it to the start line without the support of 3M.

One sponsorship lead which kept rearing its head was that of Creative Fragrances, whose parent company was Spanish. Soon after leaving Chay and the British Steel Challenge, I had received a call from the friend of a friend who had a friend of a friend who was involved with marketing Creative Fragrances in Britain. The company was about to launch a new men's fragrance called Aqua Quorum, and the advertising campaign was to be on the theme of the freedom of the ocean, man's constant quest for challenge and so on. The friend of a friend wanted to add to the occasion by having a known sailor present at the launch. No budget was available to hire a celebrity, but my name came up. I was offered travel expenses and lunch on the house. I needed to get to London for the Boat Show in any case, so the rail ticket would come in handy, and a decent free meal wasn't going to do me any harm. I duly turned up, was introduced to the managing director Robert McClatchie and thoroughly enjoyed an entertaining lunch with a spirited bunch of people. I was particularly interested in the image that the company was building round the Aqua Quorum brand. If I had tried to invent a tailor-made product to link with my Vendée project I would have been hard pressed to find a better one. I spent the next four days at the Boat Show doing deals on the equipment that would be needed on the boat and returned home to bash out the sponsorship proposal Robert needed. I had a good feeling about this one.

Back in the build shed things were getting pretty tight. Gary had completed the plug and it was time to order the more expensive construction materials. I was determined to keep the build going because I knew that if we stopped it would be virtually impossible to start again. I worked even harder on both sponsorship and other sources of income in a desperate fight to keep Gary on the go. At about this time Stuart Horwood's BT Logistics came on board as a silver sponsor for £10,000. He was to be immensely valuable to the project as a close personal friend and sounding board. In addition, thanks to an introduction from Pete Calvin and Steve Whittell, I picked up Holliday Chemical Holdings as another silver sponsor. Pete and Steve never once doubted that the project was going to succeed and their enthusiasm was always an inspiration. As the project gained momentum they could see that I needed a car to belt round the country in as I tried to coordinate everything. They lured me up to Huddersfield and presented me with a very nice surprise: a brand-new Vauxhall Frontera Sport. They gave me the keys and, in their usual style, said: 'Here you go. We're right behind you, mate, go get 'em.' It was just what the project needed; they always seemed to know instinctively what would make the difference. My old VW Polo was on its last legs; it leaked so badly that I had had to drill holes in the floor to let the water out when it rained and I invariably had to bump-start it.

Many beers were drunk that night at Steve and Pete's local pub as we celebrated the new 'wheels'. Pete Calvin's BT Global Challenge was getting closer, and somehow it didn't seem right that Steve should be left behind while both Pete and I toddled off round the world in our different directions. Steve is a man who likes a bit of action and was as caught up in the spirit of things as we were. I sank another pint, pulled him aside, and asked him if he would help me sail the boat back across the Atlantic after the Europe 1 single-handed. Just about every expression in the book ran across his face. We shook on it. A dazed and happy Steve had just taken on the greatest adventure of his life and was to live it from that moment onwards. He had never been to sea before and spent the rest of that evening pinching himself to ensure it was really happening.

My team of sponsors was growing, but not nearly fast enough and I was slipping deeper into debt. However, thanks to a chance meeting some months previously with Rebecca Stephens, who was the first British woman to climb Everest, help was on the way. Rebecca had advised me to apply to the Foundation for Sport and the Arts for funds. She felt I would have a good chance of success and I wasted no time in submitting a grant application. The final date for a decision from the Foundation drew nearer and I had anxiously contacted them several times for news. The project hung on their decision. At last the news came that the Foundation had decided to award us a £50,000 grant. The relief was indescribable.

Once again the project had survived by the skin of its teeth. More materials were ordered and Gary took on two more skilled hands as he ramped up the operation for composite work. Keith Fennel, who had worked for Adrian Thompson during the pioneering years of composite construction, came on board at this point. His knowledge and experience were immeasurable and we always used him as a sounding board whenever we tackled anything new. Keith loves a problem and, as a Geordie, has very strong opinions – generally on the right track.

The response from Aqua Quorum – my main hope for title sponsor – was positive but the deal was painfully slow in coming together. Creative Fragrances wanted to go for title sponsorship at £250,000 from the outset and had put the project to Antonio Puig, their Spanish parent company. It kept being batted back and forth with more and more demands being placed on the project for less and less money. In the meantime we were once again running out of cash. In order to pay the lads' wages, we hadn't paid ourselves for about three months and there was no money for the next batch of materials. Things looked bleak. As is so often the case, Tracey came to the rescue. 'Let's sell the house, Pete,' she said. 'It will give us some time and something will turn up.' I was lost for words. This was a gesture far beyond the call of duty and something that I would never have asked of Tracey.

There was also the small matter of where we would all live. Once again fate was to play its hand. We had always wanted to live further out in the country and Tracey particularly liked a village called St Germans which was part of the Eliot Estate. Lord Eliot was keen to maintain the village as a proper community and chose to let his cottages to young local families at a discounted rate. We had had our name on the waiting list for four years and our turn came up during our deliberations. A solution was to hand.

We were fortunate to get a firm offer for our house within two weeks of having put it on the market and the sale went through quickly. The project, newly infused with what cash was left over from the sale, managed to carry on in its precarious manner. Selling the house provided a short-term solution, but it was obvious that a bank loan was the only way to dig us out in the longer term. I set up a meeting with Shane Dickson, my bank manager at Lloyds Bank, who had been constantly supportive. I first met Shane during the British Steel Challenge, as a result of a competition in a sailing magazine. The prize had been a berth on one of the yachts during the first leg of the race. The ten finalists, including Shane, were to have a trial sail with me as skipper. The trip was from London to Plymouth and we had set sail on a lively forecast which quickly deteriorated as we entered the Dover Straits. We all looked forward to an exciting ride. It blew old boots and rose until gusts of fifty knots were recorded. I battened everything down and we settled into a wild ride. Shane had loved every minute of it.

Shane is someone who does more than look at business plans and cash flows – he also measures the people, their commitment and their enthusiasm. He has the courage to stick his neck out for something that he believes in. Having shown him the numbers I asked him if he thought there was the possibility of a loan. He believed in me and said he would recommend one. However, the bank would require some form of security. If I could get the boat registered and valued then he would be able use it, along with a personal guarantee, as security. I arranged all this and ... success! The loan could go ahead. Despite the fact that I was to have a £70,000 overdraft around my neck, I slept like a log that night for the first time in months.

The build team was starting to grow in size as work started on more and more areas of the boat. Rob Crang and his lads at CSMD Hercules took on the metalwork, a particularly important part of the yacht. To produce the swinging keel alone called for exemplary skills – even with two of Rob's best welders working sixty hours a week, it took two months to make. It is an engineering masterpiece that still looks as good as new after 50,000 nautical miles of hard sailing.

Damon Roberts and his lads at Carbospars were the obvious choice to make the mast. Damon is not only a great mast builder but also a world-class sailor – he knows what will and will not work. The fact that it was 40,000 nautical miles before I changed a halyard speaks for the time, effort and quality of work that went into both the engineering and construction. It amazes me that the mast, despite being such a delicate structure, survived the conditions of the Southern Ocean.

I chose Bruce Banks to make the sails because they seemed to be in tune with what we were setting out to achieve – and had the added bonus of a wise man called Ken Rose. Ken has been a pioneer in the world of sails for many years. Not only did I want top quality sails that would do the boat justice but I also needed them to be right from the outset. There was neither the time nor the money to change sails once they had been delivered. They had to go up and stay up for the whole campaign – they would already have pushed out 20,000 nautical miles before we even crossed the Vendée start line. It was a tough job but I wasn't to be disappointed.

Alan Ashley, an expert in marine systems, proved to be invaluable. Offshore yachts are home to very sophisticated systems. A single-handed yacht calls for extra gear, much of it electronic, upon which you are totally reliant. We knew that the Vendée would be a tough race – statistics showed that fifty per cent of the fleet would fall by the wayside. Of these, many would fail because of problems with their onboard systems. I was fortunate to have Alan on the team. First, he made sure that the equipment was installed to his own exacting standards; second, he included spare parts and repair instructions for any equipment that he felt might fail at sea in bad conditions. He has an uncanny instinct for what might need to be done and later I would often offer him thanks as I quickly carried out a repair that might otherwise have taken many frustrating hours.

On several occasions I called him up during the race to discuss a problem, only to have him rattle off a solution as if he were there. 'If you open the second panel you will see that there are eight wires in front of you. You need to check the second, third and fourth from left to right; that's the white, blue and green. Got that?' It was a great comfort and never ceased to astound me.

A vital area of the boat would be the hydraulic system necessary to swing the keel from side to side. It had to be rugged enough to harness the massive loads that would pass through it and yet at the same time be light and simple. It also required a number of easily managed back-up options. These were problems that required an experienced and fertile mind with a high degree of technical knowledge. Enter Jim Doxey. I remember him, a large-framed man, walking into the shed during a particularly frenetic day and bringing with him a calm reason that enabled him to identify a problem at a glance and come up with the solution. Jim had a belt and braces approach – a highly useful commodity given our budgetary constraints. We might not have been able to afford titanium rams for the hydraulic system, for instance, but that didn't stop him getting the best out of what we could afford.

A deal was finally struck with Creative Fragrances to promote their new product Aqua Quorum. However, although they still wanted title sponsorship, they could only manage £100,000 – approximately a quarter of the overall budget and £150,000 short of what I had hoped for from a title sponsor. In addition they insisted that the boat be insured during the race. This would cost £20,000 and meant that the actual project would see only £80,000. If I turned the offer down, we would be finished. I shook hands on the deal, knowing that I still had to find more sponsors and perhaps sell advertising space on the mainsail and spinnakers. Nevertheless, it was great to have Aqua Quorum on board as it gave the project a firm identity – and the boat a rather attractive name.

As word of our endeavours spread – often beyond the confines of the yachting magazines and into newspapers, television and radio – so more and more people wanted to help. They were fascinated by the new technology on the boat. People were drawn to the adventure of one man against the elements and attracted by the idea that we were taking on the mighty French budgets with British ingenuity and grit on the smallest boat in the fleet. Several of the new sixty-footers in the race had budgets of £3–4 million, compared to our £450,000 or so. Even the fact that Tracey and I had given up our house seemed to grab their imagination. People began to flock to the project, writing letters of support and, in many cases, giving tangible help. I was often stopped in the street and given a few words of encouragement, or a donation would be thrust into my hand.

We put out a plea on the local radio for lead in any form; two tons were needed for the bulb at the bottom of the keel. The response was overwhelming. It was a priceless boost to come home tired late at night to find a bag of scrap lead by the door with a note of support from strangers. A local church changed its organ pipes and the old lead ones found their way into our keel. It was this ground swell of support that kept the show on the road. I could go on and on with examples but one which left a deep impression was that of Yvonne Parker whom I met, along with her husband Terry, through the British Steel Challenge. They followed the race avidly, turning up to support the start and finish. Yvonne had had a fear of water all her life and she decided to help the Vendée project by overcoming this phobia and learning to swim. She managed, after much hard work, to swim a mile and raise £250 towards the project. It was a gesture that moved me beyond words. *Aqua Quorum* embodied the spirit of all these people, and it was the thought of them that later pulled me through the bad times, particularly during those cold, wet, grinding parts of the race that nobody sees. I was never alone.

Accepting a title sponsor well below the going rate presented a tough challenge. I tried everything in the book to raise more money. I cancelled the time that I had put aside for race training and allocated it instead to hospitality trips on the boat. However, if I was going to charge for days on *Aqua Quorum* she would have to comply with standing regulations for fare-paying passengers. We called in John Furnley, a friend and local surveyor who worked with Bureau Veritas, a regulatory body, to see if this was possible on such a radical boat. It turned out that we could manage it provided a number of additions were made to the structure. It was a painful decision as it meant that extra weight would have to go into the boat. It would also place extra pressure on Gary, who was working at full stretch as it was. The lads somehow pulled it off and Bureau Veritas, seeing the difficulty that I was in, waived their fee. We gained our certificate, mainly thanks to John Furnley's efforts and professionalism, and I was later able to generate revenue from day after day of corporate hospitality.

Many people wanted to make donations and, to give something back in return, we set up a newsletter to which they could subscribe. For £25 they would receive a regular newsletter as the race unfolded. This was very successful. I tried a mailshot in *Yachting World* magazine, but was disappointed that only forty people out of the thousands who subscribe to the publication responded. Oddly enough, I found that most support came from people outside the sport. I suppose that the project had less to do with sailing than it did with challenge and adventure.

Netserve, a local company that had just set themselves up on the Internet, ran a website on my behalf which developed a huge following. We received hundreds of thousands of visits a month to the site. Thanks to John Collins, a local journalist, the *Independent on Sunday* ran regular features which tied in with the website. I just didn't have time to respond to all the letters of support and felt guilty about the ever-increasing pile of unanswered mail. Fortunately, towards the end of the build, Mark Orr, whom I had met many years previously during a Three Peaks Race, dropped by to offer his help. He took the newsletter off my hands.

My local sailing club was always there to help if something needed doing. We were up against it one morning when some equipment urgently needed adjusting – something that could only be done by the manufacturer. There was no way that we could spare anyone from the team. I called the club, who found a volunteer, and the equipment was on the road within an hour. It was delivered to the manufacturer, waited for while the adjustments were made and returned that same afternoon. The club also organised a number of events and raised considerable sums of money towards the project.

Ted Drewell, one of the members of the club and a model-maker, decided that he would, with the club's support, build a scale model of *Aqua Quorum* in celebration of the project. Ted creates the most amazing models – from working steam engines to yachts. He goes to great lengths to ensure that they are accurate and makes all the deck fittings by hand; the winches turn and the blocks actually work. Ted was building the model in parallel with Gary, so they shared their frustrations as the respective boats came together. However, there were times when Ted, working from Adrian's drawings, got ahead of the game. The trouble was that we in the build shed were making the odd modification as the boat came together. On one occasion Ted visited us to find that we had made a change to something that he had already completed. It meant he had to dump a week's work. We felt terrible and from then on, when considering a modification, would find out what stage Ted was at on his model. If he had already made that area of the boat we would agonise over the change. Ted became a kind of grandfather to the project and it was always with great pride that we showed him the progress we were making.

The team worked miracles as we tried to keep on course for the launch date, which Gary and I had set many months previously. The trouble was that I had, on the back of this date, booked the naming ceremony. Much organisation had already been put in place by our sponsors, who were growing excited at the prospect of seeing *Aqua Quorum* formally named. It was an important landmark in the campaign, the moment when we would officially welcome her into the world, and I didn't want to kick off her relationship with the press and sponsors by missing the party myself. I also had to have her in the water as soon as possible so that I could get to know her. The delays caused by financial problems had put us a month behind in an already ambitious schedule and it was a real old battle to catch up. Gary's work rate was impressive – I would come back to the shed after a few days on the road and be staggered by how much he had done.

The boat was starting to look and feel like a boat and I would let myself into the building at night when all was quiet to spend time on her. It is important to establish an emotional relationship with a boat and I would visualise us in the Southern Ocean. I was starting to psych myself up for the rigours of the challenge. It is something that I always do before a hard trip; I sail the course over and over in my mind, slowly building up the picture until it is 3-D, in full colour, and I can even imagine the smells and noises. I leave nothing out – from cooking a simple meal to facing the worst possible sea conditions. It is through this procedure that I make small changes to the boat, perhaps moving a grab handle a few inches from where it had been placed in the plans, for instance. I know, having already used them in my mind, what spares I will require for every kind of jury rig. I even know how I will feel after a particularly bad spell and what meal will most cheer me up. By the time the start gun goes I am taking on something that I feel I already know intimately.

Having sailed round the world a few times in my mind I then think about what will happen afterwards. It is important to have a long-term plan. There is always a bit of a downer after crossing the finish line, a kind of mourning. To end an adventure and think, 'What the hell do I do now?' is a mistake. Better to have the void already filled and be getting on with the next project.

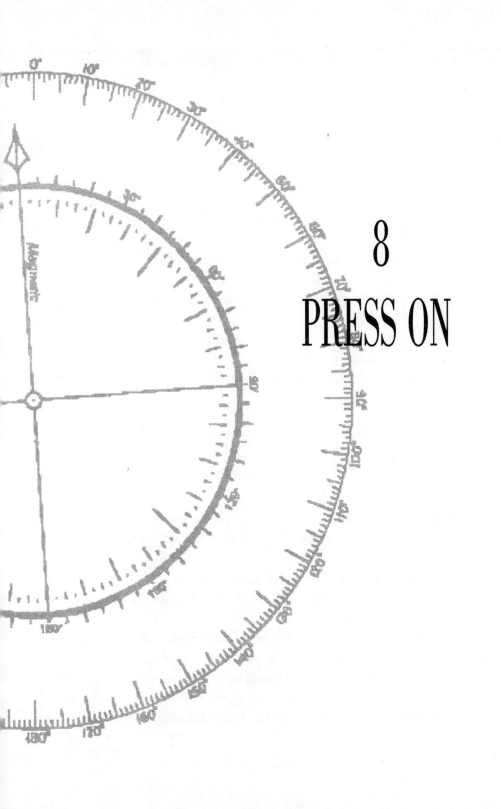

8
PRESS ON

*Nothing in the world can take the place of
persistence.
Talent will not: nothing is more common
than unsuccessful men with talent.
Genius will not: unrewarded genius is
almost a proverb.
Education will not: the world is full of
educated derelicts.
Persistence and determination alone are
omnipotent.*

This was passed on to me by Chay Blyth

The faces of the lads in the build shed became drawn and weary
as the launch date neared. The pressure was on – we had to meet
the date and everyone was reaching deep to find an extra reserve
of energy. They came to work early and left late. I hoped that I
could live up to their standards when it came to my turn to
perform.

There is a cycle to the life of a boat. First, it is the designer's
baby, conceived as it takes shape on the drawing board; then it
passes into the hands of the builders, where it is nurtured into life
until it is delivered to the outside world and into the hands of its
guardian and mentor, the sailor. Boats take on a personality of

their own. They are blessed, named and watched over with paternal pride, maturing with each knock, repair and modification. *Aqua Quorum* came from a proud and caring family.

We worked longer and longer hours until the day to run her out of the shed dawned. The crane arrived and I stood with my heart in my mouth as she was eased out – new, glistening, dramatic and with mere inches to spare through the doorway. In fact, we had to tilt her to get her out. There was a real beauty to her and she wasn't afraid to flaunt it. Her yellow hull could be seen for miles – it was like watching a tropical butterfly bursting from its chrysalis. She was breathtaking from every angle. As she wended her way through the streets of Plymouth on the back of a low-loader I felt as if I would burst with pride. She brought the city to a standstill.

We moved to an open area in Millbay Docks in Plymouth, which was kindly lent to us by Ray Escrig of Associated British Ports. Here we would finish her off and assemble all the various components that had been made elsewhere – mast, keel, sails, rudders and so on. *Aqua Quorum* was suspended in a scaffold tower high above the ground ready for the keel to be attached. I was out of cash as usual and had put a lot of jobs on hold, hoping that once the boat was named and in the water she would attract extra funding and we could tackle them then. In the meantime we would have to make do.

When it was time to transport the two-ton lead bulb for the keel from the shed where it was made to the boat, we couldn't afford proper transport so we used the furniture van that we had hired to act as a mobile workshop. We managed to lift the bulb into the back of the van with the help of a forklift truck, ropes, blocks, levers and good, old-fashioned elbow grease. The front wheels kept lifting off the road as we slowly groaned our way through Plymouth. When we arrived at the site, we applied the handbrake with some relief and set about dragging the bulb to the back of the van so that the crane could get a decent lift. There was an almighty crack, the van jumped two feet into the air and all was lost in a cloud of dust. The bulb had disappeared through the floor.

The boat grew day by day as we worked our way through the job list. The biggest event was fitting the keel. It had been designed by Martyn Smith, who had also designed *Cornish Meadow*, and Roger Scammell, and looked remarkable. It was frighteningly thin, considering it had to support a two-ton bulb, and was only two and a half inches wide at the point where the bulb was attached. All went smoothly as the fin was lowered into the boat from above and out through the hole in the bottom of the hull. It was a delicate operation and it seemed to take an age for the bearings to settle into their housing. To say we were feeling tense is an understatement – if it didn't fit we would be finished. Gary and Jim Doxey dropped the captive housing on top of the bearings and tried to run the bolts through. There was a dull thunk which echoed through the hull as solid met solid. Not a word was needed, the noise said it all. The bolts did not fit. The bearings and keel were out of alignment.

I started to think wildly about getting further funding to put the disaster right. Gary, cool as ever, sat back and quietly worked through all the possibilities. Suddenly, in a rush of noise, everyone chipped in with their suggestions. Gary, ignoring the babble, signalled the crane driver to lift the keel back up a foot or so. Jim, thinking along the same lines, ran a rag over the bearing surfaces to remove some of the grease that had been applied and then the keel was dropped back into place. The bolts shot home with a positive crack, as designed, to a tolerance of thousandths of an inch. Jim coupled up his hydraulics and did a test swing from side to side without the bulb – it worked like clockwork. Gary and

Jim, having satisfied themselves that all was in working order, gave the go-ahead for the bulb to be bolted into place. The keel, a fundamental part of the boat and the centrepiece of Adrian's creation, had finally been put to bed.

When a boat falls off a wave, it endures incalculable shock loads – and this is what might eventually destroy it. Adrian and Martin tackled the problem by fitting a sensitive release valve in the hydraulic keel system. Should *Aqua Quorum* drop flat on her side and stop dead in the water with the keel on full power she was designed to take a shock load of two Gs. Should the load exceed that figure the keel would drop, dissipating the damaging forces, before automatically pumping back into position.

The keel swung thirty degrees either side of the boat's centre-line, a total arc of sixty degrees. A simple control system meant that, having selected my chosen position, the keel would automatically stop when it reached that point, leaving me free to worry about other things meanwhile. The power pack was an electrical unit which could pump the keel from side to side very quickly. Jim had also plumbed in a hand pump so that I could still use this most vital area of the boat if the power went down. The keel was moved by two double-acting rams, each of which was capable of powering the keel on its own. I therefore had a complete back-up system.

At last, the moment to launch the boat arrived. The crane turned up – as did an encouraging crowd of friends and supporters – and we cleared the decks to prepare for the big moment. The mast arrived and we dressed it ready for stepping. I felt elated as I walked away from the boat, and turned to have one last look at her before we put her in the water. She looked stunning in the late afternoon sun and I knew that we had a winner. The keel kissed the water's surface and slowly disappeared from sight as *Aqua Quorum* descended to be embraced by her natural environment. It was a magical moment, but not without an element of suspense because you never know if a yacht, particularly a prototype, will float to its marks. It was a still, sunny evening and ripples full of reflected yellow ran across the water as the hull finally settled. The lifting strops went slack and she was in, looking a picture and floating exactly to her marks. I couldn't wait to jump on board and for the first time feel her move beneath my feet. There wasn't a face on the quayside that wasn't wearing a grin from ear to ear. The mast was quickly stepped; it was as if make-up had been applied, and she simply blossomed. We towed her to the marina and tied her up for the night. I walked away feeling elated and totally drained – we had finally, after ten years' work, made it to the water. It was time to go home for a family hug and spend some precious time together.

Adrian arrived the next day and we all stood back, anxiously awaiting his approval as he walked round the boat with an intense look on his face. After a while he stood back with a satisfied grin and proclaimed that he was happy.

My future home slowly began to take shape as I stuck up some family photos and fitted the bunks, etc. It was such a treat to make my first cup of tea below and look at the chart table and see a chart along with pencil and sharpener, rather than finding it covered with tools and boat bits. She was slowly passing into my hands and I couldn't wait to go for our first sail. Keith's dagger boards, the last piece in the jigsaw, remained on the pontoon. Between us, Adrian, Keith and I offered them up to their casing and eased them in. They fitted perfectly. It was yet another satisfying moment and I shall always remember the look of sheer pleasure on Keith's face as he pulled them up and down. She was ready.

The night before our first sail we cleared everything off the boat and made her as shipshape as possible. As everyone left for home, I hung back to gather my thoughts for the next day. I stood at the stern and ran my eyes over what had matured, in a matter of days, into an efficient working platform. The next morning was an early start and we fiddled with details until everyone arrived. I allocated jobs, asked everyone to stick to their task and refrain from letting their enthusiasm run away with itself; I wanted the boat to lead us through at its own pace. Adrian had been quiet all morning and just wanted to sit in the back of the boat and watch. It was a big moment for him; earlier he had slipped away for a cup of tea, which he then couldn't drink because his hand was shaking so much.

We slipped the lines and took a tow from some of the lads from the Royal Marines Sailing Centre, where it had all started. The mainsail was hoisted as we cleared the marina and slipped out into Plymouth Sound to catch a lift from the breath of air that was moving above a glassy sea. She found it, responded and accelerated as the staysail was hoisted. The helm came to life and she was off; I couldn't believe how game she was. There wasn't any wind to speak of and yet here we were doing an effortless six knots. We moved further offshore and it was brilliant to feel her heeling to the breeze, which was getting healthier. I handed the helm to Adrian and saw the tension slip away from him. As he sailed his brainchild, he began to smile, his eyes darting over every detail.

The wind picked up and it was time to swing the keel to windward. Adrian and I discussed putting a reef in and taking it step by step, but it was hard to be sensible in all the excitement and we both grinned. 'Sod it! She's got to go round the world. Let's go for it.' Jim did his stuff and over went the keel. It transformed the boat: she sat up, went a couple of knots faster and the helm became as light as a feather. What was already an exciting boat became the craft of tomorrow as the revolutionary design did its stuff. The log shot up to twelve knots. I just couldn't believe it and, thinking that the instruments needed calibrating, asked Alan Ashley to check the speed showing on the GPS (Global Positioning System). Twelve and a half knots, came the answer. That last half knot made it for me, the Vendée was a dead cert. Pretty soon my face ached from smiling so much.

Back to business. We spent the day identifying several snags that needed to be put right. As we fiddled away on deck, Alan spent the day below settling in the electronics, including radios, radar, computers, autopilots, wind and speed instruments, GPS and generator. There were so many beeps and whistles that you could have thought he was conducting an orchestra. He liked the music; that was good enough for me.

If there was one area that wasn't quite right it was the rudders, which were not fully balanced and could give a vicious kick. It was too big a job to tackle in the time available and was put on the shelf for a more suitable moment – the show would have to go on regardless. We ran through as many sails as we could and I was delighted with both their quality and shape. We started to bed down the rig by putting it through its paces; it was an absolute belter: light, simple and yet had the feeling of total reliability. She was a real sweetheart and I felt completely in harmony with her. I had spent so much time visualising what she would be like that I felt I already knew her. Here was a new fifty-foot boat on her maiden voyage, and I was quite happy to sail her back into the marina and alongside without the assistance of a tow. It was an indication of the kindly sea-keeping qualities that she possessed.

Towards the end of the week we had a private party on board for the lads to celebrate the launch. Hall & Woodhouse, my old Challenge sponsor, saw us right with a mountain of beer. Rob

Crang from CSMD Hercules hired a minibus to bring the lads down from Dartmouth and for the first time in ages we had a social chat. It was a great evening as we ploughed through the tinnies and laughed about all the cock-ups and the funny incidents. For instance, there was the time when we couldn't afford to hire a skip to cart away all the rubbish during the early stages of the build and, with the blessing of the lads at the depot, we tied one to the truck and towed it under cover of darkness to our shed. It made the most awful noise and lit the place up with sparks as it skidded its way down the road. We filled it and then towed it back to the depot before going home with a sigh of relief. The next morning we were horrified to find a very pronounced scrape mark from the skip to the door of our shed and back again. The evidence took ages to fade.

Of immediate concern was the naming ceremony, which was to be held in London in a few days' time. Getting there would be a close call because there was still a lot of work to be done. We were extremely fortunate in having Joanna Lumley to name the boat. Another of those strokes of luck. Back in the early days during the training for the BT Global Challenge I happened to be discussing my Vendée ambitions and plans for raising the sponsorship. It was an early morning watch and one of the crew was actress Lucy Fleming, who piped up to say that I ought to have a high profile celebrity to name the boat; Joanna Lumley was a friend of hers and she would have a word with her. I thought nothing more of it until a couple of weeks later when Joanna wrote to say that she would be delighted to name the boat. It was a very generous offer and one which no doubt played an important role in attracting the attention of the media and helping to raise sponsorship.

The crew for the sail to London arrived: Pete Calvin, Steve Whittell, *Yachting World* journalist James Boyd and Rick

Tomlinson, a top marine photographer and a seasoned sailor. The boat just wasn't ready – it was a bomb site. I was determined to sail by six that evening and sent Steve off to buy not only the food but also the pots and pans in which to cook it. Everybody chipped in and we worked at fever pitch until six, threw everything off the boat, untied it and set sail. We had just under two days to get to London.

We settled into a watch routine and attempted to catch up on sleep in the temporary bunks. It was all new to everyone and I planned to take my time and experiment with the boat, get to know her and relax a bit before the bun fight of the naming ceremony. I was going to write my speech, making sure that I remembered everyone who needed thanking.

I had seen this trip as my moment of peace between the fight to date and the even bigger fight ahead. I was wrong. Within two hours the wind went round to the east and started to rise. It was dark and I took my time as we reefed down, making sure nothing was damaged due to inexperience. The temperature plummeted and the wind kept rising, we were very quickly down to three reefs in the main and staysail as we bashed to windward. I was horrified. I like to bed a new boat down slowly. Here I was, with only about thirty miles on the log, beating into short, choppy seas and a vicious gale. I winced as if physically hurt each time we fell off a wave. I felt as if I was abusing a loyal animal that would keep giving until it could give no more.

The gale kept rising and we continued to beat our brains out, each wave shaking the boat. Dropping off a wave in a composite boat is something of an experience. Being so light and game, she leaps off the crest of each wave and becomes completely airborne until she crashes into the next trough. The bottom of the hull, little more than a fifty-foot surfboard, is as flat as a pancake and brings the boat up short in a shuddering explosion of noise. The only way the impact can be dissipated is through vibration and noise. You can see the shock waves rippling up and down both the hull and rig as the boat tries to shake itself to pieces. Each wave is like being in a car crash: you have to wear ear defenders below and the impact is so violent that you have to hold yourself down, let alone hold on. Added to this the keel bends and flops about, giving the boat the feel of a blancmange as it wobbles about on top of the fin after each impact.

The night wore on and we made little headway. Everyone was soaking wet, seasick and miserable. Progress was desperately slow as fate put the tides at their worst. The boat, designed to be steered by autopilot most of the time, has a particularly exposed steering position and we became wetter and wetter as each wave swept the boat from end to end. I was adamant that she be hand-steered. It was not in me to leave the boat to her own devices. I also wanted keen pairs of eyes on deck, both to keep a lookout for any shipping and to spot any rig problems that might come to light during her first beating.

The temperature dropped to freezing and the conditions deteriorated. James, Pete and Steve were suffering terribly from seasickness and Rick and I worked turn and turn about for as long as we could. The nearest we got to a hot drink was a mug of warm water. And I couldn't even hold that down. We could see the lights of houses and pubs ashore, no doubt with roaring fires built up against the cold, and here we were, not too many miles away, sharing a mug of lukewarm water as if our life depended on it. Not for the first time we asked: 'What the hell are we doing here?'

It took until the following night to reach the Isle of Wight, where Rick had to jump ship because of work commitments. We anchored on the south side of the island and waited for him to be picked up by an RIB (rigid inflatable boat). Everyone was ready to wrap it up and cancel the naming ceremony because of the weather. It would have been a perfectly legitimate decision given the state we were in and the fact that there was little indication of an improvement in the weather. I decided to lie up until the early hours of the morning and a fair tide and make my decision then. I was determined not to let the shore team down and chose to view the trip as a test for both myself and the boat. We couldn't afford to give up under any circumstances during the Vendée and I wasn't about to start now.

After a short respite we dragged ourselves back to work. It was even colder now and, with only myself and James Boyd capable of steering, I found it very demanding. I cut my hand open at one point and didn't feel a thing because it was so cold. It was a deep wound and should have been stitched. The worst thing about the trip was the pounding that the boat took. I could only console myself with the fact that if there were any weaknesses we would find them soon enough. It was with great relief that we finally entered the Thames Estuary, eased the sheets, felt her come upright, kick her heels and accelerate down the waves. Queasy stomachs settled and we managed our second meal of the trip as *Aqua Quorum* skipped up the river. With no preparation to speak of, she had taken it on the chin and come out on top. Quite remarkable.

We made it up the Thames with only hours to spare. Harbourmaster Ray Bateman let us into St Katharine's Dock as the day of the ceremony dawned. We grabbed a couple of hours' sleep and got stuck into cleaning her up for the occasion. She was a real crowd-puller – no one could possibly have guessed what she had just been through as she basked on tranquil waters in the morning sun. We, on the other hand, were on our knees as we worked alongside the rest of the team, who had come up by train for the big day. There were flags to be flown, logos to be applied, the bottle-breaker to be fitted, VIPs to be looked after – and everyone wanted to chat.

Just before the off I remembered my speech, scribbled a couple of words down and decided to wing it. It was a marvellous ceremony: Royal Marines buglers called everyone to order, Joanna Lumley took two shots with the bottle and *Aqua Quorum* was official. We gathered for the speeches and Joanna delivered hers with such style that it brought a lump to everybody's throat. She made the day.

The sail back to Southampton was a great success. Eddie Warden Owen of Bruce Banks Sails joined us and we ran through the sails and experimented with different settings before entering the Solent. Will Stephens came along for the ride and he and I had the boat to ourselves during the night watch. We had earned that sail and the tea tasted good that night. It was the first time that I had been able to stand on the bow and really feel part of *Aqua Quorum*'s effortless demonstration of harmony with nature as we sailed together down the moon's reflection.

Rick Tomlinson called us as we entered the Solent to ask if he could come out in his RIB and take some shots – the light was particularly good and he wanted to make the most of it. It was an excellent opportunity for me to see how she looked in the water and so I hitched a ride in his RIB as he powered around, photographing her from every angle. She looked stunning. The wind started to rise so I jumped back on board to take the helm once more while Rick carried on snapping. I really had too much sail up but held on in the knowledge that we would be bearing away for the marina once we reached Southampton Water. It was heartening to note that she remained as docile as ever, despite being over canvased. I eased the sheets on reaching Southampton Water, bore away and let her have her head. This was the first time I had had her off the wind for real and the effect was breathtaking. She picked up her bow and started to plane at a steady sixteen knots in flat water. It was very gusty and I found to my great pleasure that she simply accelerated out of the gusts with the ease of a top athlete; not once did she labour the point. I had never experienced anything like it and couldn't help letting out a whoop of joy as we planed through the BT Global Challenge Fleet, spray flying everywhere. What a boat she was, just full of surprises. And all of them good ones.

As soon as *Aqua Quorum* was safely moored up in the marina, I set to preparing her for the first hospitality sail of her career, which started the next day. There were still loads of jobs to be done, one of which was to find the foul weather clothing which had been delivered somewhere else in the marina. I only just managed to get everything ready before everyone turned up. It was a four-day charter and the plan was to put extensive day sails in and book into a bed and breakfast wherever we ended up in the evening.

The trip was a success, even if the weather was evil as gale after gale swept up the Channel. *Aqua Quorum* proved to be an excellent platform for hospitality, and people accepted and even enjoyed her frugal interior. They were fascinated by the design and felt privileged to be sailing on what was clearly a Formula One boat. She delivered a very exciting sail and yet felt safe and secure at all times. It gave me the confidence to start selling hospitality with a vengeance; it might not bring in vast amounts but at least it was something to throw at the huge debt which faced me.

I worked on the boat during the evenings. If I didn't tick a few jobs off the list every day I would never make it to the Transat start. Many of the BT Global Challenge crew would come over for a chat and help out with the chores if they had the time. I was still concerned about the rudders though – not only were they not fully balanced but they were also too big. A local yard had agreed to take on the job of reducing them, but when they saw them they got cold feet. Keith Fennel came to the rescue. I drove down to Plymouth, dropped the rudders off with him, and had two days with the family before rushing the rudders back to Southampton. They were put to the test for the first time during a hospitality sail and I was delighted. The only area of the boat that hadn't felt right had now been sorted out. An extra bonus was that now the rudders were smaller she was also a little faster.

It was a frantic period and it seemed no time at all before I was back in Plymouth and preparing for the Transat. To qualify for the race you normally have to have sailed a 500-mile passage single-handed some months before the start to prove your ability and the boat's seaworthiness. The deadline was 1 May, but the race organisers, the Royal Western Yacht Club, had given me dispensation on the date because they knew me and had kept an eye on the build. They were confident that we were both up to it and simply asked that I complete the qualifier when I could fit it in. Competitors have to turn up a week before the start to be scrutinised by the organisers and I had set aside the four days beforehand for my qualifier. It was a disaster. There was no wind, thick fog and it was unsafe. I decided not to sail because I would not have achieved anything. The organisers decided to waive the qualifying sail in my case – they considered that I was experienced enough. However, I hadn't sailed the boat single-handed yet and I was desperate to do so.

At last the skies cleared, a breeze picked up on the last of my four days and I managed to drift out at lunchtime for a five-hour sail beyond the Eddystone Lighthouse and back. It wasn't a lot but it was a start and I loved it. I used the autopilot for the first time and managed to put the heavy spinnaker up for the reach back. I would have to make do during the race as I got to know her. The purpose of the race was a work-up for the Vendée and I could always back off a bit if necessary. A result was not the be all and end all of the trip – it would be nice but not essential. I knew that I was less prepared than I had ever been for an event, but felt confident that my experience and stamina would pull it off. I knew *Aqua Quorum* could take it.

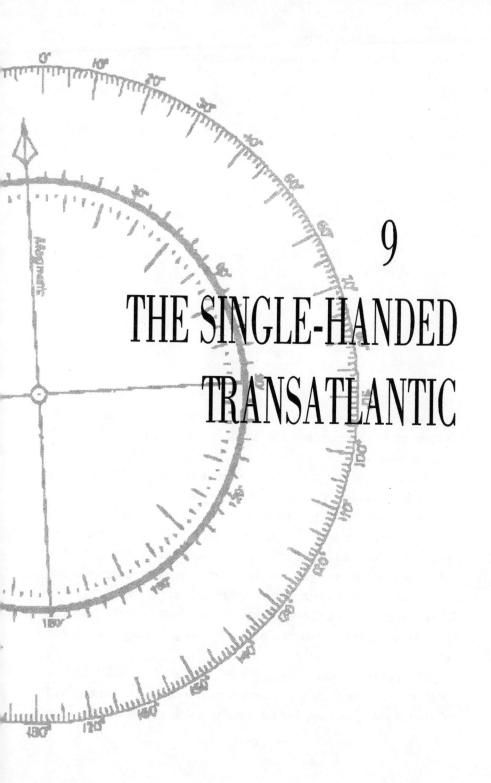

9

THE SINGLE-HANDED
TRANSATLANTIC

*It is not because things are difficult that we
    do not dare . . .
It is because we do not dare that they are
    difficult.*

Seneca

A single-handed race seems to strike a deep and emotional chord in participants and spectators alike. I think it is because the adventure of one man against the elements is something to which we can all relate. As I made my way, kitbag in hand, down to the boat at eight in the morning on start day Sunday 16 June, the world and its dog seemed to want to shake me and the other competitors by the hand and wish us well. It added to the sense of anticipation. The start was set for twelve o'clock and the other skippers and I had just emerged from the race briefing. The weather outlook was good in the short term, with easterly winds to launch us out into the Atlantic in readiness for the brute of a depression that was brewing up on the eastern seaboard. The forecaster expressed concern at what it would bring and wished us luck.

The pontoon was thronged with well-wishers and I had to push my way through the crowd, which seemed to intensify as I neared *Aqua Quorum*. Because she was a local boat there were many pinning their hopes on us and they had turned up to show their support. Sadly, much of the goodwill went over my head. I was tired and preoccupied. I was also scheduled to have a meeting with Will Stephens and my bank manager Shane Dickson on board a few moments later. Finances were looking worse than ever. I hadn't managed to reach the targets that had been set and the bank was growing concerned. The meeting was to establish whether I could start the race or not and I had a fixed grin on my face as I stepped on board to a cheer from the team, who were working on the boat. She still wasn't ready. Alan had started to fit his last piece of equipment at 2 a.m. and I didn't even know how to turn it on.

I stood in the cockpit, oblivious to the frantic last-minute efforts that were going on around me, and waited tensely. The thought of the project grinding to a halt now was just too much to bear. I felt as if I had been playing a game of poker, maintaining a calm and confident face. It had nearly worked but here I was, down to my last hand and asking to borrow the shirt off Shane's back to stay in the game. I had by now hocked everything, including my house. The tension was unbearable. I thought to myself: Christ, why the hell did I set out on this bloody awful road, when it seems to bring only misery? This race had better be worth it.

The pre-race week had been an emotional roller coaster. I was broke and yet I was spending money as we added all sorts of extra kit to the boat to bring her up to race safety standards. I hadn't entirely lost my mind, however. I had a big deal on the go with an international bank who were based in America and they were willing to pay £50,000 to have their logo on the mainsail. We had been working with a contact from the bank for about a month and he said they were ready to sign a contract. They were pushing hard because, as the finish was in America, they wanted their logo in place for the Transat. We were told that the money had already been wired into the UK branch of the bank and a director was coming down by train with the paperwork. Details were confirmed by fax and phone, right down to the logo artwork. I informed my bank that we had found the big break and not to worry, fifty big ones would be winging their way through the door on Thursday. It was close. I had been stung before and was still a little wary. Unconsciously, however, I started to spend more on the boat than perhaps I should have.

I was on my way to the railway station to meet the director – he was due to arrive at ten thirty – when my mobile phone rang. It was Will and he was spitting bullets. He had just received a fax from our contact with the bank. The deal was off. It was an amazing turnaround given that twenty-four hours ago the money was in the bank and train tickets had been booked for Plymouth. I just couldn't accept it at face value and spent an hour in the telephone box in the marina car park, eventually getting through to a big cheese in America, who made some enquiries and came back with the news that the whole thing had been a hoax. It was some sort of sick joke, a fabrication from day one. For the first time in my life I felt my spirit ebb away like a light going out. Why, after everything we had gone through to get this far, did we deserve a shovelful of shit like that? It just didn't seem fair. I could see the lads working away on the boat through the callbox window. Somehow the show had to go on, I couldn't give up now.

I walked to the café in the marina, grabbed a cup of tea and started to work out an emergency plan. I had a day and a half to come up with something. It was time for pen, paper and a list. Steve Whittell, full of the joys of spring, walked round the corner just as I started. He stopped dead: 'What's up, mate? You look like you've just seen a ghost.' There was nobody I'd rather have bumped into. Steve was a sharp businessman, knew the ins and outs of the project and was a great sounding board.

We ran through the figures calmly. We could survive on the business front, provided I didn't do the Transat. The trouble was that this wasn't just a business, it was a quest for the Vendée Globe. I had to go back to those basic principles I had set for myself so long ago: 'If faced with a dilemma just ask yourself what is in the best interests of the campaign and you have a clear and simple answer.' I had to do the Transat, my instincts told me that if I didn't I would join the ranks of those who couldn't stay the course and there was no way I was going to do that. Steve, with a huge grin on his face, said, 'Fuck it, you're going.' He pulled out his gold credit card and threw it on the table. 'No good poncing round with one of these in your pocket if you can't cane it in an emergency. This is an emergency. Come on, we're off up the bank to shove a bucket-load into your account and then we'll have a beer. We'll sort it out when you get back from the Transat.'

Steve's support got me back on the road. It was an offer I could never have accepted – it wouldn't have been fair – but I drew strength from it. Come what may, I would somehow do the race, that was what it was all about. I got back on the phone, my faith restored, and started to pull something together, anything. Everyone rallied round: Jim refused to submit an invoice for his time, just wouldn't hear of it; Mark Orr, who was doing wonders with the newsletter, took the same stance as Steve and offered to take out a mortgage and throw it into the pot. While I couldn't possibly accept that kind of offer it gave me a tremendous boost which, along with all the local support, kept me going during our darkest hours. Aqua Quorum had their pre-race party that night and it was thanks to the lads that I was able to turn up with a smile and do my bit. It had been a long, hard day. Jokes like 'You had better win this or else' fell on deaf ears. Behind the smile I felt dazed, emotionally drained and desperately tired – the Transat was a mere two and a half days away.

I was brought back to earth by the sound of my mobile. It was Will. He and Shane had been caught in traffic on the drive down from Southampton and would be with me in fifteen minutes. It was eight thirty. Three and a half hours to the start and I still didn't know if I would be able to do the race. The organisers were getting twitchy; they couldn't understand why I was dragging my heels, they wanted to tow me out, I was in the way. I could hardly tell them the truth. The pressure was building and I could feel my heart beating way above its usual rate. Time seemed to drag and my thoughts wandered back to the only tranquil time during the last week. All my boats have been blessed by the same man, Donald Peyton-Jones. He is an ex-Royal Marine working with the Mission to Seamen, and a wonderful person who had seen life at its worst during the Second World War. He had held a quiet family blessing during which he managed to slow everyone down and make us all reflect on what we had achieved and to be thankful for it. I felt as refreshed as if I had had a good night's sleep after he had finished.

Shane appeared out of the crowd on the pontoon and gave a cheery wave, which only served to make me feel worse. It was such a shame that circumstance had placed him in this position. We went below for a chat. I wasn't going to beg; he had a job to do and guidelines to follow. If we didn't fit in with them then I would be thankful for what he had done to get me this far. I laid out what little I had managed to pull together and ended by saying that I understood the situation he was in and would respect his decision. As desperate as it looked, I still believed that I could do it and whatever happened I would make good my debts. I just needed time. We talked it through to a backdrop of foghorns and cheers of support as the other competitors were towed out. It was a simple commercial dilemma; a case of weighing up the credibility that the Transat would bring to the project against dropping out and replacing it with hospitality work to bring in some money. An accountant, unable to quantify the value of positive PR, might plump for the safer option; in the real world it would be the final nail in the coffin.

Shane had to make a ballsy decision. It had to be made straight away and it was his arse on the line, not mine. He looked up and told me that it all came down to people. He had always had faith in me, still had, and there was no way that he was going to stop me going. Don't worry about the mess, he said. It was his music to face and we would sort it out when I got back. It was time to focus on what was important now, enjoy the race and go for a result. Shane's decision was delivered with dignity and sincerity. What a bloke. It was less than three hours to the start now. We shook hands, the boat was cleared apart from a scratch crew and we were off. To this day I have no idea what his head office had to say to Shane. He just smiles and says not to worry about it, but I suspect he got his knuckles rapped or whatever happens in the banking world. I sailed my heart out in that race, our skin depended on it.

The start is a haze. Jim Doxey explained the emergency back-up system that he had installed on the keel hydraulics as we were towed out. We put the main up, found some clear water and kicked in the modified autopilot for the first time. I had found it too harsh during my short work-up sail and a new set of drive gears had been added to dampen it. It seemed fine. I wrote down the basics on the bulkhead and decided to read the manual once at sea. I just couldn't concentrate – I had only known for sure that I was going to start the race an hour previously. Boats were everywhere – there were more than 70 entrants – and collision was a very real risk.

I handed over the helm, stood on the foredeck, took a deep breath and had a talk to myself. Change gear, it's only a yacht race. Put everything else aside and do a good job. You're in your own world now; this is your environment; feel the wind, get in touch with it again, work with it, relax, it's easy, you've already done it many times before, rerun the film. I'm ready, time for a cup of tea, no more talk. I might feel absolutely fucked but I'm going to take this race by the horns and push myself like I have never pushed myself before. This one's for Tracey and the team. It's time for my companions to leave. 'Cheers, guys. See you when I get back.' I feel a little distant, I've already left. They jump into the RIB and I begin to think about the start.

It was as if a great weight had suddenly been lifted. It was just me and the boat now. It was time to get to know each other and to get a feel for the competition. A number of other Vendée competitors were cutting their teeth and, being better prepared, offered an excellent benchmark. The hot competition in my class was Giovanni Soldini on *Telecom Italia* who had come straight from the last British Oxygen Challenge (BOC) single-handed, round-the-world race, in which he had competed with distinction. He was a master of his trade, his boat had been modified and he had a new set of sails. Under the circumstances I would be happy to keep up with him and learn from the pace.

I took it easy at the start. There was a decent breeze and I wasn't about to bend the boat in the confusion. I decided on a conservative rig – staysail with one reef in the main – and hung back a bit. I would be slightly late for the gun but would make sure I had a dose of speed so that I could drive through the guaranteed line of stopwatch wallahs who would claim to be first across the line but at the same time be dead in the water. Things felt good. Took a deep breath, looked round and there was the *Aqua Quorum* spectators' boat, waving flags and blowing horns. It was great to see their smiling faces. I had been a bit naughty and spent our last cent on chartering it, but it was the right decision. Everyone was there bar Tracey; she doesn't do starts, she never has. We say our goodbyes at home and I get on with it; it's a private moment that we don't like to share. She watches the start on the telly with the kids and gets on with life.

Twenty, fifteen, ten seconds. I was slightly high on the line. The keel already up, I headed for the wall of competitors barging for pole position – it was a solid muddle of confusion. *Aqua Quorum* accelerated as the wind filled her sails, a smooth, purposeful feeling. Spray cascaded over the bow in a sparkle of light as the sun was caught in what had become a fluid chandelier. I cranked in the main and flattened its shape into an efficient knife, she dug her shoulder in and surged ahead, life coursing through our veins. Twelve knots and rising. I heard the gun go off in the background as we charged for the line. Head down, there was no stopping us now, we had got the Atlantic to cross. Light broke through a fissure in the fleet to the right, it reflected off water that had been carved up by the thrashings of many. It beckoned, go for it, there was no time for second thoughts. I put the helm down further and *Aqua Quorum* leapt at the gap, accelerating by the second. She felt light, free. Christ, there wasn't room, breathe in, we hurtled for the gap full of adrenalin and burst, inches to spare, into clear air. Shit, that was good.

I was too confined to trust myself with the autopilot, I hadn't used it in anger yet and didn't know my way around the settings. The wind was up and I was getting soaked; it was a bright sunny day and the cleanest, most refreshing shower I could remember for a long time. Freedom. I would use this race to clear my head and come back to the financial hassles with renewed vigour. We were doing OK. She was fast, even with only the staysail and main. Giovanni was just ahead of us and was no faster; if anything we might have had the slightest edge. I hoped Adrian could see this, he would be just like me, happy as can be. I kept tweaking the sails, I had got to use this race to find out what made her tick, it was boat for boat. There was a huge spectator fleet, everyone was caught up in the race, waving, blowing foghorns and making our big day special. Chay pulled alongside in a big gin palace powerboat. 'Go for it, Pete. Show the bastards how it's done.' He'll never be tamed; he's still a goer and would swap places at the drop of a hat.

The adrenalin was starting to wear off. I felt cold, my eyes were gritty with exhaustion and my resistance was so low that I had minimal endurance. It was going to be a long night and a hard race. It would take a few days to get back on my feet and firing on all cylinders, but I just had to make it happen. It was time for the autopilot, now that we had pulled our way into clear water. I left the helm at the back of the cockpit and ran for the controls on the main bulkhead. Christ, which button did Alan say I had to press? It was only a couple of hours ago. The green one, the green one . . . bzzzz . . . bzzzz . . . bzzzz. It was working, and not badly, either. We were in business, the gear change looked bang on, get my head round the manual and we'd be there. I hoisted the number two and we really started tramping. What a glorious day for a race.

Looking back I can remember it clearly. You never know what a start is going to be like, it could have been a gale on the nose. As it turned out someone was looking after us. We spinnakered out into the Atlantic and, fortunately, the wind died as night fell. I was on my knees by then, and trying to keep going was exhausting. Everything was new. When I rounded Eddystone Lighthouse I rigged up the new spinnaker pole system, which Adrian had fitted on the Friday before. I did my first spinnaker gybe and generally fiddled around as I got my first feel of the boat single-handed. BT Aeronautical and Maritime had come on as a sponsor during the last fortnight and Alan had finished fitting their equipment in the early hours of the start day. Eileen Moran, a good friend and crew member of the BT Global Challenge, had organised a couple of ThinkPads from IBM to act as my link with the system. I managed to fax a quick message to Tracey to let her know all was well. It's an amazing setup, my message would drop out of our fax at home within seconds of my pressing the send button. It became a family lifeline.

I played with the radio and was able to pull in a weatherfax, which was displayed on one of the computer screens. Too tired to concentrate, I went through the motions of deciding my game plan. It was obvious that this race was going to be won or lost on tactics during the first week. There were differing opinions as to which way to go. The majority were heading straight out into the Atlantic in search of the big depression which was brewing, while a number of us, including Giovanni, opted to go north, well north, in search of a narrow easterly air stream which looked as though it might develop. It was a masterstroke which, for my part, can be credited to British weather-router Vincent Geake.

The importance of the first week of the race became obvious to me the day before the start. Weather isn't my strongest point and, being up to my nuts in mud and bullets, I was incapable of sifting through the relevant information and giving it the level of concentration it deserved. The rules precluded outside assistance during the race, but anything up to the start was kosher. I found Vincent's number and called him. It was a real cheek, I had never met the man but I simply had to do well and Vincent was undoubtedly the chap for the job. I explained my situation, and said: 'I can't pay you, so feel free to say no.' His enthusiasm for what I was doing virtually made the lights on my mobile pulsate.

Here was a bundle of energy. 'Shit, don't worry. Thanks for calling, only too glad to help, great to see someone out there doing it. I'm off to a birthday party, but I think they have a fax machine. I'll slide away, work on it and get back to you.'

That night I returned home to the best weather breakdown I have ever seen. I followed his advice and found myself, along with a few others, way out in front of the fleet and going like the clappers. The pace was staggering and we were power-reaching where one would expect to be beating – at times at speeds of up to twenty knots. Race positions came in each morning and evening and I plotted them on the chart, paying particular attention to Giovanni, who was sailing a canny race. He was always one step ahead and was an ideal foil against which to measure our efforts. *Aqua Quorum* was the faster boat, Giovanni the better sailor. He used his experience from the BOC to play his boat like a finely tuned instrument. Knowing this type of craft so well, he was able to anticipate every opportunity before it came his way and maximise every change in the weather, where I missed the odd one and was left to react. Every fix put him in a slightly better position for the next twelve hours. It was a pleasure to watch him and an even greater pleasure to see that *Aqua Quorum* was capable of digging me out of trouble each time.

After each fix I would try a slightly new sail combination and fiddle away until I was happy that I had coaxed everything out of the setup that I could for the next twelve hours. Giovanni's next position would then tell me whether it had made a difference. It seemed, thanks to Keith's dagger boards, that we had the edge when flogging to windward. However, it was when we were power reaching that we really came into our own. *Aqua Quorum* loved it and thanks to Gary was robust enough to be driven really hard. I would wind everything in and she would sit on a permanent plane with sustained speeds of over twenty knots. As the race progressed, I was able to improve on this as I got the feel of how to set her up. She just flew from the top of one wave to another in a ball of spray, noise and violent motion. It might be impossible to think, cook or relax, but the speed made every minute of the discomfort worthwhile.

I settled into good, safe routines for headsail changes, reefing the main and moving around the deck. It didn't take long for the basics to become instinctive; if we could work this well together from scratch then who knows what we would be capable of once our relationship was properly bedded down. I was pleased with progress on the water and, judging by the faxes from Amelia Lyon, who had already done such a great PR job for *Aqua Quorum*, it was much the same ashore. We all knew the importance of this race for the Vendée project and Amelia surpassed herself by making sure that we picked up the lion's share of publicity. The more attention we attracted now the better chance I would have of getting sponsors on my return.

It was tough going, though. As I became more and more tired, I found that my emotions started to swing one way and another. I just couldn't forget the financial mess at home and it perpetually niggled at the back of my mind and started to get me down. I spent a lot of time thinking myself round in circles and, as fruitless as I knew it was, I just couldn't shake it. It was like a big cloud.

The race started to go wrong as we closed the Grand Banks of Newfoundland. The deep depression had developed into a brute and had decided it was time to grace the fleet with its presence. We took a frightful pounding and the boat shook like it had never shaken before. Yves Parlier on *Aquitaine Innovations*, one of the Vendée favourites, was dismasted. Halfway through the storm I ran out of steam and was only just managing to keep going. The boat was quite happy, but for me it was a battle for survival. It was frustrating; I felt shagged out where I would normally feel boundless energy and full of fight. I love a good old ding-dong and as a result can usually guarantee gaining a decent chunk of miles on the opposition but the project had taken its toll and I had no more to give.

For the first time in my life I felt as though I actually needed a holiday. All I could do was ignore it and, taking a leaf from the Royal Marines, make my body take the punishment. Little did I know that the Atlantic was about to give me just what I was looking for on this race: the thrashing of my life. It would teach me all those lessons that have to be learnt before taking on something like the Vendée.

The wind changed direction as a front passed through. I slapped a tack in and spent a couple of hours on deck checking every detail and making a mental note of things that would need to be addressed before the Vendée. Some netting here, a rope bag there. I knocked a reef out with some satisfaction as the wind began to ease; she had pulled through and was in remarkable shape. From now on the weather should improve as we closed the eastern seaboard; the worst was behind us. I popped my head down the aft hatch to check out the back of the boat and was horrified to find it under two feet of water. It was slopping everywhere and wasn't doing the autopilot any favours. I grabbed a bucket and started to bail out the water as quickly as I could. It was full of food and all sorts. It suddenly dawned on me that this was only the beginning of the problem; it must extend further forward into the compartment under the cockpit. I grabbed a torch, knelt in the foot of water that was slopping everywhere as the boat bucked about, and stuck my head through the hatch. It was like something from a horror movie, there were gallons of water rushing from one side of the boat to the other. The water would hit the structural beam, slam up into the deckhead a couple of feet above and project itself back down again.

All my food was stored here. It should have been safe and dry but the whole lot was destroyed. So violent was the motion that the tins had ruptured. I had been popping aft every five days or so to replenish my ready-to-use box in the accommodation quarters. I had left the job until after the storm and as a result had eaten everything in the box and it was now empty. This was looking pretty serious; I couldn't use the bilge pump to clear the water because it was clogged with food and bits of packaging. I had to bail from the forward compartment into the aft one – only eight buckets at a time because I couldn't afford to get the autopilot any wetter than it already was. Climb through, bail that over the side and repeat the process. It took about four hours of concerted effort to clear. I was on my knees by the end of it thanks to the violent motion of the boat and the awkwardness of the job. My oilies had ripped on the roof, I was covered in shit and thoroughly pissed off.

The good news was that I couldn't find any holes in the structure. It wasn't immediately apparent where the water was coming from but at least I could keep on top of it with a bucket. I must have lost miles to the opposition and just wanted to get back into the competition. I shook another reef out, had a well-earned cup of tea, and took stock. I had half a tin of beans, a packet of Rolos, some crisps, half a packet of cream crackers and plenty of sugar, powdered milk and tea bags. Things were not looking good. It was a long way to the finish and I decided to pull in a weatherfax to get a handle on how long it might take. The radio was dead – the tuner unit was in the same compartment as the food and it had been flooded. I decided to do nothing but drink sweet tea for four days in order to shrink my stomach – a Rolo would feel like a banquet after that. Without any weather information I would be forced to follow the shortest route to the finish. Losing the radio was a bigger blow than losing the food – I would undoubtedly give away many of those hard-earned miles in the fickle conditions of the eastern seaboard.

I plotted the race positions to find that, thanks to fannying about bailing out the aft compartment, I had already lost a lot to Giovanni. I was determined to stay in contention. We were second in class and third overall, and if I was lucky we might just hold on to it. I got back to the job and started to feel hungrier by the hour as my body began to recover from the storm. I think the first forty-eight hours were the worst for hunger pangs, after that I just felt permanently washed out as I tried to work the boat as hard as I could. The wind died away that night, the positions showed that the leaders were slipping away and the pack behind was closing in. It was very demoralising: I was piss-wet through, cold and starving.

During the night the wind picked up from the east. I hoisted the spinnaker and we started to make excellent speed. If I pushed the boat hard enough I might just break out of the limbo I was in and join the front runners again. It was shit or bust and I wasn't going to back off for anyone. The wind kept rising. I changed to the heavy spinnaker and we were soon flying along on the edge of control. The quicker I got there the quicker I could have a decent meal. I started to fantasise about what I would eat. 'Just wipe its arse and cut off its horns, boy.' I had by now got to know the Cetrek autopilot and found that it could keep the boat on course in marginal conditions. We were reaching speeds of twenty-four knots with water flying everywhere. It was fantastic; I stood in the cockpit holding on to the cabin top with a grin on my face. If it's fun up here just imagine what those greybeards of the Southern Ocean will be like.

I popped below for yet another cup of tea with about four

sugars in it – the water-maker was working overtime. I dropped off to sleep but woke up about ten minutes later with a start. The motion of *Aqua Quorum* had changed; she was yawing a lot more and I could sense that she was starting to struggle under the press of sail. It was taking much longer for the boat to respond to the helm, she was shuddering from wave to wave and peak speeds had risen. It was time to reduce sail. I jumped on deck to find things a lot wilder, the sea angry and waves standing on end with steep faces. Everything pointed to a reduction in sail but, like a fool, I broke my golden rule and didn't follow my instincts. My blood was up and if I pushed hard I might break back into the lead group. She was coping – just. The cloud base looked angry but settled, the depression was below me and moving fast, and in theory it should start to abate.

An hour later the wind suddenly increased. I was dozing in the cockpit and opened my eyes to see a wind line approaching. I would never be able to reduce sail in time – the boat was on the edge and it would be too much to ask of the autopilot. The lesser of two evils would be for me to steer through the worst, and then put the autopilot back on and reduce sail as soon as possible. I flicked the pilot off and ran aft for the helm, just managing to catch her as the wind line ripped through the rig. Shitty death! She leapt as though stuck with a pig prod; the wind was up to forty knots and I had full main and spinnaker up. I sat on the deck, one hand on the tiller, the other on a stanchion, and braced my feet on deck fittings. The front two thirds of the boat was out of the water, the bow was up and she was touching twenty-seven knots as the gusts swept in from nowhere. I couldn't believe that she was still upright. Adrian had designed something so efficient that she just went faster and faster – there didn't seem to be any limit. The short, choppy seas made it very physical on the helm and called for a lot of concentration.

What a prat! I was trapped by my own stupidity. She was overcanvased and yet there was no way I could put the boat back on autopilot so that I could go forward and reduce sail. All I could do was helm and hope for the best. We were now climbing up the back of waves, hanging for what felt like an eternity with only the rudders in the wave top, as spume whistled away into the distance. She would then break free and I could feel the transom scudding down the face of the wave as the bow dropped and we accelerated into the back of the next one. Jesus, whatever happened now I must keep clear of the runner – the rig was going to go for sure. I held on like buggery through shuddering deceleration as the front of the boat disappeared from view with wanton enthusiasm. A wall of water swept back across the cockpit with frightening force. I took a deep breath, lying on my back to let it pass over me, as instinct and brute strength kept her on course.

I shook the water out of my eyes. Fuck me, we were about to rip another wave asunder as if it wasn't there. I glanced up at the rig to see that all was well, took a deep breath and . . . off we went again. The water was freezing cold – we'd reached the Labrador current as it made its way south from the Arctic and that must also have been why the seas were suddenly so mean. It was foggy now and I hoped there were no icebergs about; it was said to be a bad year for them. I decided just to enjoy it. No one in their right mind would have done this to a boat: the wind was forty-five knots and I had full sail up. There was nothing I could do and I started to laugh – might just as well have fun – and thought to myself that it must be every bit as exciting as windsurfing in Hawaiian breakers. I couldn't see that there was any difference apart from the fact that my board was fifty feet long. I was in the rhythm of it now, actually playing the waves for more speed. God knows what would happen when I lost it.

I had been at work for six hours now and I was feeling it. I was cold and not only were my back and shoulders cramped and knotted with the effort, but I was also starving and hadn't had a meal in ages. I reasoned that the blow had to abate sometime and felt I might just get away with it. I couldn't wait to see the positions, I reckoned I must have made miles on the others and hoped it would put me back in the running. I grinned to myself: eat your heart out, Giovanni, you won't shake us off that easily. She skipped to the left on an odd lump of water, I caught it, not quite, gave her a bit more. The rudder bit and she was going like a dingo now. There was so much pressure that I just couldn't move the rudder and I knew she was going to go over. I had enough purchase to make it slow and graceful as she leaned to windward and started to go in to a Chinese gybe. My left foot was in the water, the spray coming off it like a shotgun blast. Come on, come on, the rig would never take it if she went at this speed. She sat like that for a while and I felt I might just get away with it; every ounce of effort was concentrated on the rudder. I looked round and assessed the situation. The rudder suddenly went limp; bugger it, she was going. Time to get out of there. I launched myself at the accommodation hatch and it was a perfect dive, arms outstretched, hands together. I didn't give a shit what happened inside – it was the lesser of two evils.

I arced across the cockpit and my hands sailed through the hatch as I sensed the boom slam across. There was no chance of stopping it, given I had a full main in those conditions. The rig was bound to go over the side, and the hatch twisted in front of me as the boat started to capsize around my diving figure. Crunch! My safety strop brought me up with a teeth-rattling jar and my feet were going ten to the dozen on the deck to no avail. Laughing at the irony of it, I dumped the strop and tumbled below into a face full of bilge water, tools and – disaster of disasters – my sleeping bag. I couldn't believe it, my sleeping bag, sod the boat. I shook as much water out of it as I could and stuffed it into the starboard bunk directly overhead. She was flat on her side and the cabin skylight had become a bay window with a great view of the rig lying in the water. Waves were breaking over the top of the boat and spume was catching the light as it whistled round either end of the hull. What a shot! It couldn't have looked any more dramatic and I wasn't able to find the bloody camera in the mess. I promised myself that I would sort out a more handy stowage for the Vendée; it was bound to happen again.

It was deathly quiet now and she seemed quite happy on her side. The keel was on the wrong side of the hull and the full main was backed against the leeward runner and pinning her to the water. Damon Roberts and his lads at Carbospars were in for a pint; how the rig could still be standing was beyond me. I quietly took stock of the situation from the safety of the cabin. All the battens were broken and the spinnaker was shredded and drifting round the masthead – I decided to make that a priority because if she came up with that tangled in the rig I was in trouble. The backstay was intact. In fact, the rig looked pretty good. She was so light that the cockpit was proud of the water and as dry as a bone. I leaned out to check the water level. The canny bastard, it was exactly where Adrian said it would be – that would have pleased him no end. It was time for action so, after I'd checked my life jacket, put a knife in each pocket, and equipped myself with spanner, pliers and a couple of sail ties, I climbed into the cockpit, put the windward runner on, took up the main sheet and scrambled my way to the rig. The dagger boards were now horizontal and made a great seat as I stopped and took it in. She was content where she was for the moment, and I made the most of the opportunity to learn – it might be night next time. What a great boat.

I dropped into the water and began to fight the spinnaker. It was a real mess. I opened the forehatch, which was like the door to a dumb waiter at that angle, and started shoving the spinnaker in, the waves doing their best to drag it out again. It was three feet in, two feet out, three feet in, two feet out. The halyard had jammed despite my having flaked it out. Bugger, it was on the high side of the hull so I made the spinny fast with a sail tie, climbed up, freed it and then plunged back into the drink. It was like trying to handle a hot-air balloon full of water – it took ages and was very tiring. It was good fun, though, and I was dead chuffed with the boat, looking around, taking in all the details, and not missing anything. I was determined to make the most of the experience. As the last tatter of spinnaker disappeared into the hatch I could have cried – £4,500 down the drain. I decided I wouldn't be so stupid again. I would have to think the whole thing through and identify the critical points and decisions that caused this mess. I knew I was gung ho in not having reduced sail earlier, but I sensed that the cause of the capsize went deeper than that. I just couldn't put my finger on it.

I cleared the spinnaker pole, lashed it down as best I could, which was very difficult at that angle, and then hurried back to the cockpit. I had a bit more control now and it was time to ease the leeward runner and see if she wanted to come up. I'd already nipped over the side and the keel looked fine from the outside – I couldn't resist standing on it for a laugh. She came up slowly, the rig was out of the water but the wind was still pressing her. I felt sure that if I pumped up the keel she would right but I didn't want to put any extra load on the structure until I had established that there was no damage. Better to tackle the problem from the other end, more logically. So it was back to the rig to climb underneath and sort out the main halyard, which had been floating about for a while now and was in a real bunch of bastards – it took ages to undo. She was making about two knots on her side. 'Just can't keep a good boat down,' I told myself. I climbed to windward, dumped the halyard with my foot and started dragging the main down as she began to right herself. The main suddenly jumped and, as she came up fast, I grabbed a bit more in and ran for the tiller. The rudders bit and we were off downwind again. Bloody hell, that was close. I took my time and looked at everything in detail. Amazingly, the rig looked as good as when it was stepped.

I hit the autopilot and she was back doing her job, couldn't have been happier. I spent a couple of hours on deck making the mess good and then went below for a cup of tea. I was shaking from the exertion and lack of food. Sod the four-day abstention, it was time for a couple of crackers. It was carnage below and hydraulic oil had spread everywhere. I prayed that the keel wasn't buggered, that would be all I needed. It seemed to be fine, and I guessed that the oil was from the overflow when she was on her side. I'd have to sort that one out. I scooped the sopping wet stores out of the bilges and threw them on to the bunk; there was no time for finesse and the bunk was wet anyway. I dragged on some dry clothes, plotted the positions and saw that we had been crucified. What a bastard! That innocuous little cross on a piece of paper was quite crushing and it signified the end of my race. I had really let the side down – all the work that the lads had put in had been ruined by my stupidity. The chattering sound of the Fischer Panda generator cut into my gloom as it started automatically; it had been quietly monitoring the batteries throughout the carnage and it was time for a charge. I smiled from ear to ear; at least someone was on my side. Barry, Sean and Gary, the lads who sorted it out for me, deserved a pat on the back when I got home.

The race had now suddenly changed. It was over for me and my priorities needed to be re-established. I had done the equivalent of a twelfth of the Vendée and I felt I'd already blown it. However, it had been a priceless experience and I had to make sure that I learned every lesson I could from it. Every problem I'd experienced had a logical reason behind it and therefore a solution. Ninety per cent of what went wrong could be attributed to the fact that it was our first sail – this is what I had been out here to discover. Apart from the disappointment of losing ground, I was delighted. *Aqua Quorum* was obviously bulletproof and I knew, whatever the end result, that we had the legs for a good race. It was time to write down all my observations while they were fresh in my mind. I plotted our position to see that we were right on the edge of the Flemish Cap, where the depth was only 120 metres. No wonder the seas had built up so suddenly.

It was dark now, still blowing on deck and I suddenly felt cold and terribly weak. I couldn't afford to eat anything more, there was still a long way to go. I replaced the top battens and, feeling punch-drunk, decided that it was too dangerous to finish the job. I was starting to drop tools and it was time to back off. I put the main up with three reefs in – the rest would have to wait for daylight and a little more energy. I downed two cups of hot, sweet tea, rolled into my wet sleeping bag and dropped into a deep sleep.

I still couldn't put my finger on what was bugging me. There was something that I hadn't covered – it was important and I did a lot of dreaming. Of course! The rudders. It came to me during the night that they were still too big. The problem was that Adrian had designed such a good hull that it was able to hold on for much longer than any other boat I'd sailed. The rudders were so large that, with the aid of such a forgiving hull, they masked the danger signals. You got no warning that the boat was being pressed beyond its limits until it was too late. I needed to halve their area to ensure that alarm bells started to ring much earlier to give me time to take the appropriate action. I thought back to the race so far and the fact that I seemed to be reducing sail area much too late. I had halved the sail area at one point and still didn't lose any speed. She was so light that she didn't need a great deal of driving power. She had been gagged by the rudders. We hadn't been talking to each other and she'd been suffering in silence. Bingo!

I spent the next day tidying up, doing various repairs and replacing the rest of the battens in the mainsail. It was very disheartening to see Giovanni sail away into an unassailable lead. I was feeling very tired and really couldn't muster the energy to push the boat as hard as I would normally have done. It seemed that I had a new problem every day. I had endless trouble with the salt-water pump for the generator and spent hours trying to resolve it. The leeward runner got caught in the rigging one night as I pulled it on in readiness for a tack. I discovered by chance when I untangled the mess in the darkness that the main block had lost one of its pins. But for that chance discovery I would have surely lost the rig. I ripped the head out of the lightweight ghoster and had to climb to the masthead to retrieve the halyard. I canted the keel to leeward so that she lay well over and used the external halyards to shinny up the rig. By now I was so short of energy due to lack of food that I quickly became tired; I had to stop every now and then for a rest when normally I would climb up in one go. By the time I got back down I was light-headed and shaking like a leaf.

Every day seemed to bring a new disappointment which, because I was so tired, had a far greater effect on my attitude than it would normally have done. The generator kept playing up and I decided to sort it out once and for all by removing the keel top covers and checking the pipework underneath. I was horrified to find cracks in the top of the keel structure which were opening and closing to the motion of the boat. It was the last straw, and once again I could see the Vendée slipping away. There was no way that I could afford a big repair job anywhere – let alone in America. Indeed, I was concerned about whether or not it would hold together to the finish. I faxed Adrian with a description of the problem. Despite being very concerned, he was adamant that it wasn't life-threatening; Martyn Smith was in agreement. Take it easy on the boat and keep monitoring the keel. Adrian would meet me in Newport. Don't worry about the cost of the flight, this was on him. What a good egg.

The run in to the finish was a hard and dispiriting experience and I was delighted to close the line. I had made contact with fellow competitor Catherine Chabaud the day before finishing and we had a good old chat. She had had problems with her keel and we swapped notes. To add insult to injury, the wind died in torrential rain 400 yards from the finish. I used my last ounce of effort to row across the line – it had been a hard, shitty race. Steve Whittell and his brother Phil were the first to jump on board and when they handed me a sandwich I nearly bit my fingers off in the rush to get some food down, the first in eight days. I didn't stop eating for about twelve hours.

Newport was a busy stopover thanks to a lot of work needing to be done on the boat. Steve and Phil worked like dogs. Adrian arrived and took a hard look at the keel. It transpired that there wasn't any problem at all: what had looked like a crack across a solid member was, in fact, movement between two pieces. Resin had filled the gap in such a manner that it looked like a solid piece. Talk about getting to know your boat. I felt a bit of an idiot, albeit a very relieved one. We examined the boat to find that she had stood up to the race remarkably well. I was very pleased with her and once I had completed the necessary jobs on my return I felt confident that we would be ready for the Vendée.

We slipped for Plymouth as soon as we could and had a great sail back home. There were three of us on board: myself, Steve

Whittell and Andy Newcomb, an old friend from my Mirror dinghy days in Torpoint. Andy proved a real asset. I was washed out after the race and needed someone who could take the weight a bit. Andy was so transfixed by the boat that we couldn't get him off the helm, which enabled me to sleep a lot more than I might normally have done. I managed to fit my much-needed holiday in on the return trip and stepped off the boat feeling refreshed. Steve loved the trip and, considering that he had never sailed in his life, coped very well. We made excellent speeds, with daily runs of between 230 and 270 nautical miles being the norm; and on one occasion 314 miles were achieved with consummate ease.

We saw many whales on the trip. On a number of occasions they played round the boat – an amazing sight. In fact, we hit the first one we saw. We were in the middle of a sail change when Steve looked up and said, 'What's that in the water?' I immediately ran aft to trip the autopilot and slam the helm over. There wasn't time, and the boat shuddered on impact. I looked forward to see the bow rise a good four feet as we rode up the whale's back with Steve clinging to the bow for dear life. Goodness knows what went through his mind at that moment; his eyes were like dinner plates for some time afterwards. We came to a stop as the keel hit the side of the whale. There was a huge swirl of water under the bow, the whale turned with amazing speed and was suddenly lying alongside us. It was so big that you could have put a table and chairs on its back and sat round for a three-course meal. We slipped past with mouths open. Its tail came up just as we cleared it and then down it went. Talk about galvanising us into action: we donned life jackets and clipped ourselves to the boat and waited to see if it decided to return the compliment. I don't think we hurt it; we weren't going that fast and, as we were so light, we slid up on to its back rather than drove into it.

We sailed into Plymouth to be met by many of Steve's friends, who had come all the way from Huddersfield to see him in. His adventure had caused quite a stir up north; even the local television had followed his progress. It was a great welcome which soon made its way to the bar for a big fried breakfast and a beer. Tracey brought the kids down and we headed for home, promising to return for a meal that evening. I had put a lot of thought into my business plan on the way back home across the Atlantic and had a clear strategy in place by the time I stepped off the boat. I would need it; there were just over three months to the start of the Vendée and an awful lot to be done on both the boat and finances. The first thing on my list was a meeting with Shane to thank him and find out where I stood with the bank. I had a mountain of paperwork to plough through when I got home. The first surprise was that I was to open the Plymouth Boat Show the next morning – there went our family day. No rest for the wicked.

The rest of the mail left me with an awful, hollow feeling in my stomach; the numbers looked dreadful. I would have to show the bank some movement pretty quickly if I wanted to keep the show on the road. The longer term looked healthier as I had a lot of hospitality bookings; it was just that it would take a lot more than hospitality to balance the accounts and make up for the month without income. The press cuttings were great: Amelia had done an amazing job for Aqua Quorum, so they should be happy with their investment, and I had proof that the project could generate first-class results. As usual it would all be about getting my head down and burning the midnight oil. At least I had my energy back now and, despite the gloomy financial picture, felt that doing the Transat had been the right decision. I would keep working as hard as I could until the Vendée start line. If it all came to a halt at the last minute, then so be it. At least I would know that I had been true to myself.

We had a great meal that night. There is nothing like the

company of down-to-earth northerners, many of whom I had got to know on my visits to Pete and Steve. It was more like a reunion than anything else and the smile on Steve's face was infectious. He had truly had the adventure of his life and was enjoying every moment of the homecoming. He introduced me to Alex Kirk, his Scottish stepfather, who was very interested in hearing about the project. It was decided after a few more beers that a sail was called for – they had all travelled an awfully long way and deserved it. We made it an early morning start so that we could fit a couple of hours in before I shot off to open the Boat Show. Never have I had such a bleary-eyed crew. Steve's brain cells just couldn't take it – he had forgotten everything that he had learned on the trip back, so my hands were more than full. However, it was a great success and well worth the effort just to see the pleasure on their faces.

I said my goodbyes as I put the boat to bed, grabbed my bag and leapt on to the pontoon – I was late for the show. Alex beckoned me to one side as I rushed off; he had something to say and assured me that he wouldn't hold me up. His words brought an abrupt halt to my hopping from foot to foot. He thought the project was excellent and that I deserved to do the Vendée. He knew of my problems from Steve and wanted to help by becoming a silver sponsor. A cheque for £10,000 would be in the post as soon as he got back to the office, and he refused to take anything in return. Being a part of the family was enough for him, he just wanted to see me do it. It's not often that I am lost for words but Alex had stopped me in my tracks. All I could do was shake his hand; words seem cheap when you are on the receiving end of a gesture from the heart. Alex, being the kind of man that he is, was true to his word – and his timing was impeccable because not only did it help with the bank but it also put a spring back in my step.

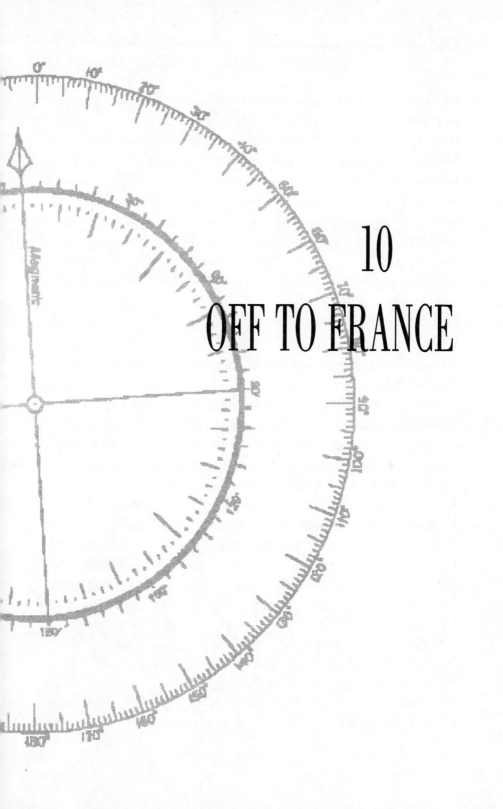

10
OFF TO FRANCE

*Obstacles are what you see when you take
your mind off the goal.*

Yachtsman Peter Blake

It was a long, hard three and a half months to the start of the
Vendée Globe and we were only just to make it. It became
obvious, a month or so after the Transat, that the only way to
tackle my overdraft would be to view the debt as long term rather
than as a problem which applied solely to this project. I would
have to use the boat to pay for itself on my return. All I needed to
do was ensure that I could keep my head above water while I was
away. I would start swimming again when I got back.

Corporate hospitality was proving very popular. I had a lot of
talks coming in and a number of other areas of consultancy work
were opening up. Indeed, the demand for hospitality was such
that I chartered *Maiden* for a month and put her in the safe hands
of Nick Booth. I now had two boats working full time; if
sponsorship wasn't looking good then at least business was. I
decided to concentrate on three things: immediate monetary
problems, race preparation and getting my ducks in order for a
hard season on my return.

I had originally set up my company Maritime Challenges not
only as a vehicle for the Vendée but also with a view to

developing my long-term ideas on my return. However, it was time to move the timetable forward a little and put some of those ideas into practice. One of the things that seemed daft was having to pay large sums to charter *Maiden* when I could own a boat of my own. I began to look for something that we could purchase and make good during the winter in readiness for the next corporate season.

Out of the blue I stumbled across *British Steel*, the boat that Chay had sailed round the world single-handed in 1971. She was lying in Portsmouth dockyard in a sorry state; you could shove a screwdriver through the base of her mast, and the engine was spread in rusty pieces over the floor. There she was, a piece of maritime history, going for a song. Because she was built of steel it wouldn't be too hard to bring her back to good condition. Seeing such a classic yacht in that state broke my heart – she was the forerunner of modern ocean racing, and I decided to give her the attention she deserved.

There was a lot of interest in her and I only had a week to pull the funds together. It sounds daft but I felt I needed to go deeper into debt to create the means to get myself out of debt. The bank was not in a position to lend me the money so I looked elsewhere. I had met Mike Garside when I trained his wife, who was one of the BT Global Challenge crew. We had much in common – a love of the sea and a spell in the armed forces. Mike was planning to do the next BOC Challenge and was keen that I give him training and advice when I returned from the Vendée. He knew I was desperate for funds, and offered to help me out by paying for the training in advance. It was a generous gesture and I wrestled with my conscience on the train up to London for a meeting with him. I just couldn't accept his offer; I won't take something on unless I can do it justice and my long-term future was too uncertain to make such a commitment.

I explained my feelings to Mike and then told him about my latest plan. He immediately offered to help by lending me enough to both buy and refit *British Steel*. The loan would be at the going rate of interest and, if it all fell apart, he would have the boat for security. The next step was to ask Nick Booth who, like me, had no wish to end his days sailing round in circles as a sail-training instructor, to take on the job of supervising the refit until we had her up and running and earning her keep. Although I could pay very little, Nick jumped at the offer. I now had two boats on the books and was confident that I would be in with a fighting chance when I returned from the Vendée.

While all this was going on I was quietly working on another future proposal – once again with Adrian Thompson. For some time I had been at a loss as to what I wanted to do after the Vendée – how could I possibly eclipse what was to me the ultimate challenge? I thought about other areas such as mountaineering, arctic exploration, building a submarine to explore the ocean bed and so on. My dilemma was solved by the launch of what is, in my view, one of the most exciting events imaginable.

Frenchman Bruno Peyron, a man of exceptional ability and vision, had announced an ocean race to celebrate the millennium. There would be no rules, apart from the course, and it would be known simply as The Race. Bruno had drawn inspiration from winning the Jules Verne trophy, when he became the first man to sail around the world in under eighty days. I knew as soon as I heard of his scheme what I wanted to do after the Vendée. It would be a global drag race in the biggest, fastest, most high-tech sailing vessels in history. Adrian's face lit up at the prospect of designing a vessel for the event – you could virtually hear his cogs speed up. We agreed on a design concept for an extremely big and fast catamaran. The Vendée was already becoming a springboard for even greater things.

Never have I worked as hard as I did during the next three months and my business diary bulged at the seams. It was a race against time and a shitty one, at that. It was not a pleasant period – nothing but long hours and a lot of stress – and we only just managed to pull it off.

I worked *Aqua Quorum* for as long as I could, hoisting her out of the water for a final refit at the last possible minute. Many jobs were put to one side for financial reasons. In an ideal world we could have done with another £30,000 and an extra month to tick off all the items on an endless work list. Despite this, she was still the best-prepared boat that I have ever sailed in, and I felt confident that I had the right tool for the job. I started to focus on the race and felt that if things went my way I had every chance of finishing in the top three.

The Vendée started in Les Sables d'Olonne and we had to be there three weeks before the start day. I wanted to leave Plymouth in full race trim in every detail, right down to the food. As the workload grew I began to rely more and more on the many volunteers who had come forward. Barry Marshall, a friend of Alan Ashley, offered to help out in any way he could. His endless energy and humour were pivotal to getting the boat to the start line and he was to join us in Les Sables d'Olonne for the full three-week work-up. Alan's wife Pauline was another who was always around to help when a pair of hands was needed. Without our helpers we would have failed to make the start on time.

My parents took on the mammoth task of preparing the food for the race – and it kept them busy for a good three weeks. They did a brilliant job. My time in the Marines taught me that the right fuel is an essential part of any campaign – particularly one as strenuous as the Vendée. It doesn't matter how skilled or strong you are, if you don't have the right grub you will slowly grind to a halt. We had a lot of help from nutritionist Maggie

Page, who is a specialist in this area. We knew that I would need a daily intake of 3,500 calories to keep up the work rate in the tropics and that this would rise to 5,500 calories in the Southern Ocean. To keep the weight down we used McDougalls freeze-dried food. I decided that to be on the safe side I would take enough for 120 days.

A six-day menu cycle was devised so that I wouldn't have the same meal every Sunday. My parents worked out the weight of each meal against its calorific content and put the measured ingredients into separate bags. A local butcher in Looe lent us the use of his vacuum-packing machine during the night, and Mum and Dad worked away into the early hours. Once the individual meals were packaged – with a label on the inside in case of flooding – day bags were made up. These contained everything I required for a twenty-four-hour period, right down to individual containers of jam. They were complemented with a six-day bag which covered a menu cycle and consisted of all the ready-to-use things that I might need during that period: vitamin tablets, toilet paper, matches and so on. It was a foolproof system and one that would see me through the race provided I stuck to a simple schedule. All I had to do was eat the day bags in numerical order and the calorific content would automatically vary as I passed through different temperature zones.

Food is not merely fuel, of course. There are times when all you have to look forward to is the next meal, and so my parents packed a surprise meal for every fourteenth day. The weight restriction was relaxed for this one so I could expect all sorts of delights, including tinned food. In addition to this they packed a real belter for my birthday, Christmas and New Year. I also had several storm bags in which there was a day's supply of food that didn't require any cooking at all, so that if it was too rough to cook I would still be able to munch away knowing that the right balance of vitamins and quantity of calories was being shoved down my neck. My cooking facilities were basic: a gimballed, single-ring camping stove, kettle, two saucepans and a small frying pan. I ate my food from a dog bowl, something I highly recommend: it has a wide base to prevent it from tipping over in rough conditions, the high sides stop food escaping and the contents seem to stay warm for longer.

At last it was time to go. Alan Ashley, Keith Fennel and I put *Aqua Quorum* back in the water, had her towed round to Queen Anne's Battery Marina to load her up – and came to a grinding halt. There was absolutely no wind, not a breath, and it was foggy. We couldn't set sail so we passed the time by trying to find the source of a persistent ingress of water in the compartment under the cockpit. All we could think of was that the water was somehow working its way into the structure where the keel exited the hull. This was a serious problem which was to plague me – it might not look much in the marina, but I had already had a taste of the consequences of a leaking hull when I was on the Transat: a failed radio and no food.

Alan decided to run the generator up only to find that it was dead. The generator was fundamental to the campaign and I was forced to delay my departure until it had been looked at properly. I didn't have the budget to fanny about in France, we had to leave Plymouth in full working order. It was a pretty grim night what with fog, rain, no wind and the fact that after all this preparation we couldn't even slip from the marina. On top of this I would now miss the deadline for our arrival in Les Sables d'Olonne and was likely to be given a time penalty. The race rules stipulated that competitors must be at Les Sables d'Olonne by a certain date. The number of·days by which you missed that date would be added on to your finish time. However, I could only be thankful that we had found the problem with the generator now rather than after the start, when it would have forced me to retire from the event.

The generator was a Fischer Panda. It was extremely efficient and could belt out a great charge with minimal fuel consumption. Fischer Panda UK Ltd supplied it free of charge. When they heard of our problem, they drove down from Poole overnight and were with us early the following morning. They traced the fault to an electronic component. There was no way I would have been able to bodge it at sea. It was a sobering thought and I decided to invest in a backup wind generator – sod the expense.

Time for the off. With Alan, Mark Orr and myself on board, we were towed out into the Sound, we raised the sails and quietly slipped out of Plymouth. I took a last look at home and wondered what the next months would bring. Would we return in one piece? Well, it wouldn't be for the want of trying. I straightened out the red ensign, this was for Queen and Country.

The wind didn't improve and we spent two frustrating days drifting up and down the Channel on the tide. There was absolutely nothing that we could do without an engine but wait. I had little experience of French sailing and as a result had no concept of the interest there was on the opposite shore. Unknown to us, our non-arrival was reported in the press and people started to worry that we had been run down in the fog. I, on the other hand, was making the most of a couple of days away from the madding crowd.

We eventually arrived off Les Sables d'Olonne, made our presence known to the harbourmaster and stood by for the tide. We'd been at sea for a few days now so we decided to smarten up a bit and have a shower on deck, taking turns to strip off and get under the bucket. Our call to the harbourmaster had set the race support system in motion: a boat loaded to the gunwales with journalists arrived to catch their first glimpse of the funny little

British entry with the big ideas. Their first sight of *Aqua Quorum* was a beautiful boat decked out with a motley crew – caught literally with their pants down.

Les Sables d'Olonne was incredible. The Vendée is more than a yacht race to the French. To them the Vendée flies the flag for the human spirit. It is a demonstration that life is about more than being pigeonholed. Solo sailors are heroes in France. An entire industry thrives on their daredevil exploits and the rewards can be staggering. Skippers are viewed as the lucky ones who have managed to make it to the start line.

Philippe Jeantot is the figurehead of the Vendée. It is his concept and he is the man who had the courage and vision to pull it off, a modern-day adventurer who has held the record for the deepest dive and sailed round the world single-handed four times. He has a wonderful family and treats the skippers as an extension of that family. He is a rock and has my absolute respect. Under his guidance the Vendée has become part of the fabric of life in the region, with everybody following its ups and downs. All the schools follow the race – during the weeks that we were there 1,500 schoolchildren visited the fleet every day. The interest was so intense that it was like living in a zoo – the marina pontoons were thick with people from dawn until dusk. We soon had a family of supporters who helped us out no end. I could happily live in the Vendée region, the people have a great attitude to life.

There was a parade of competing boats that first evening and we waited our turn for the tow. As ever with boats, the programme ran late and we missed the tide. I hitched a ride on a powerboat and we motored round the corner into the half-mile-long harbour entrance to find it ten deep in spectators. It was extraordinary. I looked up to see that one side of a huge fort had been turned into a vast video screen showing footage of *Aqua Quorum* sailing in, not four hours previously. The cheering was deafening and I started to understand that my little dream of sailing round the world single-handed was part of something far bigger. The atmosphere was intoxicating. We had made it to the start line. All those years of worry and strain just dropped away and that night we got absolutely trashed.

It was an amazingly varied fleet. Some of the bigger, faster boats had vast budgets and large support crews to polish them daily to gleaming perfection, while alongside might be an old boat which had been prepared on a shoestring and was there to fulfil an ambition to take part rather than win. There was no snobbery – all the skippers were united by a common challenge and, as is the case with seafarers all over the world, helped each other where possible. My lack of French was a handicap at times and I wasn't able to get to know all the skippers. Gerry Roufs, a French-Canadian who spoke excellent English, befriended me and often helped me out at conferences. He was a tiny man with the heart of a lion and an abundance of energy and humour.

Another engaging personality among the competitors, and one of the favourites for a place, was the Hungarian Nandor Fa. He had represented his country in the Olympics and was an accomplished sportsman. However, he had become very disillusioned during the Cold War years when his country had pulled out of an Olympics for which he had been training. Four years of dedication as a sportsman were thrown out of the window for political reasons and he just couldn't swallow it. He decided instead to sail round the world with a friend, bought an old twenty-five-footer and set off, learning as he went. The boat wasn't suitable and was frequently overwhelmed and capsized. He heard about the first BOC single-handed, round-the-world yacht race from a radio ham while he was rounding Cape Horn. It struck a chord in him and he signed up for the race at his next port of call. He completed the race in a boat he designed and built himself. It was a remarkable achievement and the forerunner to three more single-handed circumnavigations.

Isabelle Autissier on *PRB*, Yves Parlier on *Aquitaine Innovations* and Christophe Auguin on *Geodis*, were also seen as race favourites, all of them extremely competent with well-funded, top-line boats. They were master mariners and I felt honoured to be on the same start line. *Aqua Quorum*, although dwarfed by the sixty-footers, was in no way overwhelmed in concept, quality or spirit. The Vendée is like the Grand National horse race – the bookies might have their favourites but the reality of the event is that it is a race of equals once it is under way. Fifty per cent of the fleet would probably fall by the wayside but I knew *Aqua Quorum* had every chance and there was no way I was going to drop out. If I ran a good race I saw no reason why we shouldn't get a result. Call it cocky if you like, but we certainly didn't see ourselves as second-class citizens.

We had three weeks to prepare the boat and we worked every hour we could. A tight budget meant that we had to tidy up the boat each night and sleep on board. This amazed onlookers – particularly when they found us washing dishes in a bucket on the pontoon. They rallied round and were most generous; it seemed that the town had adopted us. We, in our turn, made sure that the boat was open to the public – the level of interest was so high that it became Barry Marshall's full-time occupation to receive the endless stream of visitors and keep them entertained and informed as they were shown over the 'little yellow boat with the big heart'. His personality soon overcame any language difficulties. In fact, he built up such a network of friends that he developed into an extremely efficient campaign manager – if we needed something then Barry knew somebody who could supply it.

Alan Ashley worked himself into the ground during our stay

in Les Sables d'Olonne. There was so much to sort out and his dedication to detail meant that he couldn't accept any short cuts. All was going to plan except that he just wasn't happy with the generator. It had developed bad habits which he couldn't cure. He called Fischer Panda to express his concern. Their reaction was great: nothing but the best would do and their gear wasn't going to let the side down. A new generator was despatched and they arrived in person to check it over. It was a fantastic gesture.

I hadn't seen much of Tracey or the children during the previous few months so we decided to have a five-day family break in France. Tracey had rented accommodation in the country. It was great to be together and we made the most of the break as we explored the Vendée. However, the race seemed to hang over both of us and try as I might there were times when I couldn't help being distracted by it. I knew we needed to be together and yet at the same time there was still so much that needed doing to the boat. I was also very concerned about money – I even had doubts as to whether we would actually get to the start line, so critical had the financial situation become.

We decided to visit Les Sables d'Olonne to check my mail and make sure everything was on stream. It was, as ever, a fight to get to the boat. Barry was working his usual magic with the punters and Alan was beavering away like fury. There was a fax from 3M, asking me to contact Tony Durant as soon as possible. I rushed to a phone to be told that Bob McDonald wanted to support the project further by putting the 3M logo on the mainsail. All he could muster in the time available was £25,000, and he hoped that was acceptable. What do you say to a knight in shining armour? As far as I was concerned he could have his logo tattooed on my forehead for that. The race was on! I phoned Shane to tell him the good news, called Bruce Banks Sails to order the logo and make sure it would be delivered in time – and floated back to the boat with a grin from ear to ear. 3M had come up trumps once again. That call enabled us to relax for the last few days of the holiday.

I hate goodbyes, and dropping Tracey and the kids off at the Rossolf ferry to take them home was one of the worst. We arrived early and had fish and chips in the car to pass the time. We held hands and smiled at the kids' antics in the back seat. It would be a tough few months for both of us and each was concerned for the other. Tracey gave me presents to open at various stages during the race. The start would be a relief for both of us – at least we would be able to settle into our routines and share the load talking via fax every day. I felt hollow inside as I drove back alone to the boat. For me the Vendée started at that goodbye – from then on nothing mattered but getting round the world and doing a good job.

The last week at Les Sables d'Olonne was chaos. For some reason Aqua Quorum cancelled Amelia's presence as PR representative, so I had to coordinate the press. There were over a thousand of them milling continuously around the marina and, with only sixteen skippers to go round, it was a circus. Thank goodness, Mark Orr sent his girlfriend Gaye Sarma over to help and she took a lot of the weight off our shoulders.

I have vivid memories of the warmth shown by young and old alike. I came on deck one morning to find a huge wooden case by the boat. It was a present from La Trinitain, a small town nearby; all the shops had contributed and there were CDs, champagne, tools, an epoxy repair kit, cakes, cards, lucky charms and children's drawings to stick on the bulkhead. A local diver, aware of our constraints, came along and offered to scrub the bottom of *Aqua Quorum* for free. The local supermarket Le Clerc gave those of us who were hard up a FF10,000 voucher to help victual the boat. I wanted to throw a thank-you party and, as I already had all my food in place, asked them if I could have it in beer instead. We lined the pontoon with crates and had a good old blowout, making sure that all those who had worked so hard behind the scenes on our behalf had a taste of the action. The record went to one of the security men, who looked decidedly ill the next day.

As the start drew nearer more friends and supporters from Britain came to see us off. I was amazed at how many turned up – there were people from the Torpoint Mosquito SC, sponsors, suppliers and a whole crowd of fellow sailors from the British Steel Challenge. We were so busy stowing last-minute items and running through the final check list that there was hardly any time to have a chat to anyone. Finally, the pontoon was closed to the public, the press, having made their deadlines, departed and we were left alone. Bliss. At ten o'clock I decided that enough was enough – time for that final beer and a decent sleep. The Galway Bar was a gathering place for single-handers and my adopted watering hole. This time I found it packed with wellwishers and was able to say my goodbyes properly. Halfway through my beer, the phone rang. It was for me – no rest for the wicked. I wondered who it could be at that time of night. The familiar voice of Kim Fitzsimmons sounded in my ear – she was on the beach in Copacabana in Rio playing volleyball with a load of the BT Global Challenge crew during their first stopover. The wonders of technology. I spoke to about ten of them and we wished each other well in the Southern Ocean.

I woke at five on the morning of the start, 3 November 1996, spent a couple of hours rushing through paperwork that had to be done before I sailed; packed my bag and toddled down to the boat. You couldn't see it for people – in fact, you could barely see the harbour. Security was tight and only a few guests were allowed on to the pontoon. My parents were there, bursting with pride, as were Steve Whittell and a number of others.

I gave the boat a final run-through and jettisoned a load of extras that had found their way on board during the night. There were enough treats, bottles of wine and baskets of fruit to sink the boat. I spent a few moments below revising the start procedure and studying Vincent Geake's notes on the first three days of weather.

It suddenly struck me that I was actually going to do this thing. We had made it and, suddenly, it was time to go. I now just wanted to get on with the job. It was odd. I didn't feel excited, quite the opposite, more a sense of peace. The long fight was over and all I had to do now was to sail round the world. No probs, that was what I was good at. It was as if a great weight had been lifted. I made a cup of tea, sat in the cockpit and smiled for the first time in ages. I didn't feel the least bit nervous and I knew, whatever was thrown at us, that we were somehow going to pull it off – I could feel the force. If I was put on this earth for any reason, it was the Vendée.

I looked up and down the gathered fleet. Only half would finish the race: some would have a good one, some bad, some would enjoy it and some would hate it. I felt a great surge of affection for my fellow competitors and I wanted them all to win – having managed to get this far we all deserved to. It was time to say goodbye. I jumped off *Aqua Quorum* and ran around all the boats to shake each skipper by the hand. The last boat I climbed on was that of a newcomer, a late entry who had arrived while I was away on the break with Tracey and the kids. I hadn't even had time to say hello. I found the skipper, Raphael Dinelli, and shook his hand. 'Best of luck. Be safe and have a great race.' I didn't know him but I sensed a good man.

Tony Bullimore was his usual hearty self and full of support and good wishes. We decided, being the only Brits in the race, to set up our own radio schedule for a daily chat. Good egg, that one. The kind of person you would wish to have covering your back if the shit hit the fan. The only skipper I missed out was Gerry Roufs – I asked his shore manager to pass on my best wishes. It was time for my family and friends to say goodbye, their spectator boat was about to leave. A confused mixture of excitement and emotion was written on their faces, and it was big hugs for all. Regulations allowed only two other people on board for the tow out and although I had decided that Mark and Alan were best suited to the job, I wanted Steve to come along as well – if anyone deserved a place on the boat he did. I had a chat with the driver of the RIB that was to be my guard boat until we had cleared the spectator fleet and he agreed to take Steve and put him ashore at the harbour entrance; it was better than nothing.

As each boat slipped its moorings and was towed out by a local trawler, a roar went up from the crowd. I had never been to a soccer match so I hadn't experienced before the atmosphere that large numbers can generate – it made the hairs stand up on the back of my neck. It was our turn next and the boat was cleared, with the fenders and ropes being left on the pontoon – there was no need for them, I didn't plan to stop anywhere. A RIB towed us away from the pontoon and we picked up a line from *Yovo*, skippered by Jeaneau Durandot, and made our way towards the start. We rounded the corner of the basin and entered the half-mile harbour channel. Nothing could have prepared us for the sight or noise that greeted us – 300,000 people had turned up to see us off and each wanted to be heard. There was chanting, shouting, banners, flags. I just couldn't believe the atmosphere and spent the next half-hour waving back in a daze. It was time for Steve to leave; quick hug: 'Give it rocks.'

We were out of the entrance now and a good wind was up; probably the beginning of the deep depression that was due to sweep across the Bay of Biscay that night. Mark and Alan hoisted the mainsail and I gave the thumbs-up for the tow to be slipped. It was down to the boat and the wind now and I found it strange to think that the next time I sailed into Les Sables d'Olonne I would have pushed out many thousands of miles and had the adventure of my life. It was mayhem – spectator boats were everywhere, thousands of them, and they all wanted to steam past for a wave. In fact, it was bloody dangerous and hard to keep your footing in the wash that was churned up. I stepped back and my heel came down on the starboard runner jammer, which had been left open. The handle broke off. Sod this for a game of soldiers, I thought. I'm out of here. I winched in the main, up staysail – and we were off. Mark's mobile rang; it was Ed Gorman from *The Times* wanting one last interview. Not the best of moments to do it but, like all the press, he had been very supportive and deserved it. I can't remember what I said but I know it would have been positive. My blood was up and I couldn't wait to get stuck in. It had been a long time in getting there and I was ready for it.

It was quite a distance to the start line and, because the wind seemed to be dropping, we only just made it. There were boats everywhere and I decided to hang back a bit. The risk of collision was too great for heroics and a few minutes wouldn't hurt. The RIB driver was waving frantically and pointing at his watch – shit, was it time for the lads to leave already? Alan and Mark grabbed their kit, we shook hands as they dropped over the side, an engine revved and they were gone. I was on my own. I needed eyes in the back of my head to avoid the milling spectator boats. The competitors massed near the line as the minutes ticked away. One yacht just missed me; the skipper didn't even notice. I tacked out of the way and chased up the rear, dimly aware of a lot of jabbering over the radio, of which I couldn't understand a word. Any second now, it was best to follow the others. I saw a puff of smoke from the start cannon but the noise of the blast was lost in the din of the spectator boats. We were off.

I winched in the sails, ran across the back of the fleet to pick up some speed and bore away for the first mark, which was inland and close to the beach. The noise was deafening: engines revving, horns blaring and people shouting at the tops of their voices. The wind died. I didn't have enough sail up and I was losing ground. I decided, as disappointing as it would be for the team, to stay as I was; the risk of collision if I left the helm to work at the bow was too great. Where was the bloody mark? I couldn't see it for boats. There it was, we'd overshot it. I threw in a quick gybe, winched in the sails, pumped up the keel and she came to life, alert, quivering, like an antelope sensing danger. I was determined not to be the last boat round the second mark. A gust rippled on the water, there was our chance. Adrenalin pumped vitality into every fibre as I caught the gust, bore away, made the most of it and concentrated on sucking the wind through the sails. She was tramping now. I brought her up to catch a wave and she was creating her own wind as we accelerated. I winched in the sails, she came onto a plane and we skimmed past our first rival in a flurry of spray. It felt mustard and the *Aqua Quorum* support boat went wild. Who said a fifty couldn't beat a sixty? We were racing now.

Round the second mark, I found some clear water, put a tack in and tried to settle myself down as the spectator boats began to fall away behind. There must have been fifteen helicopters in the air, what a send off. Tony Bullimore on *Global Challenger* was just ahead of me and his boat looked fantastic with the sun shining through his sails. It was time for the autopilot, a cup of tea and a sandwich. I needed to get as much food down my neck as I could – I was already feeling queasy and the gale just over the horizon was bound to bring seasickness. The last month caught up with me as the adrenalin wore off, and I felt physically and mentally drained. I sent Tracey a brief fax to let her know that I was on my way and asked her to give the kids a big hug for me. Then it was back on deck for my well-earned cuppa, I felt too queasy to stay below.

The last spectator boat to wave goodbye was that of Philippe Jeantot. I silently thanked him – if it wasn't for him none of this would be happening. He would be driving to Paris that night to head up the race centre and then be on call twenty-four hours a day until the last of his flock had returned. It was nice to know that he was watching our backs. I finished my tea, put up the number two jib and tried to doze in the cockpit. It was important that I settled into the routine as quickly as possible. The first few days at sea are always the worst – at least I had enough experience to know that the sickness would pass in a couple of days. I love my eight hours' sleep when ashore, but can reduce it to about four in every twenty-four when competing; it's a necessity if you want results. I break my four hours into twenty-minute catnaps. It's at least ten days before my system settles into it. Until then I feel old and ache all over.

The wind started to pick up and it was time to drop the number two; the mainsail was already down to two reefs. I felt a bit rusty – I hadn't had a proper sail for a couple of months and we had done so much to the boat that it was as if we had to get to know each other again. She felt very heavy with all the stores that such a long haul called for. Darkness set in over a sea that was short, sharp and unforgiving and we dropped heavily from the top of each wave. I hoped we would be able to clear the continental shelf before conditions got really bad – I didn't want to bend the boat on the first night out. I continued to doze in the cockpit, waking every ten minutes or so to look around – there were a lot of fishing boats about and I had no wish for a collision. The din below was terrible as every wave got its money's worth. I couldn't hold it down any longer and threw up.

I checked the deck to find that one of the spinnaker poles had worked its way free. I clipped on, grabbed some sail ties and inched my way forward. The sea was awful, the motion even worse and the pole needed lashing right up in the bow. It seemed to have a life of its own and I got a good soaking as we wrestled each other in the darkness. There was a gut-wrenching swoop as we climbed up the face of a big one. I was in an awkward position and felt my knee give as we came to a crashing stop. I heard it crack above the noise of the wind. Fuck it, that hurt like a bastard and I just hoped it wasn't too bad. I finished securing the pole and crawled back to the cockpit. I could bend my knee – it was just a bad sprain – and I promised myself that I would put on a support once the worst of the weather had passed through. I was still throwing up and couldn't face the thought of going below and ferreting through the medical pack. Our first night was turning into a real bastard. Another reef went in and I wondered how the others were getting on.

Aqua Quorum was going like the devil, as though she knew that this was the big one. We crashed away to windward and passed two competitors during the night, their navigation lights gyrating wildly in the darkness. If I wasn't firing on all cylinders, then at least *Aqua Quorum* was on turbo. She managed to keep storming away while I threw my ring up and felt sorry for myself. 'Good one, Ade,' I thought. His design was delivering just what we had been looking for. I tried to doze again and time slipped into a haze of misery, broken only by attention to the boat – she must always come first. I ought to have put on some more thermals and sought the comfort of my bunk for a while but the thought of going below was too much. I would probably have been thrown out of my bunk anyway. I kept being woken up by the bigger waves as the boat became airborne and slammed my head against the back of the cockpit seat on impact. I couldn't wait for the trade winds, sunshine, blue skies and T-shirts. There was only bile now. I shivered, threw up again and smiled into the darkness. 'Bite hard if a big lump comes up – it might be your arse.'

Sometime during the night the front passed through and I put a fix on the chart and decided to tack. We would just clear Finisterre, we couldn't afford to overshoot. The boat was taking a frightful pounding and I tried everything in the book to ease her way through the seas but nothing worked. It felt as though we'd done ten rounds with heavyweight boxer Mike Tyson, and it was only the first night at sea. I gulped water down to keep the fluids up as much as possible and kept fighting. On the second day there was no sign of my sea legs, which was unusual. Suddenly the autopilot went haywire and I just caught the boat before it gybed. I reset the autopilot, pressed the green button – and it put the helm hard over again. I lashed the tiller, dug out some tools, threw up, opened the aft hatch and dropped below. It was a hell hole. I knocked the pin out of the port ram, swung the starboard one across and pinned it. I scrambled on deck, urged up yet more bile, powered up the backup starboard autopilot unit, pressed the green button and all was well. I decided I would come back to the problem later, and then it was back down into the aft compartment to bail out a number of buckets of water.

I was doing my all to keep the boat up to racing speed. The wind was easing and I shook more sail out. It was nice to know that we had managed to put the worst of it behind us, and I reckoned we should be in a good race position. I didn't think I had missed much between throwing up and feeling sorry for myself. *Aqua Quorum* handled it like a trooper. The BT Inmarsat beeped – it was Amelia with news. One boat had been dismasted, another had retired with major structural problems and Tony Bullimore had had to put back because of a malfunctioning autopilot – as had Nandor Fa who had keel problems. We were doing well. Poor sods, my thoughts went out to them – I knew how I would be if I was in their shoes. It had the feel of an unforgiving race already. I gulped back a bit more water but I couldn't face food of any kind. It was back to the cockpit for a doze. Come on, sea legs, where the hell are you?

It was a tough storm and it took a long time to get over physically – it was three days before I had my first meal. All I remember is a feeling of exhaustion which left no room for emotion apart from missing Tracey and the kids. The boat took a frightful pounding and suffered a lot of minor damage, which took a long time to sort out – about ten days, in fact. The most disappointing thing was to find that all my Christmas cards, letters and presents, which were stowed in the steering well, had been destroyed by water. The loss of this link with home seemed a cruel turn of fate. Salt water had also found its way into my cassette player. Damn! I had planned to learn French for my return. The most serious thing was that the SSB radio – my main source of weather information – had stopped working. This is a crucial ingredient when racing and a vital safety feature for the Southern Ocean. Nothing more essential than to know what is brewing up and where.

Despite all this I was delighted to be on the ocean again and felt that, even if I was a little displaced, I was sailing well. The Vendée is actually two challenges: the first is to get to the start line and the second is to get to the finishing line. My mind needed time to adjust. Life, up to the start gun, had been driven by a complex, ten-year juggling act of banks, sponsors, legal issues, publicity, boatbuilding and race preparation. A puff of smoke from the start gun had suddenly put an end to it. There was nothing more that I could do – I had what I had and that was it. All that was required of me now was to sail round the world.

Simple enough, I suppose. Sort out tactics, toddle off and turn left at Cape Town and Cape Horn.

However, it was taking longer than I'd expected to make the transition from one world to the other. An additional factor was probably that the Vendée was new ground for me in terms of scale and time: the longest that I had been at sea by myself was twenty-one days; the furthest I had sailed between ports, during the British Steel Challenge, was under a quarter of the Vendée. I had mentally broken the course down into a number of milestones at which to aim – the equator, south of Cape Town, entering the Pacific, Cape Horn, the equator once more and home. To make it easier to relate to I decided to add days to this framework and used a marker to draw a crude calendar on the bulkhead so that I could tick off the days and measure my progress. I arranged my strokes, each of which represented a day, into batches of seven so that as I struck off the last of the batch I could also strike a week off. In addition I noted incidents that occurred by the appropriate day mark.

It is very easy to become lethargic when you are on your own. Dirty dishes remain unwashed, the temptation to leave that sail change for just a little longer turns into a habit, and so on. With no companion to urge you on or provide you with competition, self-discipline becomes a vital ingredient of a sea voyage. I used the striking off of a day as an opportunity to take stock of my performance. Had I worked hard enough? Was I focused on the race? Was I eating properly? Was my maintenance programme on track? I treated breakfast as the formal end of one day and the beginning of another. It didn't matter if I had been up all night, it was a fresh beginning. I would wash, tidy up, have a decent meal, cup of tea, sit in my seat, strike the last day off and reflect on how the trip was going.

Five days after the start the dreamed-of T-shirt, shorts and sunshine became reality and I was spinnakering along at a healthy ten to twelve knots. I was eating properly and felt great. I stormed through the job list and then settled down to the task of getting weather information on board. There had been some controversy before the start about the way our weather forecasts could be obtained. The Vendée rules precluded the use of an outside weather expert passing on tactical advice. The only information a skipper was allowed to use was that which was already in the public domain. Some of the wealthier campaigns were able to purchase far superior information from weather centres. Technically speaking, this was within the scope of the rules as it was information available to the public – but only at considerable cost. This, combined with very expensive software packages, enabled those better-off yachts to produce sophisticated velocity path predictions – a huge advantage because it allowed one to project the outcome of any combination of tactical options. Some felt this was an unfair advantage.

I didn't get involved in the debate – it had little to do with me in any case because I certainly couldn't afford the software, let alone the expensive information to feed it. The argument waxed and waned until a compromise was struck, Philippe Jeantot would pay for a basic three-day forecast service which would be available to all provided each skipper paid transmission costs. I felt I must at least have the facility available, but could only afford to use it when safety and tactics absolutely demanded. Nautisoft, an excellent software system, was being offered to competitors at a very cheap rate. It would process the weather information from Philippe which I received via my BT Inmarsat system. I had the program installed a couple of days before the start, signed the contract with the provider Météo France and left it to the experts to install. They had seemed happy, despite not being able to receive a test message. I had shoved the manual into the chart table to look at later.

Now that my SSB radio was down, the BT Inmarsat system was my only doorway to sorely needed weather information. So far I had managed to stick with the fleet by instinct as I blindly thrashed my way south. It was time to fish out the Nautisoft manual from the chart table drawer and discover how it all worked. No matter what I tried, despite the fact that the information had clearly been received by the computer, I couldn't display it on the screen. I had to find a solution, and quickly. Unfortunately, I am hopeless with the inner workings of computers – anything that lies behind those user-friendly windows so easily accessed by a happy little mouse is a black art to me. Added to this I was using a French system and I could barely understand the instructions.

Apart from establishing a deep-seated urge to strangle the bloody mouse, I got nowhere. I decided, after many futile hours of trying to get the screen to come to life, to contact Clive Puttock by fax. Clive used to be a ship's radio officer and is one of the best when it comes to communications – he can make the equipment sing. When you are at sea and want to have a chat with someone you contact BT Portishead Radio, the central communication station that handles radio and fax traffic in the North Atlantic. If using the radio, you tell them the telephone number you want, and they patch you through. Portishead, due to more modern direct satellite communications, has slowly dwindled in size over recent years, but the excellent standards of service have remained and the operators always bend over backwards to help. They have all done their time at sea and are aware of how important that call home can be.

One of my crew on the British Steel Challenge, Jack Gordon Smith, had promised to speak to his twins on their birthday.

Portishead couldn't make contact with his home number because the machine had been switched over to fax-receiving mode. Jack explained the problem and the operator tracked down the telephone number of a neighbour and called them to ask if they would pop over the road and alert Jack's wife. The link was made. This is one of the many stories which illustrate the compassion and professionalism of Portishead Radio. All in a day's work for the lads, but precious stuff to the many seafarers who use them.

To return to Clive, he is keen on ocean racing and over the years has become the friend of just about every ocean racer. His sparse frame barely seems able to contain his seemingly limitless energy, enthusiasm and humour. He makes his home number freely available and is often called at an ungodly hour by wives who want to contact their seafaring partners. He drove down to Plymouth on a number of occasions to sort out equipment and show me and Tracey how to use our system. He even lent Tracey a computer screen when ours failed during the Transat. I faxed Clive details of my Nautisoft problems and he acted as my link man ashore, coordinating and chivvying the various parties until a solution was found. Within a few days, my weather information system was, thank goodness, in place.

I was finally on top of the Biscay storm, back in the race and starting to enjoy life, *Aqua Quorum* was sailing like a dream and all the modifications that we had made since the Transat felt right. I was padding about in shorts with time to look beyond the guardrails and enjoy the ocean. The new sleep pattern was sorting itself out and the initial aches and pains were behind me. Life on board was suddenly extremely pleasant. What is more fantastic than to stand at the bow of a boat that you helped bring to fruition as it surges along? And what is more invigorating than a daily shower with a bucket on the afterdeck? The water has the most wonderful hue to it and the contrast between cold water and hot sun on your skin is incredibly refreshing. How better to experience the hours of darkness than at the back of your boat with a cup of tea in hand as she forges through the water, painting excited light on to the inky black as phosphorescence bursts into life at the bow and slowly fades its farewell in the wake? The deck is like a reflection of the stars in the sky as the phosphorescence glows in its random resting places. I feel so alive when I am out there with an unblemished horizon and the musical rush of water passing the hull.

The size of the ocean is amazing and yet it is the detail that can often be captivating. I recall drifting becalmed off the Azores during the Transat on *Cornish Meadow*, when a discarded plastic bottle joined us. We both came to rest beside each other and I spent an hour lying on the trampoline between the two hulls watching the little community which had developed beneath the bottle. What had started out as slime had evolved into a life-giving support system, and about two feet of weed was trailing in the water by the time we met. This was infested with tiny crabs, what looked like some form of shrimp and a whole range of other little creatures. These fed a shoal of small fish, which in turn fed the occasional passing larger fish. It is fascinating to think that nature can transform litter into something so productive.

The race rules obliged us to pass through a square-mile box which lay just to windward of the Canaries. The reason for this was so that the media would have an opportunity to photograph and film the fleet as it passed close the coast. It would be the first time that we were to see land since clearing Finisterre and I was looking forward to it. It would concentrate the fleet in one area and provide a clear indication of how we were doing. I was pleased with our performance – we were very much in the race and I felt I was getting more from the boat by the day. I was expecting to arrive by evening and started the day with a decent breakfast, shower and detailed deck check. Deck checks are all about catching a problem before it happens. I nipped up the mast to cast my eye over the halyards. All was well and I stopped, as I often do, on the bottom spreaders and scanned the horizon.

I spotted a sail behind us. It could only be Gerry Roufs. He had had a bad start and had dropped way back in the fleet. Gerry, an excellent sailor with one of the best boats in the race, was storming up through everyone at a rate of knots. I slid down the shrouds and called him on my VHF radio, the range of which is limited to the visual horizon, to be rewarded with a cheery shout from Gerry. 'Hi, mate! How's it going? Been wondering about your absence from the daily chat show, hear your SSB radio's buggered. Great day, isn't it?' We must have spent an hour chewing the cud and it was great. I hadn't spoken to anyone for eight days and, without race positions, was feeling out of touch. Gerry passed on the fleet gossip and updated me on everyone's positions. We were doing well and managing to hang in there with the bigger boats. Gerry made that morning for me and I like to remember him by that conversation.

In fact, it was a good day for communications as a whole. Now that I felt I was getting on top of my own little world, I wanted to know what was going on out there in the real world. Tracey sent a lovely long fax with all sorts of news; we call it 'Tracey Trivia'. It is the bread and butter that keeps me in touch with those I have left behind. So-and-so got married, the kids made a cake and Eliot managed to get food dye all over himself. Alex has received a star at school, Livvy has painted a picture for me and so on. The nice thing about the BT Inmarsat system is that it is confidential, effectively E-mail by satellite, which enables us to express thoughts and emotions in privacy. I received messages from many friends: Steve Whittell passed a pad and pen round his local, The Farnley Cock, one Sunday lunchtime and faxed me the result. Very funny, very rude – and very uplifting.

Gerry and I had a chat every couple of hours or so as the day progressed. The chances of someone being within my visual horizon after the Canaries were nonexistent and I wanted to make the most of this link while I had the opportunity. The wind started to die away as we approached the island of Gran Canaria and I was soon needed on deck full time to eke the most out of what we had. The island loomed majestically up above the horizon as I neared the waypoint in the square-mile box – which was slap bang in the middle of a glassy patch of windless water that one would normally avoid like the plague. The area, thanks to changes in the weather, was getting bigger by the moment. I felt as though I was walking into an ambush, every instinct screaming against it, yet I was left with no choice. *Aqua Quorum* lost her speed and started to wallow. I cursed.

To my right I could see Gerry Roufs and Marc Thiercelin, who had managed to slip through and were just able to keep in front of the ever-growing and windless area. I stopped, there was not a breath of wind, and watched the opposition slip away. Gerry and Marc were making their way round the right hand side of the island; this seemed to be the way to go but the current was carrying me to the left and I couldn't generate enough speed to counter it. I decided that I might as well assist the inevitable and add point one of a knot to what seemed to be destiny. I put up the spinnaker and steered left. The sea tends to make you philosophical about these turns of fate. I could have stood on the deck screaming, kicking winches and pacing up and down but it wouldn't have helped. I had a final chat with Gerry, wished him well, put the tea on, faxed Tracey and waited. And waited and waited, as I slowly drifted past Gran Canaria.

It was one of the worst nights of the race for me. *Aqua Quorum* was floating in circles and I spent all night trying to generate the tiniest bit of speed out of the sails as they banged back and forth in the swell. The wind finally settled in at dawn and it was a great relief to feel her come to life again. However, the relief was short lived. The wind backed round to the southwest and quickly rose until I found myself bashing into a gale with three reefs and the staysail. A small depression had formed and here I was struggling to clear the African coast when I should have been swanning along under the spinnaker. To make matters worse I discovered that Gerry was in different conditions altogether and making fantastic speed for the equator. The fleet had split and I had just missed the break – indeed, I was so close I had seen it.

We had fallen back into a different weather system from the leading group and the race was practically over in terms of boat to boat competition. The disappointment was like a physical lump in my stomach and it took a lot of dealing with. I got really down about it and took a good two weeks to work it through. What most pained me was the feeling that I had let everyone at home down. Here we were, just into the race, and I was out of it already. Even if I was to sail like an Olympic gold medallist from here on, the laws of physics precluded a jump into the weather system ahead that the competition was enjoying. It was the inevitability of it all that I found so demoralising. What was the point, why should I bother with that sail change? It wouldn't get me where I ached to be.

It was time to give myself a good talking to. I was on the adventure of a lifetime and all I could manage was to feel sorry for myself. No one at home would want that – we had all set out to get a fifty-footer around the world as fast as we possibly could and that is what I should do. Stick at it. Go for fifth place, at least. But, most important of all, enjoy it. I decided to forget the leaders, treat them as another fleet altogether, and focus on the others. There were four of us in the second group, which was enough for a good race within a race: Catherine Chabaud, Raphael Dinelli, Patrick de Radigues and myself. Then there was poor old Tony Bullimore who was back in the race but miles behind, as was Thierry Dubois.

I came to terms with my disappointment and got back into the race with renewed vigour. I was by now enjoying trade wind conditions and, putting one day aside for the task, decided to have a go at mending the SSB radio. Starting with the aerial, I slowly worked my way back through the system, checking every connection. I worked through circuit board after circuit board until I finally reached a contact which looked a little shaky. I made it good, put it all back together, took a deep breath and switched on. My old friend the BBC World Service knocked me off my feet at full volume.

At last! Something positive had been achieved and the door was once again open to a rich mine of weather information and communications. I celebrated with a cup of tea on deck and looked forward to hearing Tracey's voice that evening. I felt heady with success. Life was back on the right track, the sun was out, we were surfing at sustained surges of speed of up to twenty knots and were flying south for the equator with the spinnaker up. The autopilot was having to work hard in the short seas but was managing to hold out very well.

Having spent the day sweating away in sweltering conditions below, I decided to make the most of the moment by sitting in the bow and taking the dousing of my life as we dropped into the troughs and disappeared under a shower of refreshing spray. I thought I might just as well make the most of it and nipped back below for a bottle of shampoo. It was easier to dive into the little store behind the battery box to save dripping all over my clothes in the kitbag, but I lost my balance in my haste, fell against the main breaker switch and knocked it to the off position. A deathly silence fell as the hum of the autopilot was snuffed out – a void quickly filled by the accelerating, menacing rush of water as we surged down another wave. 'Diiiickheaaaaad' echoed through the boat as I flew into the cockpit, making sure that I didn't trap my marrying tackle in any of the many bits of equipment that festooned the deck. I didn't care what else happened, I wasn't losing that for anyone. I flicked the dead man's switch, grabbed the helm and just managed to avert a monstrous broach.

The relief was intoxicating and I burst out laughing at the absurdity of it. What the hell, it was a lovely day and I hadn't helmed the boat for ages. I spent the next few hours on the wheel for the sheer pleasure of it. The sun was behind the spinnaker and caught the spray that was thrown up from the bow as we flew along on a permanent plane. Flying fish scattered at the bow and glinted in the sun like jewels as they fled our sleigh ride for the equator. She really was a big dinghy *Aqua Quorum*, and I never ceased to marvel at her ability to deliver an exhilarating perform-ance in such a kindly and forgiving manner, a manner which enabled me to leave the helm and dash below to turn the power back on without mishap.

We were fast approaching the doldrums and I viewed the prospect with apprehension. If there is one thing that drives me round the bend at sea it is a lack of wind, and I had already suffered badly in the race as a result of this. Some people seem to thrive on it and enjoy nothing more than tweaking an extra tenth of a knot. I can do it – sometimes you have to – but it's not something I enjoy. And so I was dreading the doldrums, particu-larly as we had taken a real mauling there during the British Steel Challenge. As it was, the wind was a little fickle at times but other than that it was not a bad passage through the notorious area. The wind went round to the port bow as we picked up the South Atlantic high and started to buck our way towards the equator, the doorway to the southern hemisphere.

I used any spare time to prepare the boat for the Southern Ocean and paid particular attention to the mast and rigging, because I knew that once we entered that inhospitable area there would be little chance of climbing the rig in safety. The Southern Ocean was starting to fill my thoughts. I couldn't wait to get there and have a blast in my fifty-foot surfboard, yet it was also an intimidating prospect. The Vendée was much more of a marathon than any other race I had undertaken to date – not a pit stop to be seen. The odd small job during a normal ocean race can usually be left until the end, when a major refit will take care of it, whereas in the Vendée you had to be more disciplined. Attention to detail was crucial. Problems had to be identified and nipped in the bud before they had a chance to mushroom into an issue that was beyond a single-hander's strength and scope. Failures, no matter how small, had to be addressed straight away before they set off a chain of events. It was like a game of chess – each move arrived on the boat unannounced, as if from an outside opponent. You had two options: win or lose.

As the trip settled into a routine so I felt the need for outside stimulus and I became an avid listener to the BBC World Service. The radio also gave me a link with the race and I enjoyed my daily chat with Philippe Jeantot as he worked his way through the fleet and talked to each skipper. There was a set time for this call and I would sit down and sip a cup of tea as I awaited my turn. In fact it became a bit of a joke in France as my response to 'How are you, Pete?' was inevitably that all was well and that I had a cup of tea in hand – very English in their eyes. I also had a chat with Tony Bullimore every evening.

My contact with the other skippers was very limited, thanks to my poor French, until I started to chat to Catherine Chabaud each day. Our friendship started as we closed the equator. It was obvious that we were going to cross at about the same time. The sun was setting and *Aqua Quorum* was romping along at a rate of knots. I had a wash, tidied the boat, got a bottle of wine ready and called Catherine to see how she was doing. It looked as though I would be slightly ahead and we took turns to count down the hours until our crossing – the crackle of the radio unable to mask our excitement as the navigation systems jumped from north to south. I toasted Neptune, Tracey and the kids. Not twenty minutes later Catherine raised her glass too. Her English was far better than my French and, as our daily chats went on, she grew more and more fluent. It was nice to share the ups and downs of the race with a kindred spirit who was going through the same experience. We came to the conclusion that there was an invisible piece of elastic attached between our two boats. We drew strength from each other and became each other's minder.

I plotted the fleet positions every night. It seemed that the four of us in the second group had similar boat speeds and it was always rewarding to see that extra bit of effort show up as a few miles knocked off the opposition. I was having problems with equipment – it all reached some kind of invisible service date at the same time. First, and most worrying of all, was when I came below to find water in the accommodation. It seemed to come from the generator, which was merrily purring away. I opened the case and was horrified to find that it was flooded and water was being sprayed around by the motion of the alternator which was half submerged. I quickly turned the generator off. My heart was in my mouth. I was out of the race if I lost power at this stage of the game. I shut down as much of the electrical system as I could and sat down to work out the problem. It took a couple of hours

The beginnings of Raphael Dinelli's storm in which I was to beat back 160 miles in hurricane-force winds

Aqua Quorum struggling up after a knock-down during the storm that wiped out Raphael's boat

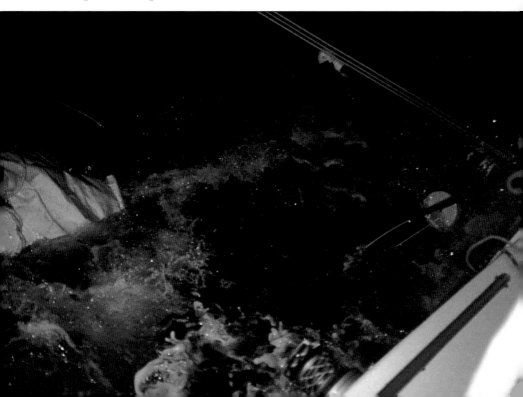

The rescue. The Royal Australian Air Force flash their landing lights to pinpoint Raphael's position

Raphael standing on his sinking boat, *Algimouss*

Closing on the raft. What will I find?

Got him! I pulled Raphael on board and made a friend for life

Raphael's ordeal is over – his eyes and fingers say it all

New Year's Eve: we pledge that we will race together when things are on an even keel

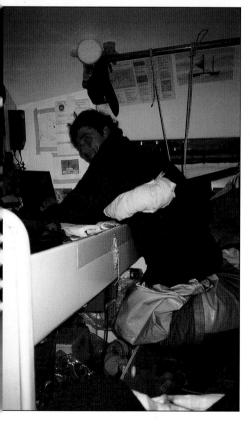

I rigged up a way of suspending Raphael from the deckhead so that he could fax Virginie and begin to write his story

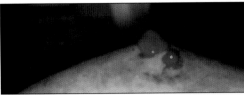

My painful elbow has ruptured – time for action

Instruments and instructions laid out

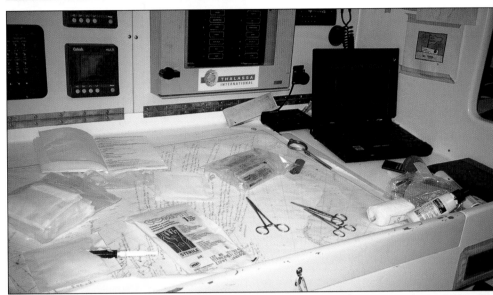

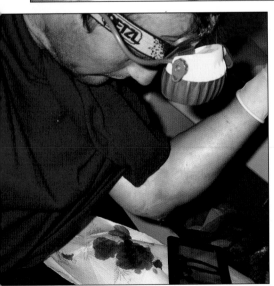

Getting on with it

Daily life in the accommodation area

Crossing the finishing line of the Vendée Globe in March 1997.
I was completely unprepared for the tumultuous welcome from
150,000 people

Tracey and I manage our long-awaited hug

I love this photograph of my family: Olivia (7), Eliot (4), Tracey and Alex (9). They were dropped on board by the Marines as I returned to Plymouth after the Vendée

My parents sight *Aqua Quorum* as I close the finish of the Vendée and we are able to have a chat on the radio

France's President Chirac presents me with the *Légion d'Honneur* – from the heart of France

With Raphael Dinelli before the 1997 Jacques Vabre transatlantic race

Raphael and I get our teeth in to the planned race – we came first in class

The design for our 115ft catamaran for The Race – a non-stop round-the-world drag race in the biggest, fastest, most high-tech boats ever – starting at midnight on 31 December 2000

The whole Goss Challenges team with the two hulls of the new boat in the build shed at Totnes. The catamaran, which shares technology with the Formula One car shown here, will be ready for trials mid-1999.

to establish that it must be a crack in the exhaust mixer box in an area that was out of sight.

The engine would normally be removed from its mounts for the repair but this was not an option. The boat was crashing from wave to wave and I didn't fancy having a weighty generator rolling around below. It took ages to work out a method whereby I could reach and then remove the exhaust box. I eventually succeeded in finding that there was indeed a crack in one of the welds. A lasting solution was to prove very elusive and it took twenty-four hours and two attempts before I had a repair that seemed to be at least temporarily up to the job.

No sooner had I got on top of this than the boat did a crash gybe and came up to the wind with the spinnaker pinned across the rig. It was a four-hour nightmare to sort out the mess. I climbed the rig, slowly untangled the knotted sail and got it down, desperately trying to avoid tearing the material. I got her back on course and pressed the green button on the autopilot. The helm went hard over and we immediately crashed into another gybe. Damn! Autopilot number two was down.

I still hadn't had a chance to repair the first autopilot, which had failed during the Bay of Biscay storm. I was now faced with no autopilot at all and cursed the fact that hard-earned miles were about to be lost by the shedful. I set the sails so that the boat would sail by herself and began to work my way through the electronics. The first thing I did was to change the fluxgate compass unit in the autopilot – the symptoms suggested that this was where the problem lay. The job took ages because I had to clamber with my tools through two watertight compartments to get to the forward hold. The boat was bouncing about too much so it was back on deck for a couple of reefs in the main to slow her down. Back to the job but the screwdriver that I had brought with me didn't fit so it was back through two bulkheads to dig out the right tool and then scramble back up forward. It was a fiddly job and the boat was still jumping about. I had to connect so many terribly thin and fragile wires and it was best done at the steadying moment at the crest of each leap. Job done, I clambered back aft, powered up the autopilot, pressed the green button and the helm went hard over. I took a deep breath, forced myself to stay calm, be logical, and go back through the system and check all the connections again. It was easy to make a mistake. Back on deck and the bloody thing put the helm over again. I set the boat up once more, got a cup of tea going, pulled out pen and paper and worked out an approach that I hoped would eventually isolate the gremlin. I spent the next four hours working through every combination possible, using every compass that I had on board. I was getting very concerned. If I couldn't find a solution the race was off.

I called up Cetrek and talked to Roy Pritchard. He made notes and came back with a series of suggestions. Back I went into what I now called the hell hole to give them a shot, then back on deck and the helm went hard over again. This process was repeated a couple of times before Roy came to the conclusion that more drastic action was called for; we were into circuit boards and microchips now. I had to power up the unit and, using a meter, work my way through a number of chips and check that the tiny amounts of current across them were correct. Every time I managed to keep the contacts in place as we bounced about, the meter fell off my knee. I taped the meter to my leg and started all over again until I found a connection that wasn't giving the right figure. I had three compass units so I poached a chip from one and fitted it. I powered up the unit and the bloody helm went hard over again. I could have screamed. I shut the power down and went through the whole process once more using the chip from my last compass. 'This is it, fruit gum. If this doesn't work we've had it.' Back to the cockpit, powered up the unit, said nice things to it, pressed the green button and winced. It felt as though I was throwing the switch on an electric chair – my own. The helm responded and all was back to normal. The relief was indescribable – I could have kissed the autopilot.

I got full sail back up in a frenzy of effort, heaven knows what we had lost to the others and every moment counted. I settled her down, put a fix on the chart and went cold – we must have lost miles. I had a cup of tea and a quick bite to eat and then set about getting *Aqua Quorum* back up to scratch. There were tools all over the place, the deck was a mess and the tears in the spinnaker needed patching. I was still at it well into the night and exhausted. I just couldn't keep my eyes open and thanked old Neptune that we had a fair wind. I checked the deck and fell into my bunk for a four-hour sleep. It was the longest I had had since the start and I woke up at sunrise feeling great. I dived under the bucket and then ate a huge meal.

I was concerned about my repaired fluxgate compass. I had no more spares and I hadn't even made the Southern Ocean yet. Roy Pritchard shared my concern but assured me that the problem was unusual. However, it was a long time before I stopped feeling uneasy every time the boat seemed to go off course. I spent the day cleaning up the system and making plastic covers that would keep water off the unit should any find its way into the forward compartment. I slowly worked my way through every system on the boat to reacquaint myself and at the same time make sure that there were no signs of wear and tear. I serviced the generator, changed the oil and gave it yet another good clean – the dousing of salt water it had taken seemed to have done little damage.

I had spoken too soon. The generator shut itself down. It had overheated and I traced the fault to the pump that supplied the salt water to keep it cool. The impeller was buggered and I put a new one in, which was OK for a couple of days before it shut down again. The pipe connection to the top of the keel supply had come off and refused to go back on. I spent a day poaching another piece of pipe from elsewhere and bonding it on. All seemed well until the generator once again shut down. This time it was the impeller housing: the inlet connection had broken off and I didn't have a spare. Another day spent on a repair job – I just didn't have enough fingers to plug all the cracks at the moment and every day lost to big jobs was a day lost to general maintenance and boat speed. I couldn't afford to drop behind on either.

The problems kept coming. Next thing was that the screen on one of my computers went dead and, despite Tony Durant passing on a stream of instructions from IBM, would not come back to life. Of even more concern was my left elbow. I woke up one morning to find it stiff, swollen and very painful. By the next day I was starting to show a fever and generally feeling off colour and tired. The race doctor, Jean-Yves Chauve, was brilliant. He had spent many years developing a medical system for use offshore and specialises in supporting single-handed sailors. At Les Sables d'Olonne the competitors were given a comprehensive medical box which held everything from lip salve to dental gear, morphine and surgical equipment. A previous competitor had had to sew part of his tongue back on. Jean-Yves had developed a brilliant booklet which leads you through an ailment in coded steps that clearly describe the symptoms, which are then relayed back to the doctor for diagnosis.

However, we seemed unable to put my elbow right whatever we tried. There were good days and bad days. The boat needed tending constantly and most jobs, such as sail changes on the foredeck, needed both hands. I tried to favour the arm, but there were moments where I might lose my balance and have to grab something to catch myself. These sudden movements were the ones that set off the most awful pain for days on end. I learned to live with it as best I could.

I think I was simply having a run of bad luck, which I was fortunate to get out of the way before entering the Southern Ocean. At least I was able to work my way through the problems in steady trade winds and the warmth of a tropical sun. I tracked the depressions as they passed to the south and tried to get a feel of the weather in the Southern Ocean and what I would do if I were in this position or that. The fleet up ahead were well into their first depression by now and making amazing speeds. Catherine would pass on their war stories during our evening yarn on the radio; things were hotting up.

I wasn't the only one who was having problems. Other competitors were falling by the wayside: Thierry Dubois lost one of his rudders, as did Isabelle Autissier and Yves Parlier, and they were all three forced to retire. Despite the fact that they were now officially out of the race they decided to restart after the damage was repaired and complete the course. Adrian's and my feeling that the sixty-footers were perhaps a little more vulnerable was proving to be true and, although I took no pleasure in their misfortune, it was nice to see that we were still in there fighting. If anything, I was starting to feel that we were coming into our own, as if the leg down the Atlantic was my final training run. It takes ages to get on top of one of these boats – for race leader Christophe Auguin it was his third single-handed, round-the-world race and the teething problems that I and many other new boats were experiencing were well and truly behind him. He was pulling away at a blistering pace day after day with what appeared to be consummate ease. I plotted his daily runs and marvelled at them. It was a one-man race, this Vendée.

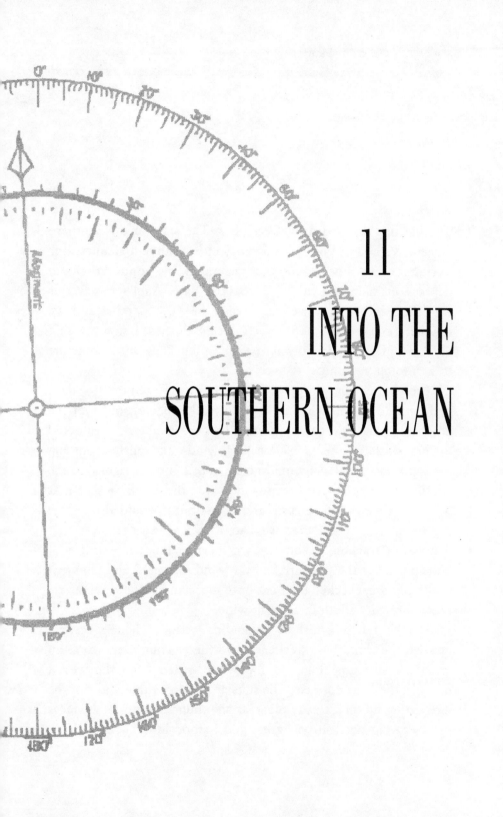

11
INTO THE
SOUTHERN OCEAN

The big day dawned on 5 December. The start of the Southern Ocean. We had dawdled through a South Atlantic high and came out the other side into wind generated by Southern Ocean depressions that were driving across our path. Appropriately, this was the wind that carried us across the 40th parallel and we officially entered the notorious Roaring Forties. I saw my first albatross gliding gracefully across the water. These birds bring life to a desolate region.

The temperature dropped like a stone over the next few days and I found myself wearing my Musto thermals throughout the day to keep warm. It was also wet on deck as the boat gathered up her skirts in the ever-increasing winds and pushed out big speeds. I decided that I would go far south and get right into the depths of the Southern Ocean – not only did I believe that that was where we would perform at our best but it would also reduce the number of miles that we had to sail. I watched our first depression tracking in on the weatherfax and felt a tingle of anticipation as the pressure fell, the wind increased and the swell built up. I ate, checked the boat once more and reduced sail as we pressed further south in a rising wind.

The boat had a feel of impending action. The air became heavier, the cloud base thickened and the heaving ocean took on an oppressive grey hue. As the wind settled from the west I brought the boat up, eased the sails and let her run – and run she did, sitting up on a steady plane as she thundered down the faces of a very big swell. It was great and I stood in the cockpit for a couple of hours and savoured the sailing with Tina Turner belting through my Sony Walkman. I decided to wang up the spinnaker to see what would happen. It was a stupid thing to do really, but I had a couple of months down here so I might as well find out what the boat was comfortable with. It was blowing thirty knots and I hummed and hahed about which sail I should shove up. I set the autopilot on a very broad reach, eased the main and clambered forward to drop the number one headsail. This became a bit of a handful when it went into the water and took a good ten minutes to retrieve. I hanked on the number two – if the shit hit the fan I didn't want to be wrestling with a bigger sail. I rigged the bowsprit, made off the spinnaker lines, took a deep breath and hoisted the spinnaker in its retaining sock.

I went back to the cockpit and, uneasy, mulled over the decision once more – the boat was going well as it was and I questioned whether I should have been doing this at all. My instinct said no and yet this was my first time down here with the boat and the only way I was going to find out what it was all about was to go for it. Perhaps I was influenced by all the old-timers who talk of keeping their spinnaker up down here. There were six hours of daylight left and I decided to treat this as a training run rather than part of the race, bung it up, see what happened, fiddle about with settings and find our feet. If it all went belly up I had six hours of light to sort myself out. I checked every line and detail one last time, stripped off my heavy thermals so that I was more agile, donned my sailing gloves, made my way to the mast and clipped on. I mentally ran through everything again before I untied the sock and started to pull it up the sail. The wind immediately filled the foot, the sock ran away and the check line burned through my fingers. The spinnaker filled with a bang and we started to lay over. I ran aft as *Aqua Quorum* leapt forward and the autopilot struggled on the edge of control as we zigzagged across the wind and waves.

It was bloody hairy now and we drove down a wave at twenty knots and disappeared beneath the water. I eased the spinnaker and the sheet shuddered under the load. That was better, it was a little more comfortable now, but it was relative. We were leaping from wave to wave, the wind was thirty-five knots and gusting. We were going like buggery but I wasn't happy – trouble was just round the corner and I questioned whether I would be able to drop the spinnaker on my own. I told myself not to rush, but to stand and watch, soak up as much information as I could – it would stand me in good stead later.

I got below and made a cup of tea – I needed to get used to life down there with the boat on the edge. I had to learn to relax even when things were marginal. The boat needed to be pushed – it was a race, after all – but I had to resist the urge to leap on deck every time she felt as though she were about to go. She hadn't lost it yet and I should leave her to it. The feeling below was awful. We were screeching along on the edge of control and I had to make a cup of tea and go about daily life. Each time she rolled at speed I felt the bow coming up and I willed the autopilot to put the helm over – it seemed an eternity before it did. It played on my nerves as we yawed from side to side and I made myself shut it out, fill the kettle and get used to it.

I saw that there was a message on the satcom (satellite communication system) and called it up. It was from Amelia Lyon. I hadn't forgotten the article for so and so, had I? They were getting twitchy, the deadline was in four hours' time. Shit! The message had been sitting there for the last hour. Writing an article was the last thing I wanted to do. I bashed away at the laptop but I couldn't concentrate. *Aqua Quorum* talked to me. 'Come on, dickhead, you know you shouldn't have this amount of sail up. There are two months of this and if you push me this hard we'll never finish the race.' Bollocks, I thought. We're here to race and race we will. By the end of the Southern Ocean this will feel normal.

Suddenly we were on the back of a big wave and accelerating like fury, the wave was steep and we started to come up. The boat heeled, I could hear water rushing across the side deck as we lay over. The log climbed . . . twenty . . . one . . . two . . . three. I looked aft and saw that the helm was hard over. I marvelled at the power of the autopilot and knew that if we pulled out of this and the rudders bit, she would drive herself into a crash gybe. I braced myself and reflected on the lesson that I was about to be taught. Prat. The hull was bouncing and banging across the water. At this speed it felt as if I was driving down a dirt track in a car with no suspension. I could feel the shocks running up through my legs and bent my knees slightly to absorb the impact. The noise was deafening and the moment was bloody marvellous. The wake disappeared over the top of the wave, narrowing at the crest like a country lane over a hill; the spray off the hull cascaded out to the sides. We suddenly decelerated at the bottom of the wave, the brakes were slammed on and the boat submerged.

I braced myself for the worst and mentally ran through the setup – halyards in use, winch handle location, runner, preventer, knife in pocket and so on. We galloped off to leeward. The back of the mainsail curled, the keel was now on the wrong side and we sagged to windward. The autopilot whirred away and the helm went over. She suddenly felt dead in the water, as if she had accepted the inevitable and decided to give up. The main half gybed. I gritted my teeth, this was going to be a belter. Where was the camera? Missed the last one on the Transat, but this time it was handy in a bag by the hatch. There was a crack. I looked up from freeing the camera to see the main slam back in place. Come on *Aqua Quorum*, you can do it.

The bow lifted and it felt as if a couple of tons had been

released as she bounced up and we were off again. I couldn't believe she had managed to pull out of it as I leapt on deck and eased the sheet, thinking 'I might just get away with this'. The spinnaker flogged, shaking the boat as if it were a toy. I scanned the horizon and saw a big cloud on the way. I had to get the spinnaker down before it arrived. As I ran forward the wind seemed even stronger up there. I braced myself against the mast, which was banging around like a child's fishing rod, and pulled on the spinnaker sock which snuffed out about six feet of sail before it filled again and was forced back up to the head. The rope burned my hands. A glance over my shoulder was enough – I pulled like a bastard, the cloud was looming larger by the minute. We careered off down another wave and I found myself up to my knees in rushing water. The boat lay over and started to go into another gybe – this was going to be a shitty one. The spinny suddenly collapsed behind the main. 'Go go go go!' As the sock came down hand over hand, something tugged at my feet. I glanced down and saw that the lazy line from the sock had wrapped itself round my leg. Time stopped. The boat was coming up for another run, the spinnaker was about to be slammed full of wind and I was going to be strung up with a large sail lashed to my ankle in a tidy gale. For the first time in the race I was scared. I daren't let go of the sock line. I had half the sail tamed and yet I needed both hands to untie the other end round my leg. Shit! I just couldn't free it. The main filled. I watched the brightly coloured spinny flutter gaily out from behind the shelter of the main, swallowed and waited for a lot of discomfort.

The spinnaker filled with a crash and the sock line whipped taut in my hand. I was lifted off my feet and came up short as my safety line tightened. I could feel every sinew and tendon stretching as my body took up the strain. I tensed the muscles across my back and shoulders. My duff elbow hurt but it was the thought of my shoulder coming out of its socket as I dangled in mid-air that worried me. There was no way, however much it hurt, that I was letting go of the line and unleashing the spinnaker – the consequences were unimaginable. I shut my eyes and shouted 'bastard' at the top of my voice, and started to feel breathless as the strain took its toll. My right hand fumbled for the knife I always carried in my left pocket, but I couldn't reach it. My grip was weakening and I could feel the line start to run. I had to do something. Dump the halyard – break every rule and dump the halyard. Heaven knows what would happen but it couldn't be worse. The jammer was just out of my reach. I concentrated my gaze on it, even the burning in my left hand was forgotten. The boat came up, the sail really pulled now and started to run away. I was losing the fight. The boat lurched and at last the tip of my index finger touched the jammer and I managed to hook it free. The halyard ran – thank heavens I always flake my lines out to avoid tangles. I hit the deck and ripped the line from my leg – I had to get it off before the dumped sail filled with water. I was free. I leapt up to jam the halyard, hoping to save the sail yet. We came up to the wind and stopped with the sail filling beyond the masthead as we lay over. It shook the boat like a rag doll. I dumped the tack, ran aft and winched in on the sheet. It was enough to kill the sail. Good old *Aqua Quorum* came up and ran off downwind with ease. The spinny was sheltered behind the main now and she was quite happy with such a reduction in sail area. It was as if she was saying 'Told you so'.

I dragged the spinny in under the boom, taking care to ensure that I didn't get caught up in it. Wrapping a load of sail ties round it, I dumped it below and closed the hatch – it felt as though I had imprisoned a dangerous criminal who had been running amok. Then it was back to business, a quick stretch, nothing broken, although my shoulder would be tender for a while. I slapped a reef

in, tidied the deck and checked that everything was as it should be.
I rigged up the pole and prepared to goosewing the number two; I
had to keep driving the boat and I now knew when the spinny was
a bad idea. I hoisted the number two under the main, returned to
the cockpit and winched it across to the windward side. The boat
loved it and flew along. It was time for a cuppa. I had been on deck
for a good eight hours and felt very tired and cold.

The warmth and light of the stove was great company. I put
my heavy thermals on and stuffed a ready-cooked meal into the
kettle. It's a great system. I poured the boiling water into my pint
cup with four sugars in it, dragged the bag out, cut the top off
and dived into a meal of beef stew with dumplings and a handful
of cream crackers. Just what the doctor ordered. I polished it off
quickly, food didn't stay warm down there for very long. I banged
a fix on the chart and was relieved to see that we had made a
good run despite the day's antics and turned in feeling pretty
pleased with myself. I had learned a good deal that day. How she
pulled out of some of those broaches I shall never know. Good
old Ade, and well done Cetrek, was all I could say.

I lay back, braced my feet on the end of the bunk so that I
didn't slide off it every time we decelerated at the bottom of a
wave and wedged myself in. I had my hat, gloves, thermals and
Walkman on inside my best sleeping bag. Warmth worked its way
back into my bones and with it a heavy weariness. The Walkman
was essential because it drowned out much of the noise of the
boat as she thundered along. My tastes are varied – Tina Turner,
Vivaldi, Abba, Queen, country and western, anything that grabs
me. I was also very lucky to have a load of tapes made up for me
by radio reporter Dennis Skillicorn. He spent hours recording his
best interviews from the past forty years for me. There are
thousands of them and they are fascinating. An old tramp on the
Isle of Wight, Lord Mountbatten, Blondie Hasler's Cockleshell

Heroes, an old farm labourer, a poacher, the list goes on and on.

I dropped into a deep sleep and woke with a start two hours later, rolled out of my bunk and dropped into my Mustos, which were hanging nearby ready for action. It was dark, cold and wet and the prospect of going on deck wasn't at the top of my list but it was something that had to be done. I checked the voltameter, which looked good and flicked the decklight on. A burst of light opened up our little world – I patted the boat, good girl, keep it up. Clipped on with hood up, I eased my way through the hatch and into the cockpit. I glanced at the instruments and watched the waves for a few moments. It was obvious what had woken me – the wind had started to go round and a gybe would be called for some time during the night. I could have done it then but I wanted to push further south and opted to change course instead. I clambered about the deck; a sail tie had come undone but otherwise all seemed well. I shone my spotlight into the rigging, it looked great. I adjusted the course by ten degrees and spent a few minutes with her to make sure that she was happy with this new heading, taking pleasure in watching her surf off under the decklight. It seemed to heighten the experience. Wind, spray, noise, rain and waves got their moment as they swept on and off stage, entering the spotlight at random and becoming larger than life in their moment of glory. Sheets of spray, thrown up by the bow, seemed solid in the harsh light but were cut off as soon as they ventured beyond its circle. I spent an hour glorying in it as I let her settle down.

It was time for tea. I shook off my Musto jacket. *Aqua Quorum* is a wet boat and being on deck when she was really tramping was like standing under a pressure hose, and yet I always remained dry. I first used Musto gear during the *Cornish Meadow* Transat when I slept on deck all the way. I have used it ever since and feel privileged to have done my bit in passing back ideas for improvement. Keith Musto decided a few years ago that the material Gore-Tex was the way to go and, with his son Nigel, developed a new benchmark in offshore clothing, the H.P.X. System. Gore-Tex is absolutely waterproof and yet able to breathe, thus venting condensation. It is very light and supple and lets me spend my days sitting about in water while remaining dry and warm.

It was two in the morning but this meant nothing now that my twenty-four-hour body clock was up and running. I munched a slice of Mum's fruit cake, swigged back the last of a cup of tea, and pissed in the keel box, checking the colour of my urine. It is easy for a single-hander to become dehydrated at sea without realising it. Golden urine is a sure sign of this problem, which can creep up just as readily in cold climes as it can in the tropics. I drink tea as a pastime – it is a ritual, a moment for reflection or a time of contemplation before a job that needs to be done. It's no good getting to the end of the boom and finding that the job requires a tool that is sitting below. Better to think it through first and make sure you have it before starting. I have saved myself many wasted hours and energy by cups of tea.

I could make out a big squall in the distance and there was no point in going to bed. I wedged myself in front of the chart table and wrote an article for the *Daily Telegraph* back in London. I was a bit reticent when Amelia fixed up a series of articles for me to write as the race progressed. I had never written before and the prospect seemed a bit daunting. But I found I enjoyed it and could bash out a rough feature in an hour and a half. Even Tracey liked the articles, and if anyone is honest she is. The cloud passed over and I could see another coming up. I was going to have to sleep at some time and pondered whether to get my head down regardless. I tried dozing in the chair, but it just didn't work. I was still not able to relax down there as the boat thundered on.

I kept pushing south and was soon the southernmost boat in

the fleet. It was bloody freezing with driving snow and became difficult to work on deck. My feet developed chilblains. Philippe Jeantot kept reminding me that it was a particularly bad year for icebergs. I was fatalistic. I hadn't seen any ice yet and my instincts told me that there was nothing to worry about. I kept a lookout but stuck to my usual laid-back approach – if a berg had my name on it then I would hit it. I was wearing full thermals, hat and gloves below by now, there was bitter snow on deck, and sail changes were particularly painful to the hands. There was a strong smell of diesel and I traced the problem to the sail locker. *Aqua Quorum* has a large diesel tank which is supplemented by plastic jerry cans. I discovered that the tops were made of a different plastic from the can itself – they were contracting at different rates in the cold and the tops had split, leaking diesel on the sails. It was these little details that I found so interesting. Like the chance discovery that pressurised canisters for inflating life rafts were unable to work in those temperatures – they froze as they decompressed – and a different gas was needed.

The race was not going to plan. I had dropped a touch too far south in my haste to get down quickly and was starting to pick up adverse winds while Raphael Dinelli and Patrick de Radigues were storming away to the north of us. I was a bit put out by this and made sure that it didn't happen again. I heard something rattle and bang along the hull. Ice! Shitty death! I was up on deck like a shot. It wasn't a big piece but it could have been the precursor to a decent-sized berg. It was hard to see in the blasts of snow. I turned on the radar but all seemed fine. It took a while for the hairs to settle down on the back of my neck, though. The desolation of that place was suddenly underlined. I couldn't see any point in slowing down – better to sail like the devil and push through the area quickly.

The longer I was away the more I missed my family. Tracey's

faxes were a daily lifeline. The BT Inmarsat system was so good and immediate that we could have a written conversation. I spent a lot of time working on next year's business and sorting out details that were left undone in the frantic last-minute preparations at the start. Nick Booth and his wife Sarah were making progress with the *British Steel* refit and I felt sure that with the two boats we would be able to keep in front of the overdraft. I had managed to sell a couple of days' hospitality on *Aqua Quorum* while I had been racing. It wasn't a chore, in fact it was nice to have something to work on outside the routine of the race.

People tend to think that a race like this is an endless series of adventures. The reality is that it is eighty per cent hard graft and twenty per cent excitement. The outside world focuses on the thrills, but they don't hear about the three grinding weeks of gale after gale. Three weeks' hard work boils down to a series of plots on the chart, that's it, nothing more. A disaster becomes a highlight, a break from the routine, something to write home about.

We emerged from the cold spell one morning to be welcomed by a crisp, sunny day with a northerly breeze. My spirits soared, the headwinds were behind us and I intended to drive myself to the bone until I caught up with Raphael and Patrick, who were now many miles ahead. I knew we could do it. I spent the day working on the boat and paid particular attention to the sail locker. It took hours to clean up the mess caused by the leaks – a little diesel goes a long way. The decks were as slippery as hell and no amount of scrubbing would take off the greasy film. I just had to be careful as I moved around. It played havoc with my elbow as I slid about. No matter how hard I tried I had to use both hands to stop myself slipping over. It was starting to swell more and the relentless, throbbing pain stopped me sleeping.

I stuck my head out the forehatch with yet another bucket of dirty water, and a 'growler' – a piece of iceberg about the size of a house – quietly slipped by with the sun reflecting off its many faces and making it look like a giant jewel. I hadn't seen anything solid outside the boat for ages and I stood watching it glide away and wondered how many others I had just missed. Back to work, there was another depression on the way and I wanted the boat tiptop.

The pressure dropped and the wind rose. This felt like our first proper depression, a classic Southern Ocean version rather than the patchy things we had had to endure so far. We crossed the 50th parallel, really in among it now and feeling good. It was not so cold now; in fact, I had been through the coldest part of the race during the past few days when the jerry can caps had split. I'll not forget it either, bloody grim, the warmest place on the boat was below – and that was zero degrees.

The wind picked up and we had a steady forty knots blowing. I had been progressively shortening sail and we were down to two reefs, staysail and the number two. *Aqua Quorum* was going like a bat out of hell and felt comfortable, despite a horrible little cross sea that kept trying to throw her off course. Apart from these odd moments I felt happy with progress and was able to get on with life below. I cooked up the biggest curry yet and shovelled some sugar into it. My sugar level felt low and I knew it was going to be a long night. I threw the pan into the cockpit – it was like a dishwasher out there, water flying everywhere as we bounced our way down the waves on a permanent plane. The white spray against the darkness was fantastic and I spent a couple of minutes looking aft at the wake as we roared off into the night. Time for a kip; I had been up too long and hadn't slept for a good eighteen hours.

I hung up my Mustos in readiness – I didn't expect to be down for long – and zipped my aching body into my sleeping bag. The feeling was fantastic and I grinned into the darkness. I was really enjoying things now, loving the rough and tumble and the fact that it was all down to me and my wits. I banged some Tina Turner into my Walkman, settled down and waited for sleep to overcome the noise and motion. I woke up and checked the instruments every twenty minutes or so and popped up on deck every now and then. The wind was starting to go round and I would need to gybe the boat sometime during the night. I didn't like the cross sea, it was giving the boat a hard time, the wind had gone up a bit but I decided to hold on to what sail I had up. We were going like a rocket.

I was woken by a dull thump on the side of the hull and felt the boat yaw to the left and accelerate down a wave. Shit, shit, shit, she was going to crash gybe, I just knew it. The boat heeled to leeward as the wind came further aft and I clawed away at the zip on my sleeping bag which had jammed. I couldn't free it. I heard the battens slam back in place, they had half gybed, bending double before crashing back. We hit the bottom of the wave and round she went. I gave up on the zip, shut my eyes and gritted my teeth. Crash! Over she went, my face was pressed against the hull and I was thrown out of my bunk. It was bloody freezing. Poor old *Aqua Quorum* was flat on her side and beam on to the wind. The keel was on the wrong side and I pictured the main across the runner, pinning the boat down. It was quiet now apart from the wind whistling over us and waves breaking on to the hull.

Take your time, I told myself, we've been here before. It was familiar ground. I worked the zip free, turned on the cabin light and found that my trousers had fallen into the water. I couldn't believe my bad luck, I had managed to keep the inside of them dry for months. Still, at least they would dry out as I wore them. I threw on the decklight and began a by now well-rehearsed sequence of actions. I used the opportunity to lean well out and check the keel. I decided not to perform a jig on it as I did in the Transat – it was pitch black and I didn't feel quite so cocky down here. I flaked out the number two halyard and dumped it, threw off the main halyard and wrestled the sail down the mast. She was coming up now, reacting in the kind and predictable manner that I had come to expect. The rudders suddenly bit and we accelerated off downwind again. The autopilot caught and she settled down on course.

The wind had gone round a bit – not too much, but the combination of that and a larger than usual cross sea was enough to cause the gybe. I sorted out the runners, swung the keel over, gybed the boat properly, heaved the number two on deck and lashed it down. A couple of hanks had ripped out. I put in another reef and spent a further two hours on deck squaring everything away. Below was a mess and I sorted that out, made a cup of tea and rolled into bed absolutely exhausted. We could have had a little more sail up but the time had come for some rest. I would have a big breakfast and resume work at daybreak. We'd done enough damage for one night, thank you very much.

I had an hour's deep sleep and bounced out of bed refreshed. In normal society, everything is geared to that eight-hour sleep. Transport, shopping, radio, television – it goes on and on, ruling your life, confining you like a straitjacket. At sea my sleep pattern varies with the weather and although I feel tired for much of the time I am not debilitated. Physically I feel lean and mean. My pain barrier rises considerably and a knock that would have hurt like buggery ashore is shrugged off as if it were nothing. There is the odd day when my limbs feel heavy, my eyes are gritty and I catch myself gazing into space in a kind of exhausted trance. Then I know it's time to have a good curry and follow it up with a decent kip.

I was very tired after the capsize but I spent the day mending the damage that it caused. All the battens in the main had broken and I took the opportunity to go over the sail with a needle and thread, touching up where necessary. The number two took an hour to repair and the rest of the day was spent sorting out below and writing an article that was well overdue. I managed to keep the boat on the boil though and ended the day with a serious look at how I was running my race. It took a glance at the chart to see that we hadn't even scratched the surface of the Southern Ocean and we had already suffered a lot of damage. If I wanted to stay in the race I would have to adapt to the environment and modify my pace.

Head down, I ignored my elbow, which did a lot of work during the capsize and was aching like a bastard, and got on with the job. *Aqua Quorum* was performing like a dream: each time the race positions came in I saw that we had pulled decent miles out of the opposition. I ate, slept, worked and kept the boat up to speed, driving her hard but not so hard that we sustained damage. A sixth sense picked up the warning signals and we didn't get caught out again.

The one thing I always insist on is reassuring Tracey that all is well. However, I was very tired after the last capsize and, although I informed the race organisers of the incident during the daily chat show, I forgot to fax the news to Tracey that night. The incident quickly hit the press and sounded worse than it was. The first a worried Tracey heard of it was a call from a journalist. I was not pleased with this slip-up on my part.

We were really pulling our way up the fleet now. I was caught in a high shortly after the capsize and two records were set that day. Christophe Auguin had a record run of 375 nautical miles – and I got the record for the least. Fourteen comes to mind. That was all behind us now, and we were the fastest boat in the fleet for a full seven days, which was topped by a blistering twenty-four-hour-run of just over 344 miles on 20 December. Philippe Jeantot informed me that this was a new record. I was well chuffed because I knew that the boat was capable of doing even better.

I was overjoyed to see that our wild dash had put us back up with Raphael and Patrick. I knew we could do it and spent a few hours pondering the weather information. My next target was to catch up with Eric Dumont on *Café Legal*. It was a tall order but I believed that we could do it. He had had some problems and did not seem to be on the pace as much as he should. I decided to keep pushing on – our performance hadn't cost us too much in terms of damage and I felt we had at last found our pace. The only cloud on the horizon was that Catherine had had a rough time with a bad knockdown and suffered a lot of damage. She was now a long way behind. I felt for her and hoped that she would be able to find her stride again. I was sure that she would become the first woman to finish the Vendée. She had the depth of character to overcome her problems and see it through to the end. I wished her well on the radio and acted as a link between her and the shore. It was the last radio call I would make before mine packed up.

The radio had died on me. It had received a good soaking in the capsize and, although it kept going for a couple of days, it was now silent. Never mind, I was quite happy out here and the less outside influence there was the better. It was as if the radio was my last link with society and I was unable to settle into this life of total self-reliance until my last crutch had been knocked away. The BT Inmarsat system did not have this effect – I called up its messages when I was ready for them, it was communication on my terms. Happy solitude.

The shallow bank of the Kerguelen Ridge presented a tactical dilemma. If it is blowing there the Southern Ocean waves can build up into a raging mess. I had a taste of it during the British Steel Challenge and had no wish for a repeat performance. Put simply, the bank has an island at either end, Kerguelen to the north and Heard Island to the south. My track would take me slap bang between the two. I didn't like it and decided to duck further south in order to avoid the area completely. I might lose a few miles but Raphael and Patrick were welcome to them in this case. As it happened the dogleg cost us little and I was glad to see that the others had cleared the area without mishap.

It was 22 December, my thirty-fifth birthday. I was fifty-five degrees south, the Kerguelens were well behind us and I felt great. It was time for a treat. I warmed up a bucket of water and had a shower in the cockpit under the cuddy. I put the heater on for an hour to dry the cabin, stood naked in the accommodation to let the warm air get to my skin and checked myself over. Loads of bruises, elbow hurting, but otherwise in good shape. No rashes or sores, the diet was obviously working. I slipped into a clean set of thermals – absolute luxury – and celebrated by trimming my moustache. The beard, if you could call it that, would stay because it stopped wet, salty clothing from chafing my neck.

Thirty-five years. I couldn't believe how quickly it had gone, it had been great. I had managed to fit a fair bit in so far and couldn't wait to grab the next thirty-five by the horns. Tracey and the kids sent a lovely fax, they had baked a birthday cake and eaten it for me. The race was going our way, we were catching the opposition and here I was fulfilling a lifelong dream. What a lucky man I was.

The next two days passed without a hitch and I carried out some routine maintenance and eased up on myself a little. I found that I was tired after working so hard to catch up with and pass Raphael and Patrick. I spent the odd extra hour or so in bed and made sure that I ate well. When I looked at the chart I was awed by the scale of this race – I had already packed in adventure after adventure and yet the halfway mark was still days away. Nevertheless I felt good – *Aqua Quorum* was bedded in and I knew that we would keep on improving our performance as we went on.

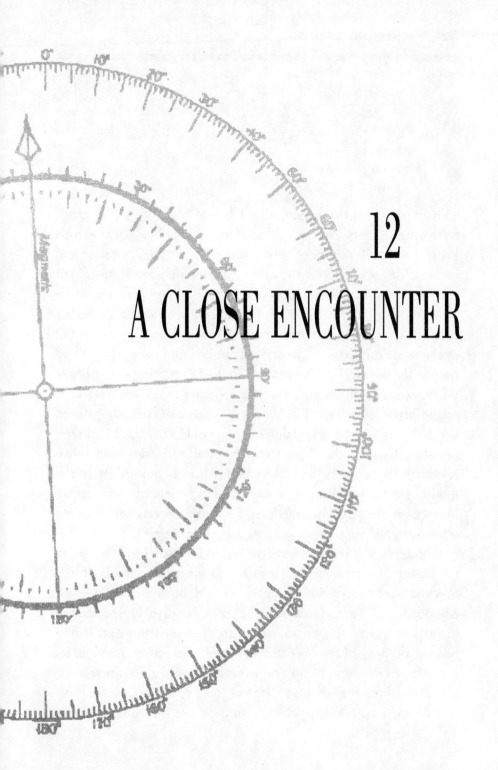

12
A CLOSE ENCOUNTER

Christmas Day 1996 began with a bright blue sky and a crisp, refreshing, twenty-knot wind from the north. My position was about 1,400 miles south of Perth, Western Australia. Perfect. I had been making good speed all night under the number two, staysail and one reef in the main as we surged along over the large northerly swell that had set in. It would have been idyllic if it hadn't been for the barometric pressure, which was dropping fast. A fall of thirty-six millibars in twenty-four hours, and most of that had been in the last twelve. The forecast looked horrifying – the isobars on the weather chart were so close together that they seemed to merge into a solid black line. I had a deep sense of impending doom and felt very uneasy – I couldn't settle, couldn't relax. I had seen livestock back in the West Country bunch together and move restlessly about the field before a bad storm; I could relate to the feeling, except I was on my own. I had experienced many severe blows over the years but this one, for some reason, held a heavy sense of foreboding. I could almost taste it in the air.

Thoughts of Christmas were pushed to one side. I tried to ignore the feeling of uneasiness but it followed me around the boat as I checked that everything was as it should be. Fear was not an emotion which I associated with the sea. Of course, I respected the ocean but for me it was no longer an alien environment, it had become my way of life over the years and I was comfortable in its presence. I knew that *Aqua Quorum* and I were up to the job – it was the waiting for what were bound to be pretty grim conditions that brought on the whispers, the anxieties. It was time to have a cuppa, get busy, apply logic. Once the storm arrived the rest would be easy.

I could feel it now. I togged up and got on deck. The wind started to back – within three hours it had gone round to the southwest and was rising at an alarming rate. I could only just keep up. No sooner had I gybed and sorted everything out than the number two needed dropping. And I mean dropping, it was over the side and in the sea. Damn! It was a real struggle to drag it on to the deck as we hurtled along. I folded it up and left it lashed there. I knew it should have gone below but I just didn't have time – the wind was rising faster than I had ever experienced. I clambered back to the mast, put the third reef in and still the wind rose. Hell's teeth! I reduced the sail area and immediately it was too much and needed reducing further. I could sense the autopilot struggling to cope as we hurtled along. No time to tidy the reefing lines. I flaked out the staysail halyard and freed the clutch; couldn't afford niceties. The sail flogged like a bastard as we careered off down an odd sea, often submerged. It was hard work to manage the most basic of jobs and my elbow was playing up, too.

I whipped off the staysail and shoved it below taking loads of water with it – so much of the stuff was sweeping the decks that it was hard to judge a good moment. I made the staysail halyard off on the storm jib, thankful that I had already hanked it on in readiness for the occasion, made my way back to the mast and tried to pull it up. It was no good, the wind was too strong. I had to winch it all the way. It felt very hot inside my Musto oilies, I'd been hard at it for a couple of hours now. I went back to the cockpit for a breather to find that the wind was up to forty-five knots and rising. Fuck me – and it was only just beginning. The hair stood up on the back of my neck.

I forgot about taking a breather. I had to get the main down and get it down quickly. Up to the mast, I flaked out the halyard, checked everything over; if it went wrong now I'd have a hell of a job getting it back under control. Not happy with the sheet, I nipped back, winched it in a bit and eased the halyard. The sail fell away and jammed on the spreaders, pinned by gusts of goodness knows what strength. It was a real old struggle and I had to work between the gusts that were whipping the water into a white frenzy. I tied it off with enough rope to moor the *Queen Mary*, removed the halyard, made it off on the end of the boom and took it up tight. I then rigged up a couple of lines from the end of the boom to either side of the cockpit and winched them up bar tight.

I worked my way round the boat, tidying everything away and making sure that all was shipshape. I pulled both dagger boards up and added a line to stop them falling out if we got rolled upside down. I tied off the blades on the wind generator as the automatic brake didn't seem man enough in these conditions. I knew the number two sail should be removed from the deck and stowed below but decided to leave it – the bow was under water most of the time now and discretion was the better part of valour in this case.

I had to crawl on hands and knees back to the cockpit. The wind was still rising and I felt as though I was a passenger in a car, with the driver pressing hard on the accelerator with no regard for a rapidly approaching corner. I rolled from my knees into the cockpit and clipped on my additional safety line before releasing the other. The wind was a screaming banshee lashing the ocean into a frenzy of spume and spray that felt like a shotgun blast on my hands and face. It had settled at a vicious fifty knots, topped up with regular gusts that blasted their way through us at sixty knots, flattening the sea as they passed. Still the storm hadn't settled – it continued to rise.

I stumbled below and for the first time in my life fitted the washboards in anger. I shook off the worst of the water, grabbed a Mars bar and once again called up the weather chart. There was nowhere to go, the best thing was just to run before it and hope the storm dissipated before inflicting too much damage. Looking at the chart I suspected that Raphael and Patrick might be experiencing even worse conditions and I silently wished them well – we were all caught up in something far greater than we had ever experienced before. The energy of the storm was incredible – they were hurricane conditions. The hull hummed and shook as we surfed off down a wave at twenty-seven knots. I braced myself for the impact at the bottom and we dropped for what seemed an eternity before the crash came. The wind in the rigging rose and fell from a high-pitched screech to a low and sorrowful moan that worked its way into my soul.

I clambered back on deck and marvelled at the conditions as we flew along under the storm jib alone. The sail was little more than the size of a tablecloth and yet the sheet was tight and as unyielding as a steel rod. It resonated when I hit it with a winch handle. There was a roar as a big sea broke behind us. I ducked beneath the canopy and held on for grim death as good old *Aqua Quorum* accelerated out of it. This was fantastic. I grabbed the camera and fired off a few shots for the kids. I had never managed to take a good wave shot in all my years at sea. The lens somehow flattened them out, but I suspected that these monsters might be impressive. And still the wind rose.

My main concern was the waves. A large and menacing sea had been whipped up from the southwest and was being made worse by a northerly swell which would take a while to dissipate. Individually they presented nothing more than one would expect – it was when they combined that they erupted into an unpredictable brute of tumbling water. At times we were planing across the face of a northerly swell, leaning to windward on the occasional steep face when a southwesterly sea slammed into us. The transom was lifted by the combined force of the two waves and we turned and dropped dangerously into a pit. I spent a while finding the best line, set the autopilot and tumbled below. There was no steering out of the bad ones. I was better off shut below in the safety of the hull.

I was worried. I felt my control of the situation ebbing away as the conditions deteriorated. Unusually, the first knockdown was to windward. Two waves erupted on my port quarter, *Aqua Quorum* slewed round until she was dead downwind, the keel on full power pulled her over and the wave did the rest as we accelerated into what felt like a brick wall. I was braced against the chart table, hands against the cabin roof, feet on the floor in a star position, and I watched through the skylight as the spreaders dragged in the water. They pulled her back to windward, she was up, the storm jib filled and she was off again. Water poured into the cockpit and cascaded below.

I considered going to bare poles to slow the boat's headlong rush but instinct told me that speed, alarming as it may have been, was the one defence I had. We hurtled into a hole at forty-five degrees and stopped dead. I waited for the seemingly inevitable pitchpole as we went completely under. The cabin went dark as the sea cut out the light. I was thrown against the chart table and looked out of the back of the boat at the sky as gallons of water poured into the accommodation from the cockpit. The flare box hit me on the shin and the pain gave me something to focus on, dispelling the fear as *Aqua Quorum* struggled to recover. The rudders were out of the water and I held on and hoped. There is always one bad blow on any long race and you know that if you get through it you will make the finish. I had no doubt that this was the one.

There was a tremendous crash and *Aqua Quorum* was knocked down again. I was thrown across the cabin as the boat groaned under the strain. Through the din I heard the satcom system bleeping away. I couldn't believe it was still able to work on what had practically become a yellow submarine. I struggled across to the chart table and called up the message. Mayday, mayday, mayday. It was a distress call being passed on by Marine Rescue and Control Centre (MRCC) Australia. The vessel in trouble was the yacht *Algimouss*. Poor sods. I wondered who they were and hoped I wouldn't be joining them. I assumed that she was somewhere near the Australian coast. I extricated a chart from the mess, plotted their position and did a double take. They were about 160 miles away. Who the hell would be daft enough to be down here? It never occurred to me that it might be one of us. The name *Algimouss* meant nothing to me as race communications had used the name of the skipper rather than the name of the boat. ·

The satcom bleeped again. This time the message was from Philippe Jeantot. The mayday *was* from one of us. *Algimouss* was Raphael Dinelli's boat and he was in trouble. Philippe asked if I could help. I took another look at the chart and realised that things were pretty bad: not only was Raphael 160 miles away from me but he was also to windward in atrocious conditions. But I had to go, I knew that. It was that simple; the decision had been made for me a long time ago by a tradition of the sea. When someone is in trouble you help.

However, I needed a minute to grasp the enormity of it. How could we make headway in this weather? Would *Aqua Quorum* hold together? The reality of what lay ahead grabbed at my guts. It was a cold and clammy grasp. Having made the decision I sat down to contemplate the consequences. It was only for thirty seconds, a minute – I'm not sure. I thought about what I was about to put on the line: my family, my boat, my life. In my own little world it was a profound moment that I shall never forget. To me, and I am sure it is different for everyone, if you keep chipping away at life you will eventually get to a clear and simple crossroads. I knew I had to stand by my morals and principles. Not turning back, whatever the stakes, would have been a disservice to myself, my family and the spirit of the sea. I fired off a quick fax to Philippe and expressed my doubts as to our ability to make our way back to Raphael – but I was going anyway.

I ventured on deck and the fight began. I had to think of it as a fight. I shouted at the wind and waves, and the anger helped to strengthen my resolve. We had to gybe. Oddly it was easy and went like clockwork. I brought *Aqua Quorum* up to face the wind, feeling the full force of the hurricane, as the wind across the deck immediately increased by the twenty-five-knot speed that I had been travelling downwind. The first gust put the guardrail under and the lower spreaders touched the water. I couldn't believe the energy that was whistling past. I winched in the storm jib hard, put the helm down again and waited to see what would happen. *Aqua Quorum* was game, it was as if she knew what was at stake. The mast slowly came upright and she began to move to windward. I couldn't believe that she was making about eight knots – sometimes more – as she climbed steeply to the wild, toppling crests at the apex of each huge wave, before accelerating down the fifty-foot slope on the other side and into the next trough. It wasn't quite the course I needed – eighty degrees to the wind was the best we could do – but it was a start, and the wind would ease soon. It had to.

Meanwhile it screamed deafeningly through the rigging, sounding like a jet taking off, as *Aqua Quorum* gamely struggled away. It was impossible to breathe if I faced windward – the breath was sucked from my lungs – and I couldn't open my eyes.

Now that we were committed, I knew that we would do it somehow. The things I learned with the Royal Marines took over: be professional at all times, never give up and make intelligent use of everything to hand. I had asked a lot of my boats in the past, but never this much. I decided to take no prisoners. *Aqua*

Quorum would do it or she would break up in the attempt; a man was out there and there could be no half measures. Night closed and we struggled on. The huge, breaking seas and the waves were horrifying.

I had to fire off a fax to Tracey as I didn't want her to hear about all this from someone else. I made the mistake of telling her not to worry which was something I had never done before. She told me later that it was the only time during the race that she became really concerned.

25 DEC 1996 15:56 FROM INMC VIA SENTOSA LES

```
Hi Tracey, Happy Xmas - I am in bad storm
60knts wind but fine, I stress fine. Another
competitor is in distress & I am trying to
make my way back to rescue him, I stress I am
fine & storm may just be easing so don't
worry. Wanted you to know before press start
baying. Can't tell you how much I love you.
Hope the Xmas meal/day has been good. Love to
all. Pete XXXXX
```

FROM 423420410=AQUA X 25-DEC-1996 15:56:42 MSG214085 SENTOSA C IOR

Below it was an indescribable mess: water slopped about and a litre bottle of cooking oil had burst. Everything was coated with the stuff and it was slippery. I slithered and slid about – it was getting as dangerous below as it was on deck. My infected elbow took a bad blow and would cause problems from then on. A wave swept the deck with such ferocity that all the rope clutches opened. God, what next?

I crawled into the cockpit and we were knocked down again, this time beyond ninety degrees, and I felt myself falling out of the boat. *Aqua Quorum* came up, a spinnaker pole had burst its lashings at one end, the head car metal fitting at the top of the mainsail had broken, and both the mainsail and the number two, which were lashed to the deck, were ripped. I decided not to venture beyond the mast.

I was wet and very cold as I hadn't had the chance to put on my full thermals. I was also hungry. I got below, grabbed some food and shoved it down. Raphael needed someone in good shape. Come on, keep going, take charge. I could feel the first signs of hypothermia coming on, being soaked through and not wearing my heavy thermals. I put the kettle on and dragged my warmest thermals over the wet ones. A big wave hit the boat and the kettle hit the deckhead. I re-filled it and flashed up the stove again. This time I held the kettle down but with the next big wave both the kettle and I hit the deckhead. I crawled into my sleeping bag and tied myself into the bunk before dropping into semiconsciousness. The tea would have to wait.

I awoke with a jolt as we were knocked down again. We were being knocked down every half hour or so now. I was disorientated, tired and confused in the darkness. The cabin filled with a nauseating smell. My stores under the chart table had broken free and an aerosol can of oil was emptying itself. There were big sparks coming from under the table – the can had wedged itself across the live generator terminals and was causing a short circuit. A fire was all I needed.

The wind had lost its edge; I felt the worst was behind us. Hold on, Raphael. We had eighty miles to go and I could make the course. I updated Philippe, gulped some water, ate what I could and went back to my sleeping bag. I had to conserve energy because I felt my limits were not far off. I thought of Raphael out there and wondered how he could possibly survive. The wind was easing, we had got through round one, and I needed to make good use of my time in the corner before round two began. I worked as fast as I could; the wind was down to thirty-five knots now and I needed more sail up. I checked the deck and stowed the torn number two. I tackled the repair to the mainsail, drilling holes for the needle to save time. It took two and a half hours, every minute dragging. Raphael would be in a bad way by now – he had to be. I talked my way through possible first aid treatment as I sewed.

Job done, I went below and stowed the sailmaker kit, put a quick cup of tea on and ... vrooooom ... it was a Royal Australian Air Force rescue plane. They told me over the VHF radio that they had dropped Raphael two life rafts, he seemed well and was in an immersion suit. His yacht *Algimouss* was submerged. I took her position and asked if there were any other vessels involved in the rescue. 'No, sir, we're pinning our hopes on you,' came the reply. Fine. We'd do it.

Round two began as the aircraft's engines faded into the distance. I spent a quiet few minutes working out my next actions as *Aqua Quorum* continued to bash her way to windward. I needed a new strategy because the fight had changed. My opponent was wily and I must adapt. More thought was required now and instinct and determination were not enough. I broke the way ahead into clearly defined chunks and mentally walked the course a few times. I felt as though I was actually there, each time throwing in a new problem and coming up with a practical solution. Every visualised run culminated in a successful rescue.

Phase one was a simple yacht race to Raphael's general location. Phase two would take a little more effort to crack. It was a big area and it would be like looking for a needle in a haystack, particularly as it would be getting dark. Phase three would be the pick-up. This could present all sorts of complications. No worries though. I had plenty of time for some more reruns of this phase. First of all I needed information and so I faxed Philippe and asked for a detailed twelve-hour weather forecast for my area. Philippe played a vital role throughout the operation.

Very soon a special forecast came through from Météo France: a front would arrive in the afternoon, the wind would head me all day, visibility would reduce and winds of forty knots were expected. This would add a good four hours to the passage and make it very hard to find Raphael. There was no room to manoeuvre. I just had to get on deck and sail like the devil. The rest of the day was spent concentrating on the boat speed – nothing dramatic, just sailing – and it was a relief, apart from the frustrations of being headed off the course by the hour. I continually got updates on Raphael's position and drift. MRCC Australia confirmed that an RAAF plane would aid the rescue in the morning. This gave me great comfort for we had a safety net if I couldn't find him in the dark.

Provided Raphael could cope with the cold I felt we had him. I was now twenty miles directly downwind of him and started short-tacking up his drift line. It began to get dark. This could actually be a blessing if the raft had a light as it would make him easier to spot. The wind just would not settle and the autopilot found it hard to keep as close to the wind as I would have liked in the confused seas, so I went back to the helm. Some five hours later, we were five miles downwind of where Raphael should be, given his drift. I slowed *Aqua Quorum* down and popped up the mast to the first set of spreaders to try and catch a glimpse of him. In those seas, I needed a lot of luck.

I went below and saw that another message had come in. It was a position update and it had changed considerably. We had overshot the mark by seven miles. Philippe also informed me that he had seen a photograph taken from the RAAF plane. *Algimouss* had been dismasted and was submerged. There was nothing to be seen apart from the life raft and he thought the yacht may have sunk by now anyway. There was no point in looking for a mast. The needle in the haystack got smaller.

I sailed back to the exact position I had been given and, as I was to windward, I dropped the main and zigzagged down his drift line under storm jib, keeping the speed down to between three and five knots. It was very dark and the front had arrived. A sense of desperation set in as the wind rose and visibility fell. I stood on the bow, blasting the foghorn and firing rocket flares. If only I could attract Raphael's attention, he could then let off a flare and we would have cracked it. 'Come on, Raphael. Wake up,' I shouted into the darkness. There was no response, just an enveloping greyness that soaked up my attempts to penetrate it.

I reached the end of his projected drift line. He was here, I knew it. I could feel it and yet emptiness pervaded. Come on, come on, we didn't tackle that storm for this. Give us a break, Neptune, surely we deserved one now. I decided to carry on the run until I had doubled his drift. We had to exhaust each avenue. Nothing.

Right. We turned round, got the main up and worked back. We'd bloody well do this all night if we had to. You'll never grind us down, damn you. The main kept jamming in the lazy jacks. My elbow ached and there was no strength. I had to be methodical. Persistence would pay. I nipped below and another position came in. It had changed and the drift was different. All that for nothing. I started to replot the position, but there were now two charts swimming before my eyes as if I were drunk. I just couldn't work it out. The first plot put him a crushing sixty miles away. Whoa, hang on, that wasn't right. I went on deck and stuck my head in a bucket of water. It was the first time I was thankful that the Southern Ocean was cold. I went back to the chart table and started again. It made sense now. He was six miles away and the plot was quite recent. Dawn had arrived. I rammed down some cold beans, a mug of cold water, and went back to concentrating on boat speed. It seemed an eternity before we arrived at the new waypoint and the show started again.

Slowly, slowly. Concentrate, don't miss him. Come on, Raphael, bang off a flare or something. You have got to help yourself now. I am not enough. I tried the Navico hand-held VHF in desperation. It is waterproof and I could use it on deck. I got a response. '*Aqua Quorum, Aqua Quorum*. This is Rescue 252. We have started our descent and should be with you in four minutes.' Thanks, guys. The relief was heady. Soon the RAAF plane flew past. They had a visual. He was three miles away and they would drop a smoke flare by him. I still couldn't see him. They turned and flew back towards me. As they passed over Raphael they flashed their lights. I took the best bearing of my life. They informed me there were two life rafts, Raphael was in the first and he had waved at them. Good lad, he must have the constitution of an ox. Phase three suddenly became simple.

I dropped the main, felt the wind and . . . there he was! As the life raft came into sight I judged the best approach. Port side. I had grablines all round the boat and a long line with two fenders on it aft just in case I overshot. Fifty, forty, thirty, twenty metres. It was going to be a good one. Thank heavens for all the practice. I ran forward and threw off the headsail halyard. Raphael gripped the grabline. Got him!

Wow, a true professional here. He insisted on passing me three distress beacons and a box of stores. There was a bottle of champagne. Oh go on, then, seeing as you've brought a drink. We both heaved and he was on deck. Just like that. The best Christmas present I've ever had, all wrapped up in an immersion suit.

My new passenger lay face down on the deck and tried to move, but he was too stiff and cold. It was hardly surprising – he had spent two days waiting for me to rescue him. I gently turned him over to reveal a nose and two very inflamed eyes surrounded by thick, yellowish wax. A feeble 'thank you' could be heard from inside the immersion suit. All I could see was his eyes and I shall never forget them. I had no idea that a pair of eyes could convey such a depth of relief and gratitude. I was cheered to see that Raphael could converse and that he tried to help himself – the last thing I wanted was a medical case. I dragged him back to the cockpit by his ankles; his feet were agonisingly painful because of the cold, and he couldn't walk. We worked together to get him under the cockpit overhang. I nipped up to the foredeck and raised the storm jib to steady the violent roll of *Aqua Quorum* in the swell. I set the autopilot and got back to Raphael.

His survival suit was inflexible and encrusted with salt, and it took five minutes to undress him. His hands and feet were in the worst condition: cold, colourless and useless. Skin came away on contact and I wondered if there would be long-term damage. The next step was to get him below through the small hatch, which was difficult to negotiate at the best of times. He was very stiff – it was as though rigor mortis was setting in – and it took a couple of attempts before he tumbled through. Now he was below in my cramped, wet little hell hole. It was a palace to him and he smiled weakly. I gave him a quick clean with wet-wipes and towelled him down – no major injuries, just bruising.

I put a dry set of thermals on him, pulled a woolly hat over his head and eased him into my best sleeping bag. He couldn't straighten out so I propped him in a sitting position against my kitbag and put a support under his knees. Every movement was slow and painful for him. I bunged on the kettle and informed the RAAF plane of the casualty's condition and thanked them for their help. They asked my intentions. Crumbs, I hadn't thought that far. I'd probably drop him off in Hobart. I asked the RAAF what I should do with the life raft. Leave it, they said. I went on deck and cast it off – it would probably bob around the Southern Ocean for ever. The kettle was boiling and I made a very sweet cup of tea in a cyclist's drinking bottle; I had it on board for just such an occasion as it has a nipple on the top and you can't spill the contents. I helped Raphael slowly and painfully wrap his frozen hands round it. He took a sip and a look of pleasure lit up a face haggard beyond its twenty-eight years. He told me later that it was as though he had landed in England.

I filled my grandmother's old hot-water bottle and placed it under his feet. As Raphael began to warm up he started to talk in a mixture of broken English and French, which I found hard to understand. He wanted to share his ordeal, repeating himself many times during the telling of how he fought off death for forty-eight hours. I told him that he was a very lucky man to have survived. It was strange to have another human on board after so long by myself. It was both a pleasure and an intrusion. I had a bizarre urge to start tidying up. *Aqua Quorum* could certainly do with it. What a boat! I felt a great surge of pride at the fantastic job she had done.

Raphael was very weak and stiff and unable to get out of his bunk without help. His body had seized up after days of being huddled in a life raft in icy temperatures. Going to the toilet was a major task – I had to carry him to the bucket and support him there. The race doctor was a great help during this time, prescribing medication and giving advice. I administered muscle-relaxant drugs and gave Raphael physiotherapy in the form of stretching. It exhausted him but improved his mobility, and after five days he could get out of his bunk unaided. When he slept, the roll of the boat seemed to bring back memories of his ordeal and he had the odd nightmare.

The fax continued to pour out an endless stream of messages. Many were from Raphael's family and he did his best to translate them for me. His parents said that I was now part of the Dinelli family and a fax from his elder brother in Paris said: 'We have another brother now in Pete.' I was very touched by the warmth of those messages.

Four days after the rescue Raphael proposed by fax to his girlfriend Virginie on her birthday. I think that perhaps his close brush with death on the deck of *Algimouss* made him realise what was important in his life. She faxed back her acceptance and suggested that I be best man. I was honoured. It was time to have a go at the champagne. The satcom had endless messages for us and demands for our story poured in from the press. It appeared that our little adventure had caused quite a stir. For the moment I only communicated with the race doctor, Jean-Yves, about Raphael's condition. I was also concerned with trying to get the damage on board sorted out before I arrived in Hobart. I wanted a quick turnaround so that I could get on with the race, having lost many miles and a lot of time. I was told that the race committee would give me an allowance for the time lost during the rescue, but I felt it was all a bit hypothetical.

Apart from a quick handshake at the start of the race, I didn't really know Raphael, but we hit it off immediately. I was to discover over the next days that we were kindred spirits. I have since been told that it is unusual for the relationship between a casualty and the rescuer to be a successful one because of complex feelings of guilt, gratitude and debt. Not so with us. We felt we were facing the same foe. Any one of the competitors could have been in the path of the freak wave that capsized Raphael and destroyed *Algimouss*. There but for the grace of God . . .

However, all I really wanted to do once I had him sorted out and in a sleeping bag was to grab some sleep myself – I was already tired when we went into the storm, and by the time of the actual pick-up two days later I was exhausted. The trouble was that Raphael was on a survivor's high and kept rabbiting away. I just couldn't shut him up.

At first he kept repeating aspects of his rescue over and over again and it took a while to piece his ordeal together. His was a tale of quite extraordinary determination. There is no way that he should have survived for the length of time that he did. He had accepted that he was probably going to die, but he never gave up and kept pushing death before him, day by day, hour by hour, minute by minute. The man is a giant.

Raphael had been overtaken by an intense storm. The wind was blowing at hurricane strength – sixty-five knots and over – and increasing in the gusts to eighty knots. His boat was surfing on waves as high as a sixty-foot, six-storey building. It was too dangerous on deck and he was sheltering down below and trying to control the headlong rush of *Algimouss* with his autopilot. It was hopeless. He was trapped inside the upturned hull of *Algimouss* after being capsized by a huge wave which crashed across the boat, flipping it on its side and turning it upside down. He was strapped below in his seat with everything flying every-where. He worked his way free and activated his satellite emer-gency radio beacons, praying that someone would hear his mayday. The mast broke and was pile-driving through the hull – water poured in through the holes it made. After freeing himself, he spent the next three hours in the galley with the water rising up to his thighs. The diesel tanks were leaking and the fumes were making him violently sick.

The mast eventually freed itself from the tangled rigging, passed through the side of the hull and the boat righted itself. He clambered into the cockpit, which was awash, clipped himself to the submerged hull, faced the fifty-foot seas and fought it out. Each wave that struck choked and froze him, the icy water working its way down inside his survival suit. He could feel his body locking up with the cold, and started dancing on the flooded deck to keep his circulation going. 'I must have looked like a madman,' he said later.

He had nothing to eat or drink as he clung on there for twenty-four hours. Huge waves were running and each time they swept the boat he could feel her starting to give up and begin to settle lower under his feet for her final trip to the bottom. He talked to her, shouted at her, and again and again she dragged herself back to the surface. He thought about Virginie and their daughter Philippine. He made plans for the future, determined to be positive. The ropes which attached his life raft to the hull parted in the savage winds, and he was forced to watch his last hope of survival blow away.

He held out through that night and thought that all was lost until the RAAF, who played such a brave and vital part in his rescue, turned up and dropped him another life raft. He clambered on board, taking with him some food and a bottle of champagne which had washed to the surface. Inside the life raft was a message in French saying that Pete Goss and *Aqua Quorum* were ten hours away, due south. Five minutes later *Algimouss* finally succumbed to the Southern Ocean and sank beneath the waves to begin her long journey, 3,500 metres down to the sea bed. Then began the struggle for survival in the life raft until we finally arrived on the scene.

For me it did not end with picking up Raphael. It was probably the toughest physical and mental ordeal I had ever been through and I didn't realise the extent of the toll it had taken until a few days later when I was sitting on deck, enjoying the sunshine and the brightness of the day. I had just given Raphael a decent physio session and he was asleep. Suddenly I found tears rolling down my cheeks. I don't think I was crying in the normal sense of the word – I certainly wasn't grieving for anything. It was a release of the tension that I had bottled up during the previous five days. I was thoroughly exhausted. I had been shocked when I changed out of my thermals after the rescue – I barely recognised my body for bruises and weight loss. I reckon I lost at least half a stone in thirty hours. The tears didn't take long to clear. I had just explained how I felt in a fax to Tracey:

29 DEC 1996 05:27 FROM INMC VIA SENTOSA LES TO 001441503230779

Hi Tracey, Raphael is asleep. I have just given him a physio session & he is improving although still not well. I just wanted to express my feelings to you as a shoulder to cry on . . . I feel quite traumatised at the moment, very tired & a bit emotional about the whole thing. It was a very bad experience & I now have to get myself back together, drop off Raphael and try to start all over again having lost my stride. I don't think it will be easy & I'm not looking forward to it . . . I'm on top of it but it just helps to share it. AQ is fine & I do little repair jobs every day – she is brilliant & it was she who saved the day . . . Tell the kids I love them loads & thank them for the cards they sent me. I had a good Christmas because I saved a man's life & he is OK. I am sailing home as fast as I can to give them a big hug. Thanks, Tracey. I feel better now, you know how it is. Love you loads 'n loads. Pete.

FROM 423420410=AQUA X 29-DEC-1996 05:28:14 MSG232858 SENTOSA C IOR

There was a language barrier between Raphael and me – he spoke only schoolboy English and I couldn't speak French. At first we communicated by using pictures and sign language but by the end of the ten days that it took us to get to Hobart we were having pretty deep conversations. As the journey went on Raphael's English grew better and better, the words just seemed to come. First, his understanding of what I was saying increased, and then, he began to reply more and more fluently.

We talked about our families and pretty much everything else – from life generally, to boat design and the ideas he had in mind for his next Vendée, and personal relationships. Sometimes it would take a whole day to get one fairly simple point across, but we would always get there in the end.

Our paths leading up to the Vendée start line were pretty similar. Like me he had been endlessly beset by one financial crisis after another. I told him about having to sell our home, and how I was worried about how Tracey and I were going to manage to pay the heating bills when I got back after the race. England was in the grip of a particularly vicious winter and Tracey was struggling to keep our rented cottage warm. Raphael told me about his struggle to find a boat and fund his campaign – only to be refused official status in the Vendée at the last moment by the race committee because he hadn't been able to complete his qualifying passage. He decided he would sail the course as an unofficial entrant, an outsider. Nothing was going to stop him taking part in the Vendée. Like me, he had dreamed long and hard about the race.

As Raphael gradually became a little more mobile he busied himself below with some light tidying up and trying to sort out the mess caused as *Aqua Quorum* fought her way back through the storm to find him. Food packages had burst and the contents were strewn everywhere. While he was putting my stores in order he found a number of cassette tapes which were hidden away along with some other surprise Christmas presents – my other tapes had long since been destroyed by water cascading below during a storm. The Walkman was still working and so Raphael and I took turns in enjoying the tapes – we discovered a shared pleasure in music. Next he came across a Christmas card from my children which had survived the soaking that had put paid to all my other Christmas cards, along with the presents, early in the race. When I read the greetings from Alex, Olivia and Eliot I had a lump in my throat.

I had my share of finds as well. While I was working on the generator on New Year's Day I stumbled across a shrink-wrapped Christmas pudding wedged up in a corner of the engine. Perfect timing. We celebrated New Year's Eve with Christmas pud and some half-bottles of wine that had escaped the bashing. Raphael and I got very drunk. Among the Christmas presents were a couple of party hats – a pair of headphones dressed up like a Christmas cracker with the word 'BANG!' printed across them for Raphael, and a bobble hat with rude words and funny sayings sewn on for me. As midnight neared we pledged that we would race together in the future when things were on a more even keel. The constant crashing and bouncing caused by the gale which raged outside barely seemed to matter as we toasted in the New Year. It was a great party.

On one occasion I decided to give Raphael a treat by cooking some popcorn for one of our evening meals. I poured a little oil into a saucepan, heated it up on my single-burner stove and popped in a couple of handfuls of corn. He didn't eat much and sat there waiting for the next course – he thought the popcorn was an appetiser. When I managed to make him understand that that *was* the meal, he seemed a little disappointed. It tasted good to me anyway.

I don't think Raphael was all that impressed either with my cooking skills or my cooking facilities. On board *Algimouss*, a much larger vessel, he had had a spacious, fully equipped galley. My camping-style stove seemed very limited to him. After all, he was a Frenchman, with a little Italian chucked in, and gastronomic matters were high on his list of things that mattered. As his strength returned, he began to experiment with some pasta dishes. He found some Italian-style sauces among my supplies and cooked up some pretty good meals. He called them Pasta Dinelli.

Raphael was very interested in the fact that *Aqua Quorum* had been built by the team and myself. His boat, formerly called *Crédit Agricole IV*, had been owned by Philippe Jeantot, the Vendée organiser. Raphael had bought her and then refitted her for the race. I talked endlessly and proudly about *Aqua Quorum* and the team, explaining how she was constructed and showing him all the innovations on board. We spent days talking about boats and ideas we would like to see on them – particularly safety features. I think the experience Raphael had been through prior to his rescue had given him a special interest in safety. He drew sketch after sketch of his ideas and we worked together on designs for keels, masts and dozens of other things. We came to the conclusion that ocean racing skippers should pool their hard-won knowledge, rather than encourage the cloak of secrecy that often surrounds new ideas on boats.

Raphael was back on his feet but he was still shaky, both physically and mentally. I made a special seat and suspended him from the deckhead so that he could use the laptop to fax Virginie as well as bash out his story. He couldn't work for more than forty-five minutes at first and suffered for quite a long time afterwards as a result of his efforts. Nevertheless I was amazed at how quickly he pulled himself together. The fact that *Algimouss* had disappeared from the daily race results was particularly painful for him and we spent a lot of time talking about the Vendée. There was never any doubt about what was next for Raphael. Nothing short of crossing that finish line at Les Sables d'Olonne would satisfy him. I look forward to being on the pontoon to take his line when he does. He is very determined and my bet is that he will be in first place.

The rescue was still generating an amazing amount of interest around the world. The satcom buzzed endlessly with requests for information but at least I could always switch it off if it became too much. On the other side of the world Tracey wasn't quite so fortunate – she was being inundated and couldn't do anything about it. The phone rang throughout the night. Journalists tracked her down at home and buttonholed her on the doorstep. The fact that I kept my head down for the first couple of days after the rescue only served to aggravate the situation. She was even getting calls from the race officials regarding the time allowance I would be given for the rescue and the fact that they felt I should drop Raphael off in New Zealand rather than Hobart. I was glad to be out of it. The word 'hero' was being bandied about too much for my liking and I was thankful that I would be at sea for a good two months yet. By then all those newspaper headlines would be wrapping up fish and chips . . . or so I thought.

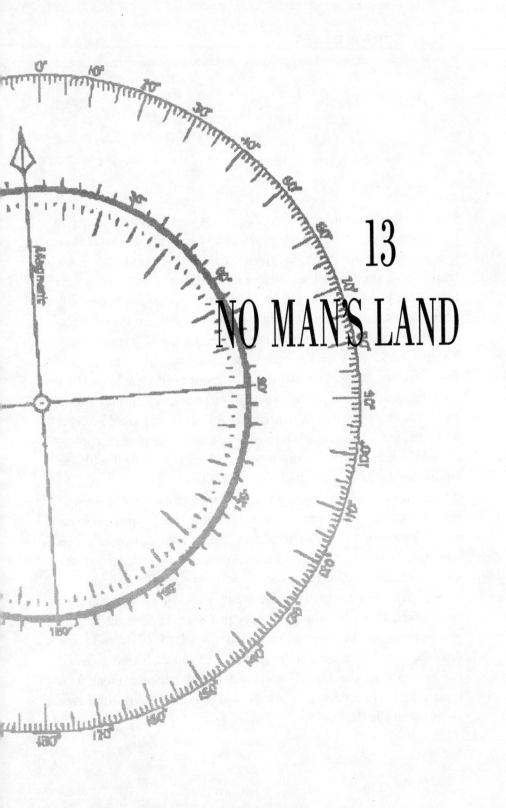

13
NO MAN'S LAND

I had decided to run for Hobart because it was the logical place to go. Fremantle was the nearest port but it was on the wind – Hobart was in a favourable direction, given the prevailing wind conditions. In any case, I had been there before and, because I had no charts, a little local knowledge would be invaluable. As we made our way north out of the Southern Ocean the sun emerged and the temperature rose. Raphael pulled together by the day and I started to give him the odd job on deck to keep his mind occupied. The story of the rescue was huge in France and all sorts of deals were being done on his behalf, including an exclusive contract, which meant that the demands on him when he arrived back on shore would be fierce and complex. I encouraged him to get as much sleep as he could – he would need all the strength he could muster to deal with the circus that I was sure awaited him on dry land.

Ten days after the rescue I could smell the eucalyptus trees as we closed the Tasmanian shore. I made the approach with extreme caution taking care to steer clear of the dangerous reefs which lie offshore. When land hove into view, we sailed down the coast, avoiding the outlying rocks and keeping well offshore. The final approaches to the River Derwent, which leads into Hobart, are flanked by rocks which are only just awash. As night fell the wind rose and the waves quickly increased to 20 feet. In the distance I could see occasional glimpses of the reefs that guarded the entrance to the river. We passed safely between them to a calmer and sheltered sea as we felt our way slowly up the River Derwent in the darkness.

I was told by the Australian immigration authorities to contact the motor yacht *Frontier*, which would be standing by to meet us. The plan was that they and only they, as there was a government representative on board, would take us in tow, pick up a mooring and then process Raphael and take him ashore. I called up *Frontier* on my VHF radio but got no response. *Frontier*, unbeknown to us at the time, had gone offshore in an attempt to pick us up out at sea and had missed us. I contacted the harbour authority, explained my predicament and asked them to pass my position on because they had a more powerful unit. Suddenly, all hell let loose. Having picked up our position from the conversation, fishing boats, packed to the gunwales with journalists and television crews, converged on us. They took hundreds of photos and shouted their questions across the water that separated us. The media was out in full force.

I reduced sail and put out every fender on the boat, threading my way uneasily through the ever growing armada of small boats that had come out to welcome us. The fax and the VHF radio spewed out a nonstop, jabbering rush of welcome, questions, messages, demands – in both English and French.

It was all a bit confusing and quickly got out of hand. The people who had negotiated an exclusive deal with Raphael's agent wanted to board us there and then. By the time *Frontier* finally showed up it was a chaotic scene and poor old Raphael was in the middle of it. I fended off the press by saying that the law of the land stipulated that I take a tow from *Frontier* and that no one was allowed to board *Aqua Quorum* under both immigration and race rules.

Raphael agreed to give the television station that had secured the exclusive deal a live interview from the back of the boat as we sailed along. The *Frontier* caught us up, I took their tow, had a last word and a hug with Raphael as he left the boat and let them get on with it. I looked on as Raphael was given a quick medical, rubber-stamped into the country and then whisked away with a bemused look on his face and a trail of press behind him. The saddest thing was that his girlfriend Virginie was not allowed to be there to welcome him back. She was secreted away somewhere so that the photographs of their reunion would be exclusive.

The one oasis in all this chaos was the skipper and crew of the *Frontier* who, being seamen, knew what the score was. I was very tired, hungry and displaced. They gave me a decent meal, my first fresh food for months, towed me to a secluded mooring and left me to it as the sun rose above the mountains and lit up my old friend Hobart. I couldn't sleep, so I sat on deck with a cup of tea and started to sort out the jumble of emotions that the rescue had stirred up and thought about my next step. I had completely lost my stride and had been so focused on getting Raphael back that I was now faced with a huge void and no plan in place. I made a list which seemed to go on for ever.

Poor old *Aqua Quorum* had given her all and needed a lot of work before I could venture back into the Southern Ocean. The first thing I did was to crawl all over the boat with a torch and check the structure for any telltale cracks. She seemed to be as good as new. Amazing. There were times during the apex of the storm when I had questioned whether *Aqua Quorum* would stand up to the onslaught. I was thrown about so much that I had no option but to strap myself in and let the boat get on with it. On one occasion I said, 'It's over to you guys now,' meaning Adrian, Gary and the rest of the lads who had put the boat together. I later discovered that two of the engine mounts had been ripped in half by the boat's violent shaking. That storm was the build team's finest hour. I have an immense sense of pride in being one of them.

I have no doubt that one of the key factors in *Aqua Quorum*'s ability to pull through was Adrian's swing keel design. With the keel out to windward and both dagger boards up there is nothing in the water to trip the boat. She is able to dissipate the impact of beam-on forces by sliding sideways at anything up to ten knots before finally lying over on her side if it is a particularly bad wave. The good thing is that the rudders had the strongest grip, so the bow would always fall off to leeward. The swing keel was a breakthrough in yacht design and I feel sure it will become a standard feature on future yachts.

Meanwhile I found myself in a kind of no man's land. Officially, I was still racing; the race committee had agreed that I could remain on a buoy for repairs and, provided I didn't get off the vessel and no one got on, they would recognise my passage as unassisted. The reality was that the shore, bustling with life, was about 100 yards away. The many friends I'd made when I was in Hobart for the stopover on the British Steel Challenge rowed out to see us and we had a chat over the guardrail. By mid-morning the press were back for more interviews.

The *Frontier* returned, this time with replenishment stores – I was allowed to replace what had been lost as a result of the rescue. The best bit about this was that it came in the form of fresh food – bread, bacon, peaches, a couple of slabs of beef and much more. I gorged myself and my bucket took a real pasting because of the change in diet. Max Sarma, Gaye's brother who lived in Hobart, was a great help and he became my minder ashore. My ThinkPad laptop had started to go on the blink as a result of the rescue. IBM had sent a replacement but it got lost somewhere in the system. Max worked long and hard to locate it and managed to get the customs to rush it through.

It took two days' hard work to get *Aqua Quorum* up to scratch so that we could leave in a seamanlike manner. One of my greatest concerns was my elbow, which was playing up after the bashing it had taken and seemed to be getting more inflamed by the day. I was still very tired and bruised. There was no way that I was going to give up the race but I was completely thrown. I concentrated on dragging myself away from the womblike comfort and safety of Hobart and stomped on deck with a purposeful glint in my eye. One of the things I had to do was to climb to the top of my mast to check and replace some of the instruments which had been damaged during the knockdowns. By now my elbow was particularly painful and I was not looking forward to the ascent. I donned my harness and gritted my teeth in readiness for the discomfort, only to be distracted by the revving of an engine and a shout. It was Raphael coming out to bid me farewell. He passed me a Tasmanian T-shirt and a promised pizza and we said a brief goodbye, which was spoilt by a television crew who did their utmost to turn it into a Hollywood-style set piece. I got back to my job and it was only when I glanced back to catch a last glimpse of a forlorn Raphael in the boat as it disappeared behind a headland that I realised with a pang of guilt how insensitive and dismissive I had been when I said goodbye. My only excuse is that I had no room for anything but the rest of the race. I was single-handed once more, I had shut out the world.

As I slipped my mooring I sent Tracey a fax and managed three link calls on the VHF radio before leaving the range of Hobart's coastal station. I thanked Mark Orr for the tremendous support he had given me during my stay in Hobart; I called Aqua Quorum, who seemed pleased with all the publicity; and I finished off with a call to Adrian Thompson. I tried to thank him for the boat and what it had done for Raphael and me in the Southern Ocean but I became too choked up. It was the last conversation I was to have until I reached Cape Horn.

The rescues of Tony Bullimore and Thierry Dubois were still fresh in my mind. Tony spent four days inside the upturned cabin of his capsized boat in the storm-tossed Southern Ocean before HMAS *Adelaide* found him in a dramatic mercy dash that had never before been attempted so far south. Television viewers around the world watched in amazement as the rescue crew approached the wreck in an inflatable and Tony's head suddenly popped up beside the upturned hull of his yacht, as it wallowed in huge waves. HMAS *Adelaide* had already picked up Thierry Dubois, who had been marooned on the hull of his upturned yacht.

While I was overjoyed by the news of their rescue, it served to underline that the Southern Ocean was a threatening and forbidding place. The fact that the rest of the fleet was by now too far away to come to my assistance, should I need it, did not escape me either. I was truly on my own. It was with a heavy heart that I pointed *Aqua Quorum* towards Cape Horn.

I was still feeling the effects of rescuing Raphael and my resolve was at a low ebb. Fortunately, the first week at sea brought with it quiet weather and I was able to tackle outstanding repairs. I was still very weary, thanks to a seemingly endless list of little problems, which meant that I was unable to settle into a routine. *Aqua Quorum* was very tired in places and it took time for the effects of the battering she had taken to become apparent. It took six days to repair the number two – the sail I used more often than any other. I had just finished this task when I heard a bang on deck as the staysail halyard fitting that had carried the storm jib during the rescue ripped out of the mast. Where was it going to stop? My elbow was getting steadily worse and the pain was starting to cloud everything I did. It was also preventing me from sleeping.

One day the keel began to make an unusual noise. Alarmed, I checked everything through from keel bolts to hydraulics. There was obviously something amiss under the boat and it sounded awful as it moaned and groaned. The discovery that it was merely a piece of kelp caught on the fin and banging on the hull brought with it an intense sense of relief.

As I skirted New Zealand the bad weather returned and it was back to the Southern Ocean routine of cold, grey skies and gale force winds. If sails can be described as the lungs of the boat then the winches are the muscles and the generator the heart – and it was the latter that was now to give trouble. It had not been itself since the rescue and it finally broke down during my second week out from Hobart. It is hard to describe the horror of those next three days as I desperately tried to find the problem. It was like sitting in a prison cell awaiting execution. I stripped the fuel system three times and replaced many of the components. The batteries did not have enough power to run the autopilot and at one point I had to take down the sails and let *Aqua Quorum* drift while I worked below on the problem.

At last I found a crack in the fuel tank supply pipe and carried out a hasty repair. The following twelve-hour charge of my batteries came just in time. A deep depression had formed to the west and was coming our way. The pressure dropped forty-six millibars in twenty-four hours and all the classic signs of Raphael's storm repeated themselves.

To say that this put the fear of death into me is an understatement and I prepared for the worst. I really got the wind up when Philippe Jeantot faxed me to say that both he and Météo France were worried. The fact that they were having a sleepless night on the other side of the world served to fuel my concern. The crux of the problem, despite what my common sense told me, was that I didn't have absolute confidence in the boat. Had she sustained structural damage? Was the keel in good shape? Had the mast really come through unscathed? My imagination chased itself in circles round the boat.

As predicted, it was a bad storm with sixty-knot winds and massive seas. Once the boat is made ready all you can do is get below and ride it out. It is during these periods of inactivity that your imagination can run away with itself. On this occasion mine did just that. They say a man who has time to consider the consequences cannot be brave. Well, I did a lot of considering and didn't enjoy it. As ever, though, *Aqua Quorum* came up trumps and we pulled through with no damage.

The turning point for me was riding out that storm. I wrote on my chart afterwards: 'Wind up to sixty knots with huge waves – a fantastic and frightening sight all at once.' It put me back in the saddle and the relief that came with its passing was intoxicating – a feeling that was heightened when I was joined by dolphins. I sat beneath a blue sky, content for the first time since receiving that mayday call, and watched them cavort about my boat putting on a private display for me. There were about a dozen of them and they jumped out of the water belly to belly, wrapping their tails around each other, twisting in mid-air, breaking away and diving back in the water. They whistled to each other and squealed with delight, the noises echoing and reverberating through *Aqua Quorum*'s hull like a jabbering foreign language. The magic scene heightened the relief that I felt after the storm.

The generator was an ongoing problem and was to plague me for the rest of the trip. I spent day after day stripping and reassembling the fuel system. No sooner had I cured that than other parts broke down. The cooling water was pumped by an ancillary electrical pump which was falling apart and needed stripping and reassembling after every charge. The two remaining engine mounts that had survived the rescue finally failed and it took nearly two days to make new ones. Thanks to the continual dunkings that the generator had had to endure, the main terminals started to corrode and I had to bypass them. And so it went

on, day after day. Each time I started it up to charge the batteries
I winced, tensely awaiting the next problem.

The water pump, after many days of struggling, eventually
packed in completely a few days from Cape Horn. I had no
alternative but to replace it with a hand-operated bilge pump.
This added dramatically to my daily workload – I had to squeeze
myself into a sitting position in front of the generator as it ran,
and pump away for four hours every day. It was most uncomfortable and physically demanding, particularly when *Aqua Quorum*
was bouncing about as she bashed to windward. It also meant
that other duties were neglected – once the unit was running, I
was captive. If the sails needed trimming, I couldn't nip on deck
and trim them, they just had to wait. I eventually split the daily
four-hour charge cycle in half and tackled it morning and
evening.

Throughout this my elbow was worsening. It became so
painful that I was unable to sleep – every time the boat bounced,
shooting pains arced through the perpetual aching throb. I
experimented with a sling suspended on elastic above my bunk to
help me sleep but it was no use. The race doctor Jean-Yves
suggested painkillers but I was loath to take them as I felt they
might impede my ability to think clearly and interfere with my
coordination on deck. My elbow had now swollen to the size of a
small melon and I couldn't bend it beyond ten degrees – it
brought new meaning to the term 'single-handed'. The words of
the kind woman in Plymouth who had knitted a good-luck
jumper for me for the Carlsberg Transatlantic came back to me.
She had been concerned because she thought that taking part in a
single-handed race meant that one arm was tied behind your
back. I had chuckled to myself at the time, but perhaps time and
circumstance had proved her right.

I was obliged to sail under the main and staysail alone as I crossed the Pacific – manhandling the much heavier headsails was just too much for my elbow. It was frustrating that I wasn't able to do the boat justice. She could have sailed much faster and I wanted the best result that I could get – I was, after all, still in a race. We were lying last out of the six that were left and I had set my heart on coming in fifth. Catherine Chabaud was in fifth place at that time, many hundreds of miles ahead.

I often thought of Gerry Roufs on board *Groupe LG 2* during this time. He had suddenly vanished from the communications net while en route for Cape Horn during a bad blow on 7 January. He had been lying in second place at the time and I was still in Tasmania. Efforts to contact him had failed – the automatic satellite beacon which gives the position of the yachts had not responded since that night and we all feared the worst. His silence could mean two things: either he had suffered a catastrophic disaster or he had lost all power on board and was quietly making his way to Cape Horn in forced silence. We all hung on to the latter and dreaded the former. His last known position was in an area so remote as to deny even the use of search aircraft.

A number of merchant ships had diverted to look for him as had fellow competitors Isabelle Autissier, Marc Thiercelin, Hervé Laurent and Bertrand de Broc, who were upwind and to the west – but all to no avail. Without a positioning beacon the task of finding him was virtually impossible. It was a cloud that hung over all of us. Three had survived capsize and been rescued – could not a fourth? Our hopes rose when a Chilean aircraft reported a weak radio transmission from him near Cape Horn. It was a euphoric moment and I celebrated with a special meal for Gerry and toasted him with one of my Tasmanian tinnies. But the hopes faded as time passed and no more was heard of him. On 17 July 1997 a freighter sighted the wreckage of a yacht drifting off the coast of Chile. It was later identified as Gerry's boat. The sad reality of his death sank in. We shall never know what happened and it was a tragic loss for everybody – particularly for his wife and young family.

I wondered whether we had the right to head down into the Southern Ocean and in so doing sometimes put the lives of others at risk. The rescue services are fantastic, jumping at the cry for help without thought for their own safety. Having been in the services I knew what they would be thinking as they donned their gear ready for the takeoff: 'Bloody great! This'll be a good one.' I was grateful to them and the chance to make a gesture presented itself when a television crew had contacted me for an interview during the ten days when I was making my way up to Hobart. A member of the crew, Margie Bashfield, seemed to be a good egg and I asked her if she would mind punting my articles round the Australian newspapers – if she could raise any money I wanted her to buy a mountain of beer and drop it on the doorstep for the lads at MRCC Australia and the RAAF rescue services. Margie pulled it off beautifully and, what's more, kept it quiet, as I had asked her to. I wanted it to be a private gesture, not just another PR stunt. There had been enough of that around the rescue already.

On 31 January, halfway between Hobart and Cape Horn, I felt something wet trickling down my arm as I worked away yet again at the generator. The skin at my elbow had ruptured and two hernias of soft tissue had squeezed out. I dressed it as best I could and then went on deck to reduce sail to a minimum as the wind went round to the east and rose to thirty knots. We pounded to windward through the night and I lay sleepless and wracked with pain in my bunk. The prospect of self-administered surgery loomed closer.

I wasn't too fussed about getting stuck in to the job. I felt that now was probably a good time to go for it as the risk of infection in these cold climes would be reduced. If I left the wound open until I reached the tropics it would surely become even more infected than it already was. I mulled it over for a couple of days and waited to see if it settled down. It didn't improve so I came to the conclusion that now was as good a time as any. If it was dealt with straight away it would have twelve days to heal by the time I neared the Falkland Islands. If it grew worse in that time then at least I would have the option of making use of the hospital facilities on the Falklands.

Jean-Yves, a number of his fellow surgeons and I kicked it back and forth until the morning of 4 February when, independently, we all decided the moment had come. I had fallen over on deck and knocked the elbow. The pain was excruciating. I crouched in a corner of the cockpit for half an hour waiting for the waves of pain to subside. It was time to do something about it.

I sanitised the surfaces in the accommodation area as instructed, dug out all the instruments, laid them out in order of use and read the instructions that had been sent by Jean-Yves on my computer screen. Once I had the surgical gloves on I wasn't to touch anything other than my elbow. This obviously ruled out the use of the scroll button on my computer. Back to square one. I copied the list of instructions on to the back of a chart, strapped on my head torch, fastened a mirror to my leg and rehearsed the operation a couple of times so that I knew what I would be up to. There would be only one run at this and I couldn't afford to cock it up. I was to cut into the flesh at the elbow and drain any fluid I found there.

Jean-Yves recommended that I smear the area around the elbow with an anaesthetic cream which would act as a surface painkiller, but I was reluctant to use it as the instructions said that it shouldn't come into contact with flesh – which was precisely where I wanted to get stuck in with the scalpel. I smeared some on the surrounding skin in any case, but decided that I couldn't be bothered to wait the twenty minutes that were needed for it to take effect. So I wiped it off, took a deep breath and made my first incision with the scalpel.

I was amazed at how sharp the scalpel was – it was like cutting butter with a hot knife, far easier than carving the Sunday roast. As I came to the end of the first cut blood welled out and dripped all over the mirror. Sod's law. I couldn't see a thing. This was beginning to remind me of a comic sketch for television. Jean-Yves had warned me to expect a lot of fluid to come out but no matter how deep I cut I just couldn't find anything of significance. In fact, I began to worry about going in too deep and cutting through something that I shouldn't.

I have to say it felt rather odd slicing away at myself but once I had made the first incision I became completely detached and absorbed in the job – it was as if I was working on someone else. There were two of us on board *Aqua Quorum*. The surgeon on the one hand, observing details in the bloody mirror – such as the fact that my pupils were twice their normal size – and the other part of me that was worrying about the race and whether this would call it to a halt.

I wasn't happy with the lack of fluid and I faxed Jean-Yves, who was on standing by. I typed with my bad arm while I held a pad on the elbow with my good one, holding the scalpel handle between my teeth to keep it sterile. 'Dear Jean-Yves, not going to plan . . .' No, I don't believe it. I had been faxing him for two months now without a problem and his fax machine chose this moment to break down. I contacted the race office and asked them to call Jean-Yves and then settled down to wait for a response, which was probably going to take at least half an hour.

Not being one for sitting around for too long I ran through the list to see that I had to take painkillers at the end of the operation and decided to get on with that part of it now. I easily identified the two large tablets but could not read the instructions which were, of course, in French. A big wave chose this moment to knock into the boat and the instruments fell to the floor. Shit! What next? I popped the tablets into my mouth as I stumbled about recovering the instruments from the floor. I was pretty alarmed when froth began to foam and bubble at the corners of my mouth – too late I discovered that the tablets were effervescent and should have been dissolved in a glass of water before being taken. It was quite a struggle to swallow them down against my laughter.

I gave the elbow a final and enthusiastic doing before cleaning it up and applying a dressing. Next came a cup of tea with two sugars, a sluice down of the accommodation with a bucket of water and into bed. The painkillers were very effective and I slept well for the first time in weeks. I changed the dressing regularly during the next seven days, the pain easing all the time. Although it continued to drain during that time not once did it show any sign of infection. I was soon able to start giving the elbow physiotherapy and getting it working properly once more. I had my race back.

Cape Horn, my exit from the Southern Ocean, was fast approaching. The anticipation was intoxicating and I worked the boat like the devil as we struggled through a spate of squalls, headwinds and a south-southeast wind which was blowing straight off Antarctica and was bitterly cold with snow and hail. At one point it went so far round that I found myself on a lee shore and was wondering whether I should tack so as to clear the coast. As it turned out I was able to bounce my way down what must be one of the most magnificent coastlines in the world until I could just make out Cape Horn in the distance.

The sight of land after so long was thrilling and I was amazed, not four hours from Cape Horn, to feel the wind ease and see the sun come out. I heated up some water and treated myself to a birdbath in the cockpit. This was one rounding that deserved the very best. I tried to call up the lighthouse and was surprised to hear an Australian voice reply. Pretty soon a converted ice-breaker full of Australian tourists sailed by to say hello. They were exploring the region. They crowded the rail taking photographs of *Aqua Quorum* and promised to send prints off to Tracey. What a great day. I had Cape Horn, sunshine, company and champagne. Thanks to the combination of antibiotics and champagne, I got very, very drunk.

14
THE HOME RUN

*If I have seen further it is by standing on
the shoulders of giants.*

Sir Isaac Newton

I had a shocking hangover the next morning. As I cleared Cape
Horn the wind went round until it was on the nose and
blowing at thirty knots. The conditions were terrible with fog,
rain, cold and the most awful sea state. We were now on the
continental shelf which, being shallow, was throwing up a very
short, steep sea. No matter what I did *Aqua Quorum* leapt
from the top of every wave and plunged into the face of the
next with a boneshaking crash. I decided that I would never
drink again – until the next time that is.

For the next six days we plugged away under storm jib and
three reefs with the wind blowing between thirty and forty
knots on the nose. I had made the mistake of thinking that I
had put the worst behind me on rounding Cape Horn – in fact,
the conditions became even more uncomfortable as we crashed
and shuddered our way to windward. We still had 7,000 miles
to go and I was, despite rounding Cape Horn, still below
fifty-five degrees south. I felt tired, run down and at a low ebb.
Poor old *Aqua Quorum* was taking yet another sound beating
and I felt every blow. I tried everything to ease her through this

final harsh and unforgiving round but it was no good, we would just have to slog it out to the end.

I began, believe it or not, to think that the Southern Ocean was preferable to this. Sleep was impossible and the perpetual noise gave me a splitting headache. A daily run of problems was shaken to the surface. One night I discovered, quite by chance, that one of the leeward bottle screws that adjust the tension of the mast support shrouds had come undone. The pulpit framework at the bow started to collapse under the shock loads from the spinnaker poles. The pin holding the head of the main to the mainsail car ripped out. The tiller fixing screws vibrated loose. I had to rejig my home-made engine mounts. And, finally, the water pick-up for the generator failed and I had to bodge one together. It refused to function unless I slowed the boat speed right down. This became a daily four hours of frustration as the batteries received their charge.

Although my elbow was still making a good recovery, the extra workload and need to cling on for even the simplest of tasks aggravated the joint and it troubled me from time to time. The generator mixer box once again split and flooded the accommodation with black, oily water, which penetrated everywhere as it slopped about the boat. It made me feel thoroughly seasick. I couldn't eat properly and even my sleeping bag got a good dousing. I wasn't able to repair the mixer box at that point because to do so I would have had to free the engine partially from its mounts, and the prospect of a heavy lump of metal rolling about the hold in those seas wasn't really an option. I had to endure the fumes and pump away at my makeshift hand-operated bilge pump until the accommodation was awash with the water running from the mixer box. Then I had to shut down the generator, bail out the accommodation, start the generator again and keep repeating the process until I had managed a full charge. Each time took hours of grim, patient effort.

I received a fax at this point telling me that I had been recommended for the Légion d'Honneur by President Chirac of France. Having never heard of it, I asked what it was, to be told that it is a very prestigious French award – a bit like a knighthood. I was sure I was the victim of a hoax. 'In that case,' I joked, 'I'll only accept it if it comes with a white charger'. When Philippe Jeantot was told about this, he said: 'If Pete wants a white charger, he will have a white charger!'. I spent several days terrified at the prospect of having to ride a large white horse up the Champs d'Elysées to accept my award.

I was by now catching Catherine Chabaud, who had been 1,000 miles ahead at one point. If I caught the weather right I might just close the gap as she, unfortunately for her, was pinned against the South American coast. I was determined to cross the line in fifth place. It was only now, with my arm in working order and all the drama of the Southern Ocean behind me, that I felt I was beginning to do *Aqua Quorum* justice. It had been one hell of a learning curve – perhaps we were finally ready for a Vendée.

Six days after Cape Horn, as if we had served our time, the conditions broke. It was a blessed relief. The sun came out – proper sun that is, the kind that is revitalising and warms your bones. I took half an hour out, sat in the cockpit and soaked it up with a cup of tea. The boat was surrounded by a huge flock of small sea birds, the first birds I had seen since Hobart, apart from albatrosses. The ocean had lost its malevolence and once again was warm, welcoming and invigorating.

News came through that Christophe Auguin of France on *Geodis* had crossed the finishing line as winner and 2,000 miles ahead of his nearest rival. He had set a new single-handed, nonstop record of 105 days, 20 hours, 31 minutes and 23 seconds. Christophe compiled one of the greatest single-handed sailing sequences of all time, with victories in the Figaro Race, in both of the last two BOC round-the-world races and now the Vendée, during which he also set a twenty-four-hour single-handed distance record. A great campaign from a great sailor – it was Christophe's race from day one.

We endured one more gale on the nose until we finally picked up the trades at five o'clock on 24 February. I had been waiting all day and, as ever, marvelled at the immediacy of the wind's arrival. I saw it come rippling across the water, tacked the sails and started to cream along on a flat, glassy sea under a burning sun. It was irresistible and I had my first shower under a bucket for months. It was glorious to feel sunshine on my body once more. We had really done it. All I had to do now was to hold it all together until the finish. I couldn't stop singing to myself and grinning as I worked my way over the boat to ensure that all was well for the last 3,000 miles of the race. After all that we had been through those miles felt no more daunting than a Channel crossing.

I caught Catherine by the equator. Our piece of elastic was still in place and, unable to communicate because her systems had failed, I toasted a kindred spirit and the comradeship that comes with sharing a common challenge. I can't describe how much I enjoyed that final run for home; the sailing was glorious and I had time to reflect on the race, rescue, Southern Ocean and all that I had experienced. I had seen and learned a lot about myself, both good and bad, and decided I could live with the view.

Physically I saw a marked improvement in myself as I started to put weight back on, developed a tan and purged a few aches and pains. I felt a great surge of energy and I took pleasure in the smallest things like breathing the cool air of dawn. I couldn't wait to get back to my family. I might face a struggle financially on my return but I knew that somehow I would get on top of it. I longed for Tracey's company once more – I had served my time alone.

The run home from the equator was a busy one and I sometimes worked for up to twenty hours a day on maintenance and sailing hard. The jobs still seemed endless: from sewing a patch on the staysail to changing the power packs on the autopilot system. I spent a night sorting out the most awful spinnaker wrap that I have ever had and hit something very substantial with an enormous bang off the Azores. No damage, thank goodness, but a bit of a worry all the same – to lose the race so close to the finishing line didn't bear thinking about.

I had one final memorable night before the real world started to creep back on board. There is nothing more satisfying and moving than planing along at a steady twelve knots on a tropical night beneath a full moon that is bright enough to read a book by. The heat of the day had passed and the night chill put goose bumps on my skin. There was time to savour the moment, all was well. A streak of light appeared at the bow – a dolphin, its playful path a trail of fluorescent light, was joined by several more and they seemed to compete with each other as they frolicked about the boat. They jumped, individuals, groups, the moon reflecting off their backs. A sense of joy and wellbeing welled up from the bottom of my stomach to catch in my throat. I made a silent promise that one day my children would see a sight like this.

My tea drinking had become a joke with the French, particularly with Philippe and his race support team who by now, thanks to their solid support, had become good friends. I couldn't resist a

practical joke in my last few days at sea and fired off a message to
stoke them up.

Hi Philippe, thanks for your fax, I am well and
sailing as hard as I can. My ETA is sometime
Saturday possibly Sunday . . . all is well
except that I was forced to consider retiring to
Finisterre last night as something terrible
happened & I was worried for my physical and,
more important, mental well-being.

After a long, hard think and much agonising I
have decided to finish . . . Cheers, Pete.

My intention was to tell them later that the dreadful news was
that I had run out of tea bags. Just as I pressed the send button
the wind headed us and I leapt on deck to put a tack in and
then became preoccupied with a few other jobs. I forgot all
about the joke. Apparently my message put the shore team into
a cold sweat – not only was the fax alarming and out of
character, but their tracking system showed that, thanks to my
having tacked, I might indeed have diverted to Finisterre. The
prospect of losing a competitor who was so close to home was
too much for them to bear. What could be wrong? They pored
over old faxes for clues and discussed the matter with a
psychiatrist. After all, it's not unknown for single-handers to
lose their sanity. Poor old Philippe was beside himself with
worry and didn't sleep all night.

It wasn't until I received the most delicately worded of faxes
the next day, expressing how everyone was behind me and that if
ever I needed help of any kind etc, that the penny dropped and I
banged off a quick message of reassurance:

Hi there, the disaster was that I ran out of
tea bags . . . Sorry about the bad joke, I
feel terrible now, it wasn't intended to
worry you . . . I'll make it up with a beer.
I couldn't be happier. Cheers, Pete.

It turned out to be a very frustrating last few days as we struggled against light and fluky winds across the Bay of Biscay. The estimated time of arrival kept being pushed back and I started to wonder if I would ever make the finish. I just couldn't seem to get there. At one stage I was well north of Les Sables d'Olonne and had to beat back down south.

The highlight of this period was when, the day before I got in, Colin Ridout of 3M flew out in his own light aircraft to greet me with Tracey and my parents on board. I was beside myself with excitement and paced the deck searching the skies for them as I tried to contact them with my hand-held VHF radio. Colin appeared and put me on to my father who was navigating and in need of a position update. It was the first conversation I had had since Cape Horn and the excitement in Dad's voice was catching. He took my position and handed the mike over to Tracey and we took great pleasure in hearing each other's voices again. My abiding memory of that conversation is Tracey's first words: 'Have you shaved that beard off yet?'

Sunday 23 February. The morning of the finish. There was a light breeze. I had drifted about aimlessly all night with no wind. I hadn't slept for two days because of the fluky conditions and the need to keep watch among the heavy shipping traffic, and I was terribly tired. The sun came out and I cleared my head with a good old shower and tidy up before we got in. I knew from Catherine's last position that she was now 100 miles behind so I didn't feel under pressure. I put the spinnaker up to catch the breeze that was settling in and sat on deck with a cup of tea and quietly reflected on the last ten years and what had been the most exciting few months of my life. I suppose I was bidding a private goodbye to the Vendée and preparing myself for the bun fight that was ahead.

I really had no idea of the scale of the welcome that was building up ashore. In a sense the race had been like living in a goldfish bowl – everyone could see in but I couldn't see out. An indication of what was to come was at about sixty miles out when the first light aircraft full of press and television burst into my little world, taking pictures and demanding interviews over the VHF. I was still lost in my thoughts and it all felt terribly intrusive to begin with. The first helicopters arrived about thirty miles out and the first boats at about ten, all of which began to fuel my anticipation and excitement.

It was fantastic to see so many friendly faces and after so long alone I couldn't wait to down my first beer at the Galway Bar. The flotilla of welcoming boats just kept growing. Raphael turned up with Virginie, and Tracey suddenly popped up right beside me on an RIB with Mark Orr. I couldn't wait for my hug.

Yovo, the same trawler that had towed me out to the start, appeared with my parents and the rest of the team on board. It was incredible. It was a beautiful day and we surfed along at ten to fourteen knots under the 3M spinnaker. As we closed the line so the flotilla became more and more dense until there were a hundred boats or so scooting about and the risk of collision became a real threat.

Everybody asks: 'What is it like when you cross the line?' Well, this time I felt a real prat because at first I couldn't find the line for boats. I only just saw it at the last minute and was caught a bit short as I rushed to drop the spinnaker and head her up to the finish. As the gun sounded the ocean erupted in a cacophony of noise, revving engines, cheers, foghorns, flares and raw emotion. I crossed the line in fifth place in a time of 126 days, 21 hours, 25 minutes and four seconds. Of the sixteen who had started, only six finished. Of those who finished, *Aqua Quorum* was not only the smallest but also the only new boat – something of which we as a team are very proud.

I felt on top of the world – talk about a dog with two dicks – and I couldn't stop smiling. At last a Briton had carried the red ensign across the line in a Vendée. As I dropped the main, the lads from the marina came alongside and took me in tow for the harbour entrance. I shook my first hand. I really didn't know whether I was coming or going. Tracey wasn't allowed on board until we reached the pontoon so we sneaked a quick and elated hug off the transom as we entered the harbour. I turned round and my jaw dropped at the sight that confronted me.

One hundred and fifty thousand cheering, applauding people were standing twenty deep along the castellated walls and cobblestones of the quayside. To my embarrassment, chants of 'Pete Goss, Pete Goss' rang through the air. Some in the crowd waved huge home-made posters. 'Pete the Great is back'. 'Welcome Pete God'. They banged drums. They screamed. Somewhere in the crush a band played *Rule Britannia*. I was overwhelmed. I had been on my own for four and a half months and now this.

There were so many boats you could have walked on them from one side of the harbour to the other. At one point the whole show ground to a shuddering halt as the harbour entrance literally jammed solid. I spent the next hour waving as if my life depended on it as they tried to get the little yellow boat with the big heart to the pontoon.

Suddenly we were there and Raphael, as we had agreed in the Southern Ocean, took my line. The Vendée was over. Tracey jumped on board and we finally managed a proper hug. Raphael followed with Virginie and I was given the biggest bottle of champagne I have ever seen with which to spray the crowd.

And there was big Adrian with a grin from ear to ear. This was his moment as much as mine. Words wouldn't do for what I wanted to say so we kept it to a handshake, a hug and a 'Cheers, mate.' It was enough.

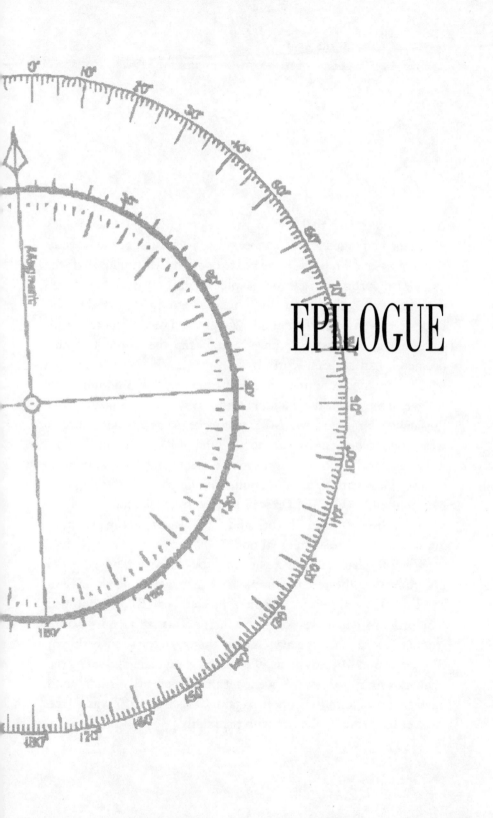

EPILOGUE

After the fuss and the fury of the welcome back to Les Sables d'Olonne had faded and a few beers had been sunk at the Galway Bar, Tracey and I retired to the peace of a flat that friends had lent us. We sat propped against the pillows in bed late that night, drinking tea, eating toast and tucking into fresh strawberries. Life, we agreed, felt pretty good. We reflected on the last ten years – the highs, the lows, the uncertainties and the triumphs – and decided it had all been worth it.

The year since the finish has been amazing. I was honoured to receive many awards, including the Légion d'Honneur from President Chirac and the MBE from Her Majesty the Queen. I was proud to be best man at the wedding of Raphael and Virginie in Les Sables d'Olonne, and they were special guests of honour at another important event – my homecoming party at the Torpoint Mosquito SC, when Ted Drewell handed over his model of *Aqua Quorum*. It was beautiful work and took twice as many painstaking hours to create as the real boat.

When Raphael and I were heading for Hobart on board *Aqua Quorum* after the rescue, we pledged that we would do a two-handed transatlantic race together. In October 1997 we fulfilled that promise when we competed in the Transat Jacques Vabre from Le Havre to Cartagena – mainly thanks to the sponsorship of BMW and Sun Microsystems. We made a great team and sailed the boat into first in class. We went into credit on my birthday and have moved in to our own home again. Christmas 1997 was all the sweeter for being by the fire with the family.

The new project for the Vendée team – still in place with a few additions, most notably Mark Orr, who is now my business manager – is a revolutionary, Adrian Thompson-designed catamaran in which we will compete in The Race, a nonstop dash round the world – starting on 31 December 2000 – to celebrate the millennium. There are no rules apart from the course, making it a global drag race in the biggest, fastest, most technologically advanced boats ever designed. The 115ft craft, which has a beam of 60ft, will be capable of speeds of up to 40 knots, and we plan to warm her up by having a crack at the Jules Verne nonstop, round-the-world record in the winter of 1999, before we line up for The Race. We reckon we can knock a week off the record. Gary Venning and his build team have taken over a large factory in Totnes in Devon and work has started on the biggest multi-hull to be built in Britain.

An education scheme is being dovetailed into the project and there will be a visitors' centre. You will all be welcome. Find out more on our website – www.petegoss.com – and come and be a part of the Goss Challenge.

Life hangs on a very thin thread and the cancer of time is complacency. If you are going to do something, do it now. Tomorrow is too late.

Pete Goss

LIST OF SPONSORS

LEVEL	COMPANY	EQUIPMENT
Title	Aqua Quorum	
Title	BMW (GB) Ltd	Support vehicles
Gold	3M United Kingdom PLC	Boat maintenance materials
Gold	Foundation for Sports and the Arts	
Gold	Sun Microsystems Ltd	
Silver	BT (UK Carrier Services)	
Silver	BT Aeronautical & Maritime	Satcom C and Mobiq Marine satellite telephone
Silver	Caltell Communications Ltd	Support vehicle and computer
Silver	Canon Europe	Image stabilised binoculars
Silver	Fischer Panda UK Ltd	Generators
Silver	Holliday Chemical Holdings	
Silver	HQ Royal Marines	Loan of building
Silver	Humana International Group PLC	
Silver	Inmarsat	Inmarsat-E (EPIRB)
Silver	Musto Ltd	Breathable waterproofs and thermal clothing
Silver	Nera Ltd	Maintenance and repair of all communications equipment
Silver	Timberland (UK) Ltd	Shoes and casual clothing
Supplier	Airex	Foam core materials
Supplier	Associated British Ports	Launching facilities in Plymouth and short-term berthing
Supplier	Avesta Sheffield	Stainless steel fabrications
Supplier	Bainbridge International	Sailcloth and sail hardware

LEVEL	COMPANY	EQUIPMENT
Supplier	Bruce Banks Sails Ltd	Design and construction of all sails
Supplier	Bureau Veritas	Surveying
Supplier	Carbospars	Design and construction of the mast and boom
Supplier	Cetrek Ltd	Instrumentation
Supplier	Concept II Ltd	Fitness training and equipment
Supplier	Eagle Signs	Signage
Supplier	Exd Services	Hydraulic systems engineering
Supplier	Frederickson Boat Fittings UK	Batten car system
Supplier	Heinsco Ltd	Carbon materials
Supplier	Hellermann Electrical	Electrical components
Supplier	Henry Iron Trades	Keel bulb manufacture
Supplier	Hercules CSMD	Keel structure and all fabrication
Supplier	Hobson Audley Hopkins & Wood	Solicitors
Supplier	Hydraulic Projects Ltd	Hydraulic steering pumps and cylinders
Supplier	IBM	ThinkPad laptop computers
Supplier	International Paints	Deck paint, exterior and interior finishes
Supplier	John Fearnley	Certification
Supplier	Lewmar Marine Ltd	Winches, racing hardware and hatches
Supplier	Lloyds Bank PLC	Overdraft and continued support
Supplier	Malcolm Roose Scaffolding	Scaffolding
Supplier	Marlow Ropes Ltd	Running rigging, sheets and warps
Supplier	McDougalls	Freeze-dried food
Supplier	Navico Ltd	Waterproof handheld VHF radios
Supplier	PC Maritime	Computer weather and routing software
Supplier	Plymouth Gin	Drink supplier

LEVEL	COMPANY	EQUIPMENT
Supplier	Power Survivor	Watermaker
Supplier	Raytheon Marine Europe Ltd	LCD Radar
Supplier	Rick Tomlinson Photography	Photography
Supplier	Scanti	HF and VHF radios
Supplier	Simpson-Lawrence Ltd	Boat building equipment and chandlery
Supplier	SP Systems Group	Structural engineering and materials
Supplier	Sparks	
Supplier	Whitlock Marine Steering Co Ltd	Steering gear
Supplier	Winsund	Wind generators
	Xelerator Internet Solutions by Netserv (UK) Ltd	Website hosting and design

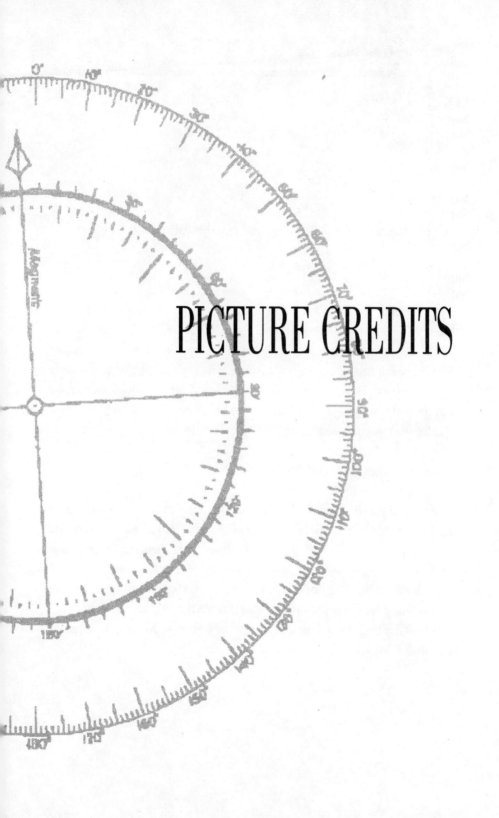

PICTURE CREDITS

All photographs by Pete Goss, except the following:

Between pages 90 and 91

Page 1 Rick Tomlinson; *page 2 yellow boat* John Goss; *page 3 Sarie Marais* John Goss; *page 4 British Steel 92-93* Pictor Picture Library; *page 5 Brian Lister* Pictor Picture Library; *page 6 Aqua Quorum* Paragon Mann; *boat plug* Daily Telegraph; *page 7 inside shell* Andrew Dare; *electronic equipment* Gautier Deblonde; *lead* Andrew Dare; *page 8 build team* Philippe Falle; *AQ launch* Andrew Dare; *Joanna Lumley* Rick Tomlinson.

Between pages 186 and 187

Page 2 Dinelli sinking Royal Australian Air Force; *closing the raft* J.McDonald/ Pictor Picture Library; *rescue* Royal Australian Air Force; *page 5 finishing line* Jacques Archambaud; *hugging* Jacques Archambaud; *page 6 family* Gaye Sarma; *page 7* Président de la République Française Services Photographique; *before Jacques Vabre* Thierry Martinez/Allsport; *starting Jacques Vabre* Allsport; *page 8 new catamaran* Paragon Mann; *build shed* David McHugh.

Index